Dirk Philips,
A Sixteenth-Century Dutch Anabaptist

Dirk Philips, A Sixteenth-Century Dutch Anabaptist

His Doctrine of the Visible Church
and Its Influence on His Theological System

INSUNG JEON

☙PICKWICK *Publications* · Eugene, Oregon

DIRK PHILIPS: A SIXTEENTH-CENTURY DUTCH ANABAPTIST
His Doctrine of the Visible Church and Its Influence on His Theological System

Copyright © 2022 Insung Jeon. All rights reserved. Except for brief quotations in critical publications or reviews, no part of this book may be reproduced in any manner without prior written permission from the publisher. Write: Permissions, Wipf and Stock Publishers, 199 W. 8th Ave., Suite 3, Eugene, OR 97401.

Pickwick Publications
An Imprint of Wipf and Stock Publishers
199 W. 8th Ave., Suite 3
Eugene, OR 97401

www.wipfandstock.com

PAPERBACK ISBN: 978-1-6667-0790-8
HARDCOVER ISBN: 978-1-6667-0791-5
EBOOK ISBN: 978-1-6667-0792-2

Cataloguing-in-Publication data:

Names: Jeon, Insung, author.

Title: Dirk Philips, a sixteenth-century Dutch anabaptist : his doctrine of the visible church and its influence on his theological system / Insung Jeon.

Description: Eugene, OR : Pickwick Publications, 2022 | Includes bibliographical references.

Identifiers: ISBN 978-1-6667-0790-8 (paperback) | ISBN 978-1-6667-0791-5 (hardcover) | ISBN 978-1-6667-0792-2 (ebook)

Subjects: LCSH: Philips, Dirk, 1504–1568. | Anabaptists—Netherlands—History—16th century.

Classification: BX8143.P45 J46 2022 (print) | BX8143.P45 J46 (ebook)

To Minyoung

אֵשֶׁת־חַיִל מִי יִמְצָא וְרָחֹק מִפְּנִינִים מִכְרָהּ
בָּטַח בָּהּ לֵב בַּעְלָהּ וְשָׁלָל לֹא יֶחְסָר
גְּמָלַתְהוּ טוֹב וְלֹא־רָע כֹּל יְמֵי חַיֶּיהָ

—Proverbs 31:10–12

CONTENTS

Acknowledgments ix
Abbreviations xi

CHAPTER 1: *Introduction* 1
   Biographical Outline 7
   Literature Review: The History of Anabaptist
     and Dirk Philips Studies 12
   The Importance of This Study 27

CHAPTER 2: *Dirk Philips's View of the Visible Church* 30
   Introduction 30
   Influences 31
   Reformers' Views of the Visible Church 50
   What Concept Did Dirk Philips Consider as
     Most Important in the Visible Church? 52
   Conclusion 60

CHAPTER 3: *Christology* 62
   Introduction 62
   The Humanity of Christ 64
   The Deity of Christ 70
   The Relationship of Christ to the Trinity 84
   Functional Christology 85
   Summary 88
   The Correlation of Dirk Philips's View of the Visible
     Church with His Christology 90

CHAPTER 4: *Ecclesiology* 93
   Introduction 93
   Dirk's View of Baptism 94
   Dirk's View of the Lord's Supper 106
   Dirk's View of Church Discipline 115
   Summary 124
   The Correlation of Dirk Philips's View of the Visible Church with His Ecclesiology 126

CHAPTER 5: *Soteriology* 129
   Introduction 129
   Dirk's View of Predestination 131
   Dirk's View on Justification 135
   Dirk's View of Conversion 137
   Dirk's View of Regeneration 139
   Dirk's View of Sanctification 145
   Dirk's View of Unity with Christ 147
   Dirk's View of Perseverance and Glorification 149
   Summary 150
   The Correlation of Dirk Philips's View of the Visible Church with His Soteriology 152

CHAPTER 6: *Anthropology* 155
   Introduction 155
   Dirk's View of Human Nature 157
   Dirk's View of Human Free Will 160
   Dirk's View of Sin, Evil, and Suffering 164
   Dirk's View of Human Reason 172
   Summary 175
   The Correlation of Dirk Philips's View of the Visible Church with His Anthropology 176

CHAPTER 7: *Conclusion* 179

Bibliography 185

ACKNOWLEDGMENTS

This book is a revision of a dissertation, written to meet the requirements of the PhD program at Midwestern Baptist Theological Seminary. I am glad to acknowledge my debt to some of those who have helped me take this project from an idea to a finished this work. There are many people to whom I need to give thanks for their care and sacrifices.

In writing the original manuscript, I am privileged to have received guidance from two great professors at Midwestern Baptist Theological Seminary. My thanks go first to Dr. Michael D. McMullen, who as chairman on my dissertation committee, guided this work always with a kind heart and strengthened this work beyond my expectations. His dedication to his students has inspired me to be a better writer and theologian. Also, I would like to thank Dr. Jason G. Duesing, who has served as the second reader on my dissertation committee. His deep insight, advice, and encouragement helped me complete this project, and he took the time to provide detailed criticism. I am also grateful to Dr. John Lee, my neighbor, advisor, and exercise partner. He has broadened my perspective of reading the Word of God.

Looking back on the past several years as I have finished my studies abroad in United States, the greatest gift that God has given me is that I made valued friends, and can continue studying in their prayers and support. I am convinced that without their encouragement and fellowship in the Lord, I would not have successfully completed my long-term study abroad. I owe them a lot. Wooil Jun, Jeahyu Lee, Jinhee Lee are friends whom I met while studying for my Th.M degree at New Orleans Baptist Theological Seminary. They are like family to me, and I will never forget our fellowship and conversations in the Lord. I am also grateful that God directed me to several good friends while studying at Midwestern Baptist Theological Seminary. In particular, I have developed previous ties with several members of the "bonfire meeting," who gathered together on every Monday evening to have a theological and pastoral conversation, particularly Kyung-Hwa Chung, Jay Kwon, and Kevin Choi. I am grateful to Kevin for reading the original manuscript and giving valuable advice. Thanks also to Nathan Huffstutler, who proofread my dissertation and gave me meaningful advice on style and form.

I would also like to thank each member of my family. They are the ones who have made it possible for me to continue study abroad. My wife, Minyoung An, is the one who has devoted more than anyone to help me complete this long journey. She is the wisest wife and mother, and she is unbelievably dedicated to her husband and family. I would also like to thank Eden and Ina, whom God gave as gifts to my family while studying in the United States. They are my joy. Through them, I am learning God's love for me. My dad, Rev. Bonggil Jeon, and mom, Seungja Lee, have long supported me with prayer and with finances. Also, through their lives of sacrifice and devotion in planting a church and serving for over 40 years, I have learned what the life of good pastor looks like. I would also like to thank my father-in-law, Jongbae An, and my mother-in-law, Suhui Park. They have always been model parents in their warm and loving words, and through them I have been able to work hard to be a better parent for my children. I also want to express my deep gratitude to my younger brother, Inseok Jeon, and his wife, Sungeun Bae, and to my brother-in-law, Hyoungtae An, and his wife, Bobae Kim.

Lastly, I would like to express my special thanks to my grandfather, Sungchan Jeon, and my grandmother, Insu Jin. They are my supporters who love and care for me more than anyone else in this world. My grandfather passed away during my PhD course, and unfortunately I was unable to attend his funeral in Korea while studying in the United States; but he was my greatest friend. Even though I was unable to say farewell to him in this world, I believe the day will come again when I will meet him in the future. The love I received from him is carved deep into my heart, and it is a great blessing to me to be his grandson. I miss him.

Insung Jeon
Wonju in South Korea
March 19, 2021

ABBREVIATIONS

BRN	*Bibliotheca Reformatoria Neerlandica.* 10 vols. Edited by Samuel Cramer and Frederik Pijper. 's-Gravenhage: Nijhoff, 1903–14.
Confessions	*The Confessions of St. Augustine.* Edited and Translated by E. B. Pusey. Waiheke Island, New Zealand: The Floating, 2008.
CWMS	Simons, Menno. *The Complete Writings of Menno Simons, C.1496–1561.* Edited by J. Denny Weaver. Translated by Leonard Verduin. Scottdale, PA: Herald, 1986.
Institutes	Calvin, John. *Institutes of the Christian Religion.* Translated by Henry Beveridge. Grand Rapids: Eerdmans, 1957.
LW	Luther, Martin. *Luther's Works.* 55 vols. St. Louis: Concordia, 1955–2011.
WDP	Philips, Dirk. *The Writings of Dirk Philips, 1504–1568.* Classics of the Radical Reformation 6. Harrisonburg, VA: Herald, 1992.

Chapter 1

INTRODUCTION

IN THE TENTH VOLUME of *Bibliotheca Reformatoria Neerlandica*,[1] which was published in 1914, F. Pijper evaluates Dirk Philips as follows:

> Het Enchiridion mag dus op ééne lijn geplaatst worden met de voornaamste uiteenzettingen der Protestantsche geloofsleer uit het eerste tijdperk. Wat de „Loci communes" van Melanchthon waren voor de Lutherschen, de „Confession" van Beza voor de Fransche, de „Leken wechwyser" voor de Nederlandsche Gereformeerden, dat is het Enchiridion voor de Mennonieten geweest.[2]

According to Pijper's evaluation, although Dirk Philips has excellent theological abilities and he was a leader who made a significant contribution to the development of the Mennonites camp, he did not receive much attention in the study of Anabaptists, and there has not been much

---

1. *Bibliotheca Reformatoria Neerlandica*, hereafter referred to as *BRN*, was published in ten volumes between 1903 and 1914. The series, edited by Samuel Cramer and F. Pijper, introduces important Dutch writings during the Reformation period. Volumes VII and X of the series provide very important data in research on Dirk Philips. Volume VII includes Obbe Philips's *Confession*, and volume X includes Dirk Philips's *Enchiridion*. Volume II and volume V of the series also provide information on the Mennonites. Volume II contains the oldest collection of Mennonite martyr letters and sacrificial songs, and volume V contains works by Melchior Hoffman and Adam Pastor.

2. The English translation is as follows: "The *Enchiridion* may, therefore, be placed on one line with the most important explanations of Protestant doctrine of the first age. What the *Loci communes* of Melanchthon was for Lutherans, the *Confession* of Beza for the French, the *Leken wechwyser* for the Dutch Reformed, that was the *Enchiridion* for the Mennonites" (*BRN*, X:4). William R. Estep and William Keeney also mention that statement. See Estep, *Anabaptist Story*, 114; Keeney, "Writings of Dirk Philips," 306.

1

research on this sixteenth-century Mennonite leader.[3] William Keeney, who has made a great contribution to research on Dirk Philips, points out that although Dirk's work has been translated into English, it has not drawn much attention to his life and thought.[4] According to Keeney, there are three reasons that theologians and historians have not had much interest in Dirk. First, Dirk was always in the shadow of another leader throughout his career as a second leader of his group, even though he had a better systematic theological talent than anyone in the group. Second, because Dirk had a stubborn attitude toward those who made mistakes, the Mennonites, which were characterized by diversity and tolerance, had relatively little interest in Dirk. The final reason is that Dirk's work is written in Dutch or a Dutch-German dialect.[5]

Indifference to Dirk Philips has resulted in a lack of research on his theology. Although there have been attempts to clarify Anabaptist theology, it is also true that there is not enough research to reveal the key to grasping Dirk Philips's theology. Among the few attempts at this, the most prominent is Keeney's. Keeney argues that Dirk's theology has two focuses: one is the word of God and the other is the incarnation.[6] Keeney's claim, at least, is superficially adequate, because in terms of the volume of Dirk's writings, it is true that the word of God and the incarnation are the most discussed. Keeney, however, did not have enough clarity to explain why Dirk's discussion of the word of God and the incarnation is more important than other theological topics. A more recent study suggests another possibility. Aaron Schubert recognizes Christ and the church as the most important themes of Dirk's theology. He says, "Dirk's central hermeneutic principle was 'ecclesiocentric,' focusing on the Body of Christ, the church."[7] Moreover, it is also true that the era of church schism led many Anabaptist leaders to be interested in ecclesiology rather than other theological subjects, and even Dirk's interest in the

---

3. Only two extended studies of Dirk Philips's life and theology have been published. One is *Dirk Philips: Friend and Colleague of Menno Simons, 1504–1568*, by J. ten Doornkaat Koolman (Koolman, *Dirk Philips*). The other is William E. Keeney's *The Development of Dutch Anabaptist Thought and Practice from 1539-1564*. (Keeney, *Development of Dutch Anabaptist Thought and Practice*).

4. Keeney, "Research Note," 557–60.

5. Keeney, "Research Note," 558.

6. Philips, *Writings of Dirk Philips*, 38.

7. Schubert, "Dirk Philips' Letter and Spirit," 41.

incarnation had the practical purpose of defending the church against the Unitarian view.[8]

It is not unique for research into the Anabaptists to claim that ecclesiology is the central theme of their theology. Although not directly concerned with Dirk Philips, several attempts have been made to identify what the key of Anabaptist theology is, finding that the key is ecclesiology. The most representative example is Franklin H. Littell, who argues that "the concept of the church [is] the essence of main-line Anabaptism"[9]; Todd Johnson also says that the most important issue of the Anabaptist movement is ecclesiology.[10] However, not all scholars agree with this view. Rollin Armor sees baptism as a key to understanding the Anabaptist movement,[11] but John Yoder claims that baptism is a secondary issue in Anabaptist theology.[12] There are also skeptical views of finding the key theology of the Anabaptist movement. William Estep argued that because of their circumstances, Anabaptists did not "erect elaborate speculative systems of theology,"[13] while Robert Friedmann claims that the Anabaptists did not even have explicit theology.[14]

Unfortunately, studies on Anabaptists so far have not been successful in disrupting misunderstandings toward the Anabaptist movement.[15] Many theologians did not recognize the diversity of the Anabaptist movement, nor did they distinguish between extreme and evangelical perspectives within the movement; in some cases, the Anabaptist movement was considered an extremely violent movement or a mystical movement.[16]

One of the most notable recent misunderstandings about Anabaptists appears in the work of Alistair McGrath. He divides the ecclesiology of the era of Reformation into the Augustinian tradition and the Donatist tradition in his book *Reformation Thought: An Introduction*. The crucial

8. Keeney, "Editor's Introduction," 52.
9. Littell, *Anabaptist View of the Church*, 46.
10. Johnson, "Initiation Or Ordination?," 70.
11. Armour, *Anabaptist Baptism*, 135.
12. Yoder, "Kirchenzucht Bei Zwingli," 63.
13. Estep, *Anabaptist Story*, 130.
14. Friedmann, *Theology of Anabaptism*, 27–34.
15. Estep argues that the reason for this tendency is due to hostile objections to the Anabaptist movement and a lack of data on the movement. See Estep, *Anabaptist Story*, 1.
16. For this view, see González, *Story of Christianity*, 2:53–60. Also see MacCulloch, *Reformation*, 204–212.

difference between Augustine and the Donatists was the question of what to do if a bishop who committed the sin of apostasy during the persecution period later repented. In such a case, the Donatists believed that "[b]y lapsing, the bishop has committed the sin of apostasy (literally, 'falling away'). He has therefore placed himself outside the bounds of the church, and can no longer be regarded as administering the sacraments validly."[17] On the other hand, the Catholic Church, including Augustine, argued, "[b]y his repentance, the bishop has been restored to grace, and is able to continue administering the sacraments validly."[18] According to McGrath, Augustine's claim is based on two things: first, that there are wheat and tares in the church of the earth, and second, that schism is a greater sin than apostasy.[19]

As a result, there are no reformers following Augustine's ecclesiology in the full sense because the reformers had caused divisions—Protestantism's divide from the Catholic Church. McGrath, however, considers Magisterial Reformers as those who supported the institutional church and follow the Augustine view, while he assesses the ecclesiology of the Radical Reformers as much closer to the Donatists' view.[20] Nevertheless, is McGrath's assertion true that the Radical Reformers are disciples of Donatus? Is it true that the Anabaptists thought that the failed believers cannot be forgiven because the church is a gathering of pure souls?

The goal of this dissertation includes the following. First, this dissertation will demonstrate the central emphasis in the theology of Dirk Philips, examining that the doctrine of the visible church is the key to understand his theology. In order to support this claim, this dissertation will explore his various doctrines, including his Christology; his ecclesiology, including his view of church ordinances and disciplines; his soteriology; and his anthropology. In addition, the dissertation explains that each doctrine is closely interrelated with his view of the visible church. Second, this dissertation, as it examines Dirk Philips's view of the visible church, will naturally prove that the Radical Reformation, is closer to the ecclesiology of Augustine's tradition than to the ecclesiology of the Donatists' tradition. Of course, in the sense that the Radical Reformers—in the same way as the Magisterial Reformers—admitted the schism

17. McGrath, *Reformation Thought*, 145.
18. McGrath, *Reformation Thought*, 145.
19. McGrath, *Reformation Thought*, 145–146.
20. McGrath uses Radical Reformers as synonyms for Anabaptists, and he chooses Menno Simons as a representative figure of the Radical Reformation.

of the church, they did not follow Augustine completely. However, the schism was an inevitable decision of both the Magisterial and the Radical Reformers—even though the Magisterial Reformers did not intend to do so from the first—in the midst of the Reformation era because they knew that maintaining biblical soteriology from the corrupted Catholic Church was more important than preventing division.[21] It would, therefore, be inappropriate to conclude that the Anabaptists followed the Donatists' tradition based on the fact that they contributed to the division of the church and did not prefer the institutional church. Furthermore, this dissertation will argue that Dirk's ecclesiology was closer to Augustine than to Donatus because he admitted that the church is a mixture of wheat and chaff, and because he accepted those who left the church when they repented and returned.

This chapter will outline Dirk Philips's brief biography and the history of research on the Anabaptist movement as well. A look at Dirk's life reveals the process of the formation of his theology, and exploring the history of the Anabaptist research that has been carried out so far will guide the direction of future research. Therefore, this chapter will present the need for this dissertation on Dirk Philips.

The main goal of chapter 2 is to describe Dirk's view of the visible church. This chapter will explore the backgrounds that have influenced the formation of Dirk's thought, and it will explore how earlier Dutch Anabaptist leaders saw the visible church as well. In addition, this chapter will point out Dirk's perspective of the visible church, which appears in his treatises and letters. This chapter also will demonstrate that Anabaptist views of the visible church have changed in accordance with the times and circumstances, and sometimes because of the interests of the leaders in the movement.

Chapter 3 will explore Dirk Philips's Christology. Christology is a very important concept in understanding his theology because Dirk developed a distinctive Christology, unlike other contemporary Christian leaders. That is why his Christology needs to be explored before his other theologies. After examining Dirk's Christology, this chapter will reveal the aspects of his Christology that are associated with his view of the visible church. In particular, his concept of the incarnation in his Christology is positioned as the most important doctrine for the saints to live a

---

21. Benjamin Warfield says, "for the Reformation, inwardly considered, was just the ultimate triumph of Augustine's doctrine of grace over Augustine's doctrine of the Church" (Warfield, *Calvin and Augustine*, 322).

holy life, because he believed that the incarnation causes humans to have divine nature in Christ.

Chapter 4 will examine Dirk's ecclesiology. Because Dirk's view of the visible church is part of his ecclesiology, this chapter will be directly related to his view of the visible church. The first part of this chapter will explore the elements of the church that Dirk has emphasized, namely the two ordinances of the church: baptism and the Lord's Supper. It will also explore his view of church discipline. Dirk regards baptism as a requirement of the visible church as a symbol of renewal—not merely the re-baptism of believers by verbal confession, but the moral intention of a promise of a deep brotherhood in the visible church. This chapter will also show that Dirk saw the Lord's Supper as another fundamental sign in the visible church, and it will discuss how Dirk looked at admonition, excommunication, and so forth to ensure the purity of the visible church.

The subject of chapter 5 is Dirk's soteriology. This chapter will focus on his view of predestination, justification, conversion, regeneration, sanctification, united with Christ, perseverance, and glorification, but more specifically on his view of regeneration. This chapter also will reveal that his soteriology is deeply related to his view of the visible church. Since Dirk believes that the regeneration of believers must lead to visible changes as well as invisible changes, his understanding of regeneration supports his concept of the visible church. In addition, because he sees the church as a gathering of saved people, he believes that it is a gathering of people with visible changes, and therefore, that the change must appear in the visible church.

Chapter 6 will explore Dirk's doctrine of man. The goal of this chapter is to clarify his doctrine of man, including his view of the human role as a new creation in Christ. By studying his view of human free will, sin, evil, suffering, and human reason, this chapter will examine what role human beings can play in establishing the visible church. Since the visible church exists physically in this world, the human role in physical space is inevitable. Thus, by examining at what Dirk thinks of human beings, this chapter will help to understand his view of the visible church.

Finally, the conclusion summarizes these findings of Dirk Philips's theology, relating them to his view of the visible church. Based on the findings, the conclusion will point out that the view of the visible church was critical in the ecclesiology of the sixteenth-century Mennonite, as well as the ecclesiology of Dirk Philips. Dirk's understanding of the church, which regarded the practice of faith as an essential aspect of the saints. In addition, the conclusion argues that the close connection between Dirk's theological system and his concept of the visible church is the basis for his recognition of the importance of the saints to live a distinguished and holy life in the earth, and it argues that Dirk believed that the church of this world is a mixture of wheat and chaff. In addition, Dirk's view of excommunication and admonition shows that he forgave repentant brethren who had made mistakes in the past, and he returned them to their original positions after their repentance. Thus, in this conclusion, it will be argued that Dirk Philips's understanding of the church is not very different from the Magisterial Reformers and follows the Augustine tradition.

Biographical Outline

There is no exact data on the birth of Dirk Philips, but he was probably born in 1504 in Leeuwarden.[22] He is known to have been the young son of a priest named Phillips, so he would be called Dirk Philipszoon, or the son of Phillips.[23] His brother was named Obbe, but little is known about their father or mother. What is known is that at that time, it was common in the Friesland region for priests to have concubines and a legal wife, and that the sons were able to inherit property from their father.[24]

Little is known about Dirk Philips's childhood, just as there is little known about his birth. Dirk seems to have been associated with Franciscans and the cloister Nieuw Galilea, which moved to Leeuwarden from outside the city. According to Koolman, Dirk would have been accepted by Franciscans in Leeuwarden and would have received a high level of education there[25] because one of his opponents despised Dirk as having been involved with one of the Franciscan clusters.[26] With the exception of this information, no data has been found to date about his early life before he joined the Anabaptists.

---

22. The most detailed and monographic form of a biography of Dirk Philips is Koolman, *Dirk Philips*. This section is compiled in consultation with Koolman's biography, as well as Keeney, "Dirk Philips' Life"; Keeney, "Dirk Philips"; Rempel, *Lord's Supper in Anabaptism*, 165–67.

23. Keeney, "Dirk Philips," 19. According to Keeney, there is a variety of spellings for the name Dirk Philips. See Keeney, "Dirk Philips' Life," 171.

24. Keeney, "Dirk Philips," 19.

25. Koolman, *Dirk Philips*, 1.

26. Koolman, "Joachim Kükenbieter," 161.

Although Dirk's education level is not known, his writings indicate that he probably attended school and had an above average education.[27] There is no doubt that he knew Latin. In his writings, he inserts some Latin sentences, and he provides paraphrases of Latin in Dutch. It is also certain that he knew Greek and Hebrew. However, it is unclear whether he had a deep understanding of Greek and Hebrew words or phrases, because the Greek and Hebrew words he used were not numerous, nor did the words he used require deep understanding. In addition, he probably knew German because he spent most of his time after 1537 in northern Germany.[28]

Dirk was baptized between Christmas in 1533 and Candlemas in 1534.[29] The person who baptized him was Pieter Houtsagher. In order to know who Pieter Houtsagher was, Jan Mathys, Houtsagher's mentor, and the Dutch Anabaptist movement need to be understood first. The Dutch Anabaptist movement began in 1530 with Melchior Hoffman,[30] but his ministry was not long. On December 6, 1531, Jan Volkertszoon, who was one of Hoffman's converts and later became the leader of the congregation, was executed in Amsterdam. In 1533, Melchior Hoffman, who had established an Anabaptist congregation in the Netherlands, was arrested and imprisoned. After the execution of Jan Volkertszoon and the imprisonment of Melchior Hoffman, the Dutch Anabaptists became confused. At this time, the emerging figure was Jan Matthys, a baker from Haarlem. He began organizing Hoffman followers and sent twelve apostles to various areas to baptize people and ordain bishops.[31]

One of the places where the Apostles traveled was Leeuwarden of Friesland. Bartel de Boeckbinder and William Cuiper, who were sent there as apostles, baptized Obbe Philips and Hans Scheerder and delegated them as preachers to lead the congregation. The two immediately began a trip around Leeuwarden to take on the task entrusted to them. When Obbe and Hans left, another apostle, Pieter Houtsagher, who Jan

---

27. Keeney argues that although there is no positive evidence, Dirk may have attended a university. See Keeney, "Dirk Philips' Life," 173.

28. Keeney, "Dirk Philips' Life," 173–74.

29. The baptism of Dirk Philips is described in detail in Obbe Philips's "Confession" (see *BRN*, VII:89–138). For an English translation, see Williams et al., *Spiritual and Anabaptist Writers*, 206–25.

30. Krahn, *Dutch Anabaptism*, 92.

31. Keeney, "Dirk Philips," 23.

Matthys had sent, appeared in Leeuwarden and baptized Dirk Philips. Both Obbe and Dirk Philips were baptized by Jan Matthys' disciple.

However, shortly after Dirk was baptized, shocking events happened to Matthys and his apostles. Three apostles who had previously visited Leeuwarden, Bartel de Boeckbinder, William Cuiper, and Pieter Houtsagher, ran on the streets of Amsterdam on March 22, 1534, proclaiming that the day of the Lord had come, waving their swords. They were immediately arrested, and they were eventually executed in Haarlem.[32]

Meanwhile, Jan Matthys led a violent revolutionary movement. He occupied the city of Münster with his believers, who supported his revolution. However, they were soon besieged by the Catholic bishop Franz von Waldeck. Eventually, in April 1534, Jan Matthys was killed by the bishop's army. Since then, there was an effort to restore the violent movement. Jan van Batenburg continued to use armed tactics with the remnant, but he was captured and executed, and eventually, the violent revolutionary movement of Anabaptists ended.[33]

There is no detailed record of the events of Dirk Philips's life after the fall of Münster. Perhaps this is due to the use of aliases or identity codes in letters and writings in an effort to avoid being found by the authorities.[34] Yet the information available for this period reveals that Dirk's importance in the Dutch Anabaptist movement seems to have increased during this time. Jan van Batenburg, after being arrested in 1538, was tortured, and submitted the name of "principal baptizers," which included dozens of names. On that list, Batenburg included David Joris first, followed by Obbe and Dirk Philips.[35]

A decisive event in this movement occurred in the late 1530s. Obbe became disillusioned with his baptism and his ordination as bishop, and left the movement. Dirk was shocked at his brother's departure, but he was unwavering, and he held himself firmly. Fortunately, the appearance of Menno Simons was crucial in maintaining the movement. Menno made a great contribution to the survival and spread of the movement after Obbe left. Dirk also helped Menno and made contributions to the movement.[36]

32. Keeney, "Dirk Philips," 23.
33. Keeney, "Dirk Philips," 25.
34. Keeney, "Dirk Philips' Life," 176.
35. Hullu, *Bescheiden Betreffende de Hervorming in Overijssel*, 252.
36. Koolman, *Dirk Philips*, 19–22.

Traces of cooperation between Dirk Philips and Menno Simons are found in their participation in the ordination of Gillis van Aken and Adam Pastor. Dirk seemed to ordain them in 1542 with Menno, at which time Dirk and Menno also sent other preachers to various places.[37] After that, Dirk was prominent in several debates. The first debate was with Nikolaas Meyndertsz van Blesdijk. Nikolaas, who was once a follower of Menno, later became a follower of David Joris, claiming that he had received special revelation. This led to controversy in Lübeck in 1546, and among those involved in the debate were Menno Simons, Gillis van Aken, and Adam Pastor. The main issues of the debate were the forms of baptism and church organization. David Joris insisted on baptizing young children and on attending Roman, Lutheran, or Reformed Church worship to avoid persecution. For him, the external form was not important; only inner faith was important.[38]

In 1547, the second debate at Emden took place. The main issue of the debate was the avoidance of those who were excommunicated. Menno and Dirk maintained a strict stance, suggesting that it is best to avoid an excommunicated person, even a husband or wife. However, they did not enforce this view by legal code. Also discussed in this debate were marriage issues outside the faith and the incarnation of Christ.[39] In fact, the debate with Nikolaas—the previous debate—revealed that Adam Pastor had doubts about the divinity of Jesus Christ. Because of this, the debate at Emden had to deal with the incarnation of Christ, and there was an additional debate in Goch later that same year. In this debate, it is clear that Adam Pastor denied not only the divinity of Christ but also the Trinity; and in the end, Adam Pastor was excommunicated. Dirk was the executive responsible for the excommunication.[40]

It is likely that Dirk's headquarters moved to northern Germany in the 1550s. It is certain that he participated in several important meetings in the region of northern Germany at this time.[41] Since Pastor did

---

37. Keeney, "Dirk Philips' Life," 177. Regarding the time of ordination, it says that it took place between 1542 and 1547 in *BRN*, VII:50.

38. Keeney, "Dirk Philips," 26.

39. Keeney, "Dirk Philips," 27.

40. Koolman, *Dirk Philips*, 34–35.

41. Koolman cautiously argues that Dirk might have stayed at Emden in the East Frisia region. See Koolman, *Dirk Philips*, 47. Keeney claims that Dirk stayed in northern Germany at this time, but he does not mention a specific area. See Keeney, "Dirk Philips," 27.

not acknowledge the decision in Goch in 1547, another debate was held at Lübeck in 1552 at his request, with Dirk also participating. However, Dirk's position on Pastor's doctrine was firm, and Dirk had already opposed Pastor's assertion in his various treatises without referring to his name.[42]

In 1554, Dirk assembled at a secret place in Mecklenburg with other elders to discuss the issue of Gillis van Aken. At some point before this meeting, Gillis had perhaps been suspended or excommunicated for having committed adultery.[43] At this meeting, Gillis was restored to his position. Another important meeting was held in 1554 in Wismar, where seven elders, including Dirk, participated, and as a result of the meeting, they produced nine articles.[44]

In 1555, an event that led to the division of the Anabaptist movement occurred. In Emden, Leenaert Bouwens excommunicated Swaen Rutgers' husband, and claimed that Swaen Rutgers must avoid her husband. Nevertheless, because she had not avoided her husband from the bed and table, Leenaert Bouwens excommunicated her as well, even though she was a devout woman. In this situation, Menno stood on Leenaert's side, and Dirk also supported Leenaert. At the meeting held in Harlingen for this matter, the extreme leadership of Leenaert was supported by leaders in the movement including Menno and Dirk and, as a result, the more moderate positions of Franekers and Waterlanders became divided from the extreme position of Bouwens and his followers.[45]

In 1565 there was a disagreement over choosing Jeroen Tinnegieter as a pastor in Friesland. The conflict between the Frisian and the Flemish caused this problem. To solve this problem, the elders held meetings in Harlingen, where it was revealed that the four churches in Franeker, Dokkum, Leeuwarden, and Harlingen had previously made a covenant called the "Ordinance of the four cities." Dirk opposed this covenant and insisted that "Scriptures alone should be the basis for the actions in the

---

42. Koolman, *Dirk Philips*, 50.

43. Koolman speculates that Gillis would have been suspended. See Koolman, *Dirk Philips*, 52. On the other hand, Keeney argues that he was banned. See Keeney, "Dirk Philips," 28.

44. Mennonite historian Nanne van der Zijpp calls the nine articles the Wismar Resolutions; others called them the Wismar Articles. See van der Zijpp, "Wismar Resolutions." A letter by Menno Simons mentions Wismar's work. See Simons, "Instruction on Discipline," 1041–42.

45. Koolman, *Dirk Philips*, 84–86.

Christian congregation."⁴⁶ After that, the conflict between the Frisian and the Flemish continued, and Dirk sent "Epistle to Four Cities" on September 19, 1566, to deal with this problem.⁴⁷ Even after Dirk's efforts to resolve the conflict, the conflict became even more intense. Dirk stayed at Emden in his later years and died there in 1568.

Literature Review: The History of Anabaptist and Dirk Philips Studies

The growing interest in the Anabaptists dates back to the mid-nineteenth century. This phenomenon was caused by the people's challenge to the state-church and the growth of the free church movement.⁴⁸ In this context, C. A. Cornelius's *Geschichte des Munsterischen Aufruhrs*,⁴⁹ published in 1855, provided an important opportunity for the study of Anabaptists. This work, unlike the writings in the past that merely attacked the Anabaptist movement, did not evaluate the Anabaptists with antipathy, but rather drew attention to their original writings. Later, *Ein Apostle der Wiedertäufer*,⁵⁰ published in 1882 by Ludwig Keller, helped many people distinguish Hans Denck as a spiritualist, and Keller did various activities thereafter.⁵¹ Since then, Ernst Troeltsch and Max Weber's publications have contributed greatly to the study of the Anabaptists.⁵²

---

46. Keeney, "Dirk Philips," 33.
47. Philips, "Epistle to Four Cities," 476–88.
48. Estep, *Anabaptist Story*, 2.
49. Cornelius, *Geschichte Des Münsterischen Aufruhrs*.
50. Keller, *Ein Apostle Der Wiedertäufer*.
51. Between 1880 and 1914 Ludwig Keller published 10 books on the Age of Reformation. Amalie Keller analyzes Ludwig Keller's writings as follows, "In all the writings he aimed to demonstrate that the reformatory movements were considerably older than was usually assumed; that the 'old evangelical' congregations had taken over ideas from the early Christian congregations and that the Anabaptist movement of the Reformation represented a widely spread phenomenon" (Keller, "Ludwig Keller," 159).
52. Hershberger provides a detailed list of Anabaptist studies published in the nineteenth and early twentieth centuries (Hershberger, *Recovery of the Anabaptist Vision*, 1–10). Eire describes Troeltsch and Max Weber thusly: "thanks largely to the work of Max Weber (1864-1920) and Ernst Troeltsch (1865-1923), founders of modern sociology, a new narrative emerged in which the dissenters were no longer on the margins, but rather at the cutting edge of the Reformation" (Eire, *Reformations*, 252).

Twentieth-Century Anabaptist Studies

The publication of "The Anabaptist Vision" in 1944 was a significant development in the studies of the Anabaptists. Harold S. Bender, the author of "The Anabaptist Vision," desired to make the Mennonite church honorable in church history and in the history of the sixteenth-century Reformation.[53] Bender, who supported Ernst Troeltsch's views on the origin of Anabaptism,[54] sought to differentiate Anabaptists from mystics and spiritualists, as well as from the practitioners of violence observed in Thomas Müntzer and the Peasants' War.[55] Bender argues that Anabaptism has suffered many misunderstandings, and he says, "Anabaptism is the culmination of the Reformation, the fulfillment of the original vision of Luther and Zwingli, and thus makes it a consistent evangelical Protestantism seeking to recreate without compromise the original New Testament church, the vision of Christ and the Apostles."[56]

In 1927, Bender founded The *Mennonite Quarterly Review*, the first North American journal about Mennonites. The journal has proliferated and has played an important role in researching Mennonites from the sixteenth century to the present. Bender's influence has gradually expanded, and a group of Anabaptist scholars known as the Bender School appeared in the first half of the twentieth century. These scholars were Harold Bender, Fritz Blanke, Guy F. Hershberger, Robert Friedmann, J.C. Wenger, Melvin Gingerich, Franklin H. Littell, Donovan Smucker, Cornelius Krahn, John H. Yoder, and Clarence Bauman.[57] These men published a number of works with vigorous activity and have consistently maintained that there is essentially no fundamental difference between evangelical Anabaptists and the Magisterial Reformers.[58]

---

53. Klaassen, "'There Were Giants on Earth,'" 233.

54. Troeltsch classifies the Anabaptists as a "sect" type and clearly distinguishes them from the "mystic" type mystics and spiritualists (Troeltsch, *Die Sozialleheren Der Christlichen Kirchen Und Gruppen*, 794–815).

55. Bender, "Anabaptist Vision," 8.

56. Bender, "Anabaptist Vision," 9.

57. The list of Bender School characters is not always consistent. See Walton, *John Howard Yoder*, 18, and Choi, "Centrality of Andreas Karlstadt," 18.

58. Research on the Anabaptists was actively conducted in the Baptist camp. These studies are about the origins of Baptists, and the main discussion topic is the extent of the relationship between Anabaptists and Baptists. According to Hudson, the early Baptists considered themselves different from the Anabaptists, but by the nineteenth century, Baptists themselves asserted continuity with the Anabaptists. However, this

As a result of this growing interest in the Anabaptists in the past few decades, essential works of the Anabaptist study have been published. The most striking work in the second half of the twentieth century is George Huntston Williams' *The Radical Reformation*.[59] Because *The Radical Reformation* contains a large amount of Anabaptist history and covers most of the major Anabaptist leaders, it is an indispensable source to the study of sixteenth-century Anabaptism. Williams gives an overview of the Radical Reformation that took place in the sixteenth century, discussing a large part of Europe where the movement appeared. In addition, the book includes an extensive introduction to the activities and thought of most of the movement's leaders. The book consists of chapters on areas and persons involved in the Radical Reformation, but it also describes the Radical Reformation chronologically. Although the book is not divided according to a specific theological theme, each chapter effectively introduces the theological controversies that the movement's leaders were associated with.

Williams also follows the Bender School tradition. He explains the characteristics of the Radical Reformation as follows: "The proponents of the Radical Reformation, espous[ed] the faithful restoration of the apostolic church," and he says that it was especially "the Anabaptists [who] were most confident in being able to reproduce the structure of apostolic Christianity from the New Testament."[60] He regards the Radical Reformation as "a wholly original collection of independent dissenters" rather than as the left-wingers or sectarians of the Magisterial Reformers, and he divides the Radicals as three types: Anabaptists, Spiritualists, and Evangelical Rationalists (Anti-Trinitarians). He also proposes various subcategories in each type.[61]

---

situation was reversed again in the twentieth century. Hudson also emphasizes the differences and discontinuity between Baptists and Anabaptists; he recognizes the Anabaptists as those who rejected the doctrine of justification by faith and original sin, and pursued biblical literalism. See Hudson, "Who Were the Baptists?," 303–12; Hudson, "Who Were the Baptists?," 53–55. Payne, on the other hand, disagrees with Hudson. According to him, Hudson's criticism of the Anabaptists does not correspond to all Anabaptists, and he claims that many groups of Anabaptists are stepchildren of the Reformation. See Payne, "Who Were the Baptists?," 339–42.

59. Williams, *Radical Reformation*.

60. Williams, *Radical Reformation*, xxviii.

61. Eire adequately summarizes Williams's argument in *Reformations*, 253–55.

INTRODUCTION 15

In 1972, Claus-Peter Clasen published *Anabaptism: A Social History, 1525–1618: Switzerland, Austria, Moravia, South and Central Germany.*[62] Like Williams, Clasen is in the line of the Bender School tradition. He demonstrates that the Anabaptists' practical life shows that the group has inherited traditional Christianity. In this book, Clasen also discusses the social history of sixteenth-century Anabaptism, discussing the Anabaptists' view of church discipline while dealing with their social and spiritual life. He describes the Anabaptists as a group who organized their congregations for a spiritual purpose. However, Clasen insists that "the Anabaptists attached much importance to the exercise of the ban, just as they did to the establishment of a congregation of true believers."[63]

One year later, in 1973, Robert Friedmann published a book entitled *The Theology of Anabaptism: An Interpretation*. In this book, he underscored that the theology of Anabaptism pursues the restoration of the gospel, reviving the theology of the Kingdom of God, and he argued that Anabaptism should not be merely regarded as part of the Radical Reformation or "Protestantism plus more emphasis on ethics."[64]

In 1975, another book essential to the sixteenth-century Anabaptism research was published. In this book, *The Anabaptist Story*, William Roscoe Estep provides the history of Anabaptist origins, their theology, and extensive information regarding Anabaptist research.[65] Estep introduces various stories that have developed from the beginning of the Anabaptist movement. Following the tradition of the Bender School, Estep argues against the failure of some scholars to differentiate Anabaptism from mysticism and spiritualists, and insists that the nature of the Anabaptists has been misunderstood because of this unclear distinction. The book focuses on a specific area and person in each chapter, and it follows a roughly time-based order. Estep thoroughly points out that the theological controversy that arose in the process of the Anabaptist movement's origin and its development was due to the conflicts and problems that they faced.

The scholars of the Bender School were not the only the voices in the study of Anabaptism in the twentieth century. Others were the followers

---

62. Clasen, *Anabaptism*.
63. Clasen, *Anabaptism*, 109.
64. Friedmann, *Theology of Anabaptism*, 159.
65. Estep, *Anabaptist Story*.

in the tradition of Karl Holl, who contended with Ernst Troeltsch, arguing that Anabaptism cannot be distinguished from mysticism.[66]

The most important figure of this group is Hans J. Hillerbrand. In his famous article "Origin of Sixteenth-Century Anabaptism: Another Look," published in 1962, Hillerbrand argues that those who influenced the beginning of Swiss Anabaptism were Karlstadt and Müntzer, as well as Luther and Zwingli.[67] In his relatively recent book, *A New History of Christianity*, published in 2012, Hillerbrand continues to hold this position.[68] In 1975, the polygenesis theory of Anabaptist origins emerged in an article entitled, "From Monogenesis to Polygenesis: The Historical Discussion of Anabaptist Origins" by James M. Stayer, Werner O. Packull, and Klaus Deppermann.[69] Unlike Hillerbrand, they argue that Anabaptism did not originate in one place under the influence of various groups, but rather in various places. According to them, the history of Anabaptist origins "must devote itself to studying plural origins of Anabaptism and their significance for the plural character of the movement."[70] In 1987, J. Denny Weaver wrote *Becoming Anabaptist*, a book dealing with the origin of sixteenth-century Anabaptism.[71] In this book, he presents an alternative to the Polygenesis theory. He acknowledges the diverse origins of Anabaptism but he sees a common denominator in their theological development. He says, "diverse movements do constitute a common historical tradition whose development we can follow to the present."[72]

In the late twentieth century, a monumental event occurred that brought about an epoch-making transition to the study of the sixteenth-century Anabaptists. It is now possible for English-language scholars and readers to read the writings of sixteenth-century Anabaptist leaders. *The Classics of the Radical Reformation* series is the translation and publication of the primary works of the major Anabaptists in the late fifteenth, sixteenth, and early seventeenth centuries. A total of thirteen books have published, each volume containing scholarly and critical editions. In

---

66. Holl, "Luther Und Die Schwarmer," 420. The book was first published in 1911, and it has been translated and published in English under the title *The Cultural Significance of the Reformation*.

67. Hillerbrand, "Origin of Sixteenth-Century Anabaptism," 152–80.

68. Hillerbrand, *New History of Christianity*.

69. Stayer et al., "From Monogenesis to Polygenesis," 83–121.

70. Stayer et al., "From Monogenesis to Polygenesis," 85.

71. Weaver, *Becoming Anabaptist*.

72. Weaver, *Becoming Anabaptist*, 117.

1973, the first volume, *The Legacy of Michael Sattler*,[73] was released, and the ninth volume, *Peter Riedemann's Hutterite Confession of Faith*,[74] was published in 1998. In addition, the series includes *The Writings of Pilgram Marpeck*,[75] *Anabaptism in Outline*,[76] *The Sources of Swiss Anabaptism: The Grebel Letters and Related Documents*,[77] *Balthasar Hubmaier: The Theologian of Anabaptism*,[78] *The Writings of Dirk Philips, 1504-1568*,[79] *The Anabaptist Writings of David Joris, 1535-1543*,[80] *The Essential Carlstadt: Fifteen Tracts by Andreas Bodenstein (Carlstadt) from Karlstadt*,[81] *Sources of South German/ Austrian Anabaptism*,[82] *Confessions of Faith in the Anabaptist Tradition 1527-1660*,[83] *Jörg Maler's Kunstbuch: writings of the Pilgram Marpeck circle*,[84] *Later Writings of the Swiss Anabaptists 1529-1592*.[85]

The Study of Anabaptist Ecclesiology

The recent increase in interest in Anabaptism has naturally led to an interest in the ecclesiology of sixteenth-century Anabaptism because that "which unites the early Anabaptists is the agenda of issues they were probing, particularly in the sphere of ecclesiology."[86] Perhaps the most critical and comprehensive publication on the subject is *The Anabaptist View of the Church*, published in 1952 by Franklin Hamlin Littell.[87] In this

73. Yoder and Sattler, *Legacy of Michael Sattler*.
74. Riedemann, *Hutterite Confession of Faith*.
75. Marbeck et al., *Writings of Pilgram Marpeck*.
76. Klaassen, *Anabaptism in Outline*.
77. Harder and Grebel, *Sources of Swiss Anabaptism*.
78. Hubmaier, *Balthasar Hubmaier*.
79. Philips, *Writings of Dirk Philips*.
80. Joris, *Anabaptist Writings of David Joris*.
81. Karlstadt, *Essential Carlstadt*.
82. Snyder, *Sources of South German/Austrian Anabaptism*.
83. Koop, *Confessions of Faith in the Anabaptist Tradition*.
84. Rempel, *Jörg Maler's Kunstbuch*.
85. Snyder, *Later Writings of the Swiss Anabaptists*.
86. Colwell, "Radical Church," 120.
87. Littell, *Anabaptist View of the Church: An Introduction to Sectarian Protestantism*. This book was revised and enlarged and published in 1958 as the second edition. See Littell, *Anabaptist View of the Church: A Study in the Origins of Sectarian Protestantism*.

book, Littell argues that the Anabaptist movement has not been treated fairly so far. According to Littell, the center of the Anabaptist view of the church is its concern for restoring the true church. Littell claims that this concern takes precedence over their theological and political matters.

Two years after this book's publication, Theron Douglas Price gave a favorable appraisal of Littell's work in his article "The Anabaptist View of the Church." He said, "it is perhaps not too much to say that Littell's book opens up new possibilities for Reformation research along with a fairly wide front."[88] In the article, Price analyzes the Anabaptist view of the church in its distinctive character, and he explains how this view controlled Anabaptists' understanding of the Christian's relationship to society. He admits that some leaders of Anabaptism held radical ecclesiology, such as Müntzer and Karlstadt, who supported social revolt. But he argues that these Radicals were only a small number of the Anabaptists as a whole. Most of the evangelical Anabaptists' ecclesiology was characterized by their emphasis on the Christian's personal life and the congregation's need for discipline. In addition, Anabaptists had a vision of discipline that was not merely for their own communities, but for the church as a whole. According to Price, they had "the vision of a corporate body in which Christ takes up habitation by the Spirit, and through which he reigns in the world."[89]

In his book *The Believers' Church: The History and Character of Radical Protestantism*, Donald F. Durnbaugh devotes the third chapter to the Anabaptists. In the book, Durnbaugh mainly deals with the history of believers' church, and he describes the Anabaptist movement as an important part of the believers' church.[90] Durnbaugh points out that since the early church, members of the church have included both believers and unbelievers, and he says that in the believers' church, people becomes a member of the church based on their confession of faith.

In 1984, Peter H. Davids attempted a more theological analysis of Anabaptist ecclesiology in his article "An Anabaptist View of the Church,"[91] which examines three major points of view regarding the church within Anabaptism. The first is the church as the kingdom of God. Since Anabaptists saw "a radical dualism in the universe: good vs.

---

88. Price, "Anabaptist View of the Church," 190.
89. Price, "Anabaptist View of the Church," 196.
90. Durnbaugh, *Believers' Church*, 18–22.
91. Davids, "Anabaptist View of the Church," 81–93.

evil, light vs. darkness, the kingdom of God vs. the world," the church is the only present realization of the kingdom of God in this world.[92] The second is the church as a foreign nation, which means that their members must live a different life from this world. Because church members are transferred from the old to the new at the moment they were baptized, they "must always be conscious of a higher loyalty than the state."[93] The third is the church as an alternative community; namely, they have their own activities and structure. To illustrate this point, Davids introduces three concepts: (1) Anabaptists prized Scripture highly; (2) they celebrated the Lord's supper; (3) they had the concept of the role of the Servant of the word.

In 1986, Ronald David Rogers insisted that the doctrines of salvation and the church closely related to the life and thought of the Anabaptists in his doctoral dissertation entitled, "The Relationship of Soteriology and Ecclesiology in Sixteenth-Century Evangelical Anabaptism."[94] In this dissertation, he examines the relationship of these two doctrines in Anabaptist belief and practice, but he limits his work by studying only four major Anabaptists leaders: Michael Sattler, Pilgram Marpeck, Menno Simons, and Peter Riedemann. Five major points of the dissertation are as follows: (1) the soteriology of the four evangelical Anabaptist leaders was found to be foundational for their ecclesiology; (2) the church was the arena for the demonstration of salvation in Anabaptist life and thought; (3) the nature of the church was largely determined by the doctrine of salvation; (4) the ordinances of the church were portrayals of salvation; (5) witness was seen as both an individual and a corporate responsibility.[95]

The following year, John E. Colwell, in his article "A Radical Church: A Reappraisal of Anabaptist Ecclesiology," examined the distinctive ecclesiological perceptions of Anabaptists.[96] According to Colwell, the practice of baptism was the most obvious distinctive feature among Anabaptist groups. The practice of baptism meant an expression of devotion to community life beyond a simple expression of individual faith, an emphasis which was different than that of the reformers. Regarding the eschatology and ecclesiology of the Anabaptists, Colwell found that there

---

92. Davids, "Anabaptist View of the Church," 82.
93. Davids, "Anabaptist View of the Church," 86.
94. Rogers, "Relationship of Soteriology and Ecclesiology."
95. Rogers, "Relationship of Soteriology and Ecclesiology," 159–61.
96. Colwell, "Radical Church," 120.

were some forms of extreme ecclesiology and eschatology, such as the views of Thomas Müntzer, but others such as Peter Riedemann, Menno Simons, Michael Sattler, and Pilgram Marpeck rejected the concept of a "sacral society" and refused to use any violence.

In 1988, William Roscoe Estep argued in his article "The Ecumenical Implications of Menno Simons' View of the Church" that there are many ecumenical concepts in the writings of Menno Simons.[97] He says that because of his departure from the Catholic Church, Menno has hardly been considered one who was eager for ecumenical dialogue. However, according to Estep, Menno's ecumenical implications are found in four areas of his thought: his Christology, his view of the Holy Spirit, his principle of voluntarism, and his view of the church.

In studying the ecclesiology of the Anabaptists, it is worth noting that in addition to two marks of the Protestant church, baptism and the Lord's Supper, their view of church discipline has attracted the attention of many theologians and historians. Why is church discipline important in Anabaptist ecclesiology? Perhaps it is because the Anabaptists understood baptism and the Lord's Supper as integral parts of the Christian life. Therefore, it is natural that theologians and historians are interested in the practical life of the Anabaptists, who had always longed to restore the holy Christian community.[98] There have been many attempts to explain Anabaptists' view of church discipline. In 1955, Robert Friedmann wrote an article entitled "The Oldest Church Discipline of the Anabaptists."[99] In this article, Friedmann examines the oldest church discipline document of the Anabaptists, which is called *Brotherly Union of Several Children of God*, commonly and briefly called the *Seven Articles*. These are the Seven Articles adopted at Schleitheim, Switzerland, on February 24, 1526.

Kenneth R. Davis examines the influence of the Anabaptists on the traditional Reformed view of church discipline in his article "No Discipline, No Church: An Anabaptist Contribution to the Reformed Tradition" in 1982.[100] He argues that the influence of the Anabaptists on the Reformed tradition can be found in Martin Bucer. Although Bucer avoided Anabaptist separatism, it is clear that he was affected by the church discipline of the Anabaptists. Calvin was also affected by the

---

97. Estep, "Ecumenical Implications," 356–67.
98. Davis, "No Discipline, No Church," 43–58.
99. Friedmann, "Oldest Church Discipline of the Anabaptists," 162–66.
100. Davis, "No Discipline, No Church," 43–58.

Anabaptists, but less than Bucer. According to Davis, Anabaptist church discipline was closely related to their views of baptism and moral intention. Thus, the ban in the Anabaptists was also an essential church discipline.[101] Timothy E. Fulop supported Davis' claims. In his article entitled "The Third Mark of the Church? Church Discipline in the Reformed and Anabaptist Reformations" in 1995, Fulop argues that Calvin's view of church discipline was more moderate than Luther's and Zwingli's, and he claims that Calvin was influenced in his view of discipline by the Anabaptists through Bucer.[102]

In 1983, Marlin Miller wrote an article that examines three major points of a Mennonite understanding of discipleship and the church. Its title is "The Church in the World: A Mennonite Perspective."[103] Miller's first point is that the Mennonite understanding of discipleship and the church presupposes a concept of grace. Unlike the view of traditional Lutherans, Mennonites perceived the reality of "grace alone." The second point is that the Mennonites viewed the life of faith as a life of discipleship. The life of faith is not merely "understood primarily in terms of giving assent to the correct doctrinal beliefs, even though right teaching remains important."[104] The third point is that the Mennonites emphasized that newly born Christians must live in relation to the life of the community. Moreover, "the Church as the community of grace is to exist not for itself but for the world."[105]

In 1992, Stephen B. Boyd discussed the life and theology of Pilgram Marpeck in *Pilgram Marpeck: His Life and Social Theology*, a revision of his doctoral dissertation. In this book, he attempted to describe Marpeck's activities, as well as the social and political circumstances that he influenced and that influenced him.[106] He also pointed out the connection between Marpeck's Christology and his ecclesiology. According to Boyd, the privotal role of Marpeck's theology is the incarnation and the cross of Christ.[107] Marpeck saw the cross of Christ as deeply related to the earthly stage of believers. In other words, a new kingdom or realm began

---

101. Davis, "No Discipline, No Church," 47.
102. Fulop, "Third Mark of the Church?," 26–42.
103. Miller, "Church in the World," 45–50.
104. Miller, "Church in the World," 46.
105. Miller, "Church in the World," 49.
106. Boyd, *Pilgram Marpeck*, 3.
107. Boyd, *Pilgram Marpeck*, 71.

through the cross of Christ, and therefore "the Christian takes on this cross, not primarily for the sake of continued self-purification, but for the sake of bringing the justice and reconciliation of Christ to the world."[108]

In the book *Erasmus, the Anabaptists, and the Great Commission*, published in 1998, Abraham Friesen introduces Erasmus' unique interpretation of the Great Commission of Matthew 28 and he discusses the impact of this interpretation on the Anabaptists. According to Friesen, Erasmus' idea had a profound impact on the Anabaptists' understanding of believers' baptism, and this influence extends to Swiss brethren, South German Anabaptism, and Mennonites.[109]

Malcolm B. Yarnell, professor of systematic theology at Southwestern Baptist theological seminary, studied believers' church in his book *The Formation of Christian Doctrine*, published in 2007. In this book, he considers the foundation of proper doctrine development from the perspective of the believers' church.[110] He chose Pilgram Marpeck, an Anabaptist leader in southern Germany, as the person who provided the foundation of believers' church theology. According to Yarnell, Marpeck's theological principles are "Christocentrism, correlation of Word and Spirit, stress on the biblical order while opposing human theological invention, and covenant ecclesiology."[111]

Simon Victor Goncharenko, in his doctoral dissertation published in 2011, "The Importance of Church Discipline within Balthasar Hubmaier's Theology," focuses on the views of one particular Anabaptist leader, Balthasar Hubmaier, on church discipline.[112] Goncharenko explains that the doctrine of church discipline is of profound importance to the theology of Balthasar Hubmaier. Goncharenko also argues that among the various aspects of Hubmaier's theology, the doctrine of church discipline was closely interrelated with his doctrines of anthropology, soteriology, and ecclesiology. Therefore, in order to grasp the centrality of Hubmaier's doctrine of church discipline accurately, Goncharenko believes that it is essential to explore the various aspects of Hubmaier's theology because of their deep connection to the doctrine of church discipline.

---

108. Boyd, *Pilgram Marpeck*, 83.
109. Friesen, *Erasmus, the Anabaptists, and the Great Commission*, 56–63.
110. Yarnell, *Formation of Christian Doctrine*, 1.
111. Yarnell, *Formation of Christian Doctrine*, 104.
112. Goncharenko, "Importance of Church Discipline."

The Study of Dutch Anabaptism and Dirk Philips

Perhaps the most notable achievement in the study of the sixteenth-century Dutch Anabaptism is *Dutch Anabaptism: Origin, Spread, Life, and Thought (1450–1600)* by Cornelius Krahn, published in 1968.[113] In *Dutch Anabaptism*, Krahn focuses on the period from 1450 to 1600. Because of its focus on this time period, this book examines with the emergence of the Mennonites as well as the deepening of the Radical Reformation that took place in the Netherlands before the Mennonites. The main reason that this book should be regarded as most important for Dutch Anabaptism research is that it deals thoroughly with the Radical Reformation in the Netherlands. Krahn deals with the emergence and proliferation of humanism that enabled the Reformation, as well as the emergence of its symbolism as the reaction against Catholic sacraments. Since Melchior Hoffman is a key figure in enabling the beginning of the Dutch Reformation, Krahn examines how Hoffman's movement spread in Strassburg and the Netherlands. Krahn also discusses some of the spiritualists, such as David Joris and Adam Pastor, as well as the connection between Menno Simons and the movement in Münster.

Another critical source on Dutch Anabaptism research is *The Development of Dutch Anabaptist Thought and Practice from 1539–1564* by William Keeney, one of the foremost authorities on Dirk Philips in the twentieth century. This book was written in 1968.[114] The main difference between this book and Krahn's work is that Keeney focuses on the Mennonites. Keeney compares the thought of Menno Simons and Dirk Philips, the two leaders of the early Mennonites, dealing extensively with the two leaders' doctrines of God, the Bible, Christ, and salvation, and he deals with some aspects of their views of church discipline. After examining the various theological perspectives of Dutch Anabaptists, Keeney concludes that there were no great differences between Dutch Anabaptists and other Christians.[115] Keeney also argues that the range of Dutch Anabaptist theology is quite wide. For example, their interpretation of the Scriptures and their epistemology, as well as their views of the sacraments, their emphasis on sanctification, and their view of the

---

113. Krahn, *Dutch Anabaptism*.

114. Keeney, *Development of Dutch Anabaptist Thought and Practice*. This book is a revision of his doctoral dissertation, which was published in 1959 (see Keeney, "Development of Dutch Anabaptist Thought and Practice."

115. Keeney, *Development of Dutch Anabaptist Thought and Practice*, 191.

church, are similar to those of the Calvinists, but some of their theology was also similar to those of the evangelical spiritualists.[116] The author also asserts that their Christocentric interpretation of the Scripture and the consequent discontinuity between the Old and New Testaments characterize Dutch Anabaptist theology as being the most distinctive feature of the reformers. In relation to church discipline, Keeney insists that both Calvinists and the Mennonites have argued for the need for discipline, but that the Mennonites' view emphasizes that the church is separate from the world.

Timothy George has placed Menno Simons in line with other Magisterial Reformers such as Luther, Calvin, and Zwingli in his book *Theology of the Reformers*.[117] In the study of Mennonites, as their name indicates, Menno Simons has been treated as the most important figure, and it cannot be denied that he made the most decisive contribution to the formation of the Mennonites. Thus, the interest in Menno Simons is natural.

However, the popularity of Menno Simons does not mean that his theological contribution is better than Dirk's. As one who established a new community called the Mennonites, Menno might have been better at leadership than Dirk in the organization, but it is not an exaggeration to say that Dirk was superior to Menno in theological ability.[118] Even though Estep rarely devotes space to Dirk's theology in his book, he sees Dirk Philips's writings as equal to those of Menno. In fact, in some respects, they are better. Estep also says, "no Anabaptist work of the sixteenth century surpassed the influence of [Dirk's] Enchiridion."[119]

The most significant achievement in the study of Dirk Philips is by J. ten Doornkaat Koolman. His book *Dirk Philips: Friend and Colleague of Menno Simons, 1504–1568*,[120] which was first published in Dutch in 1964, is considered to be most important in research on Dirk Philips, and the value of this book is unique because there are few scholars and scholarly publications on him. This is the first biographical book on Dirk, and in this book, Koolman elaborates on his life journey from his birth

---

116. Keeney, *Development of Dutch Anabaptist Thought and Practice*, 192–93.

117. George, *Theology of the Reformers*.

118. Pijper, Keeney, and Shantz all agree that, as a theologian, Dirk was superior to Menno Simons. See BRN X:4; Keeney, *Development of Dutch Anabaptist Thought and Practice*, 18; Shantz, "Ecclesiological Focus," 116.

119. Estep, *Anabaptist Story*, 114.

120. Koolman, *Dirk Philips*.

to his death. Due to the chronological narrative, this book is structured by the passage of time, but it also portrays Dirk's writings and controversy effectively. In 1964, the same year that the book was published, Koolman published a short article entitled "First Edition of Dirk Philips' Enchiridion."[121] In the article, Koolman analyzes the first edition of *Enchiridion* by Dirk Philips at the University Library at Amsterdam. According to Koolman, the second edition of *Enchiridion* was published the same year as the first edition, and although these two editions have minor differences, they have no substantial differences. Koolman claims that the publication of *Enchiridion* came after 1564 and that the other writings of Dirk were not published before 1555.

One of the most notable publications on Dirk before Koolman's book is *Writings by Dirk Philips*, published in 1914 by Frederik Pijper, a professor at Leiden University.[122] This book was a collection of Dirk's works in Dutch and was the primary source for research on Dirk until 80 years after the English translation was published.[123]

Several years before Koolman's book was published, three English-language articles on Dirk were released. In 1957, Cornelius J. Dyck wrote an article on Dirk's Christology, entitled "Christology of Dirk Philips."[124] In this article, Dyck argues that Dirk held the doctrine that Christ was both fully divine by the Holy Spirit and fully man by physical human birth. According to Dyck, Dirk rejected any radical view of Christology that denied the divinity of Christ and claimed only humanity. Dyck says that Hoffman, Sebastian Franck, and Socinianism are examples of the radicalism that Dirk rejected, but he says that their false teachings did not threaten the Anabaptist group because Dirk and his community "simply believed that Christ was the Son of God and died for them."[125]

The following year (1958), a brief biography of Dirk was published by William Keeney, who later translated Koolman's book into English and wrote the biography of Dirk in the recently published *The Writings of Dirk Philips, 1504–1568*. This article, entitled "Dirk Philips' Life,"[126] describes the life of Dirk Philips chronologically, focusing on the specific events

---

121. Koolman, "First Edition of Dirk Philips' Enchiridion," 357–60.

122. *BRN* X.

123. An English translation of the entire work of Dirk Philips was first published in 1992.

124. Dyck, "Christology of Dirk Philips," 147–55.

125. Dyck, "Christology of Dirk Philips," 155.

126. Keeney, "Dirk Philips' Life."

in his life. Early in his career, Dirk had a connection with Münsterites, and later he had one with Menno. He participated in several theological debates and conferences; among them, the most striking discussion was the conference on the subject of the ban in Wismar. According to Keeney, Dirk broke with the Catholic Church because he thought the "hierarchical authority of the Roman Church had been destroyed in favor of new freedom through the individual interpretation of the Scripture."[127] In the end, Keeney evaluates Dirk Philips's life as "one of constant struggle to hold aloft and actualize a high vision of the Christian life and the church."[128]

In the same year that Keeney published "Dirk Philips' Life" (1958), he wrote another article, "The Writings of Dirk Philips,"[129] which is an introduction to the work of Dirk Philips. Keeney primarily focuses on Dirk's writing, and he briefly introduces the relationship between Dirk's work and the events behind it, as well as the characteristics of his works.

Keeney's interest in Dirk continued to expand and develop, and his book *The Development of Dutch Anabaptist Thought and Practice from 1539-1564* was published in 1968. Keeney also published a small article in 2004, near the end of his life.[130] Its title is "Research Note: 500th Anniversary of Dirk Philips," and Keeney published it in celebration of the 500th anniversary of Dirk's birth. In this article, Keeney provides six suggestions for theologians who want to study Dirk in the future.[131]

In 1975, Marja Keyser published a groundbreaking book in the study of Dirk Philips, entitled *Dirk Philips: 1504 - 1568: A Catalogue of His Printed Works in the University Library of Amsterdam*.[132] This book is a collection of primary source information on Dirk Philips, providing information about the copies that we currently have access to. Since the Mennonite Church Library was handed over to the University Library of Amsterdam in 1968, the University Library embarked on the task of recataloguing the early printed works of the Mennonite Church Library.

In 1986, Douglas H. Shantz penned an article entitled "The Ecclesiological Focus of Dirk Philips' Hermeneutical Thought in 1559: A

---

127. Keeney, "Dirk Philips' Life," 181.

128. Keeney, "Dirk Philips' Life," 191.

129. Keeney, "Writings of Dirk Philips."

130. Keeney passed away on November 12, 2006. See "Keeney, William Echard (1922–2006)."

131. Keeney, "Research Note," 558–59.

132. Keyser, *Dirk Philips*.

Contextual Study."¹³³ In this article, Shantz discusses the connection between Dirk Philips's ecclesiology and his hermeneutical thought. He believes that Dirk's hermeneutic originated not from a vacuum but from the broader context of events in his day and from his desire to bring about a pure church through the use of proper discipline. According to Shantz, "Dirk's central hermeneutic principle was 'ecclesiocentric,' focusing on the Body of Christ, the church."¹³⁴ Dirk's desire to establish a pure church governed his understanding of Christian preaching and interpretation.

The most recent dissertation on Dirk Philips is Rempel's doctoral dissertation in 1988, "Christology and Lord's Supper in Anabaptism: A Study in the Theology of Balthasar Hubmaier, Pilgram Marpeck, and Dirk Philips."¹³⁵ Rempel effectively describes the subtle differences in the theological views of the three figures. In the dissertation, Rempel points out that although Dirk Philips's Christology was formed under the influence of Melchior Hoffman and Menno Simons, he developed beyond the thought of his mentors.¹³⁶

The Importance of This Study

As mentioned above, the most significant feature of the twentieth-century study of the Anabaptists is that it is limited to the origin of the movement or an introductory study of the movement, and it focuses on only several leaders. This may be due to the short history of interest in the Anabaptists or the low number of scholars studying the Anabaptists. Beyond the introductory work of the movement, the scholarly exploration of the thoughts and life of the leaders of each group is limited. Moreover, considering that there are many leaders or groups in the Anabaptist movement, the limitations of the previous studies are clearer, and individual studies on the views pursued in each camp of the movement are necessary to understand the Anabaptist movement fully.

In this context, therefore, the importance of this study can be considered in two aspects. The first is to explore the thought of a great Anabaptist leader and a systematic theologian who has been hidden in history.

---

133. Shantz, "Ecclesiological Focus," 115–27.

134. Shantz, "Ecclesiological Focus," 127.

135. Rempel, "Christology and Lord's Supper in Anabaptism." This paper was later published in 1993 as a book. See Rempel, *Lord's Supper in Anabaptism*.

136. Rempel, "Christology and Lord's Supper in Anabaptism," 38.

Dirk's writings demonstrate not only theological excellence but also his influence within his group. Despite Dirk's theological excellence and his important contributions, he has not been properly addressed by theologians and historians. First of all, research on Dirk Philips is very rare. A biography of him in the form of a monograph was published only about half a century ago, and only two doctoral dissertations on Dirk's thought have been written, by William and Rempel. Though they have made great contributions to the study of Dirk's thought, their dissertations do not focus entirely on Dirk; only a portion of the dissertations allowed space to discuss him. Rempel's dissertation, "Christology and Lord's Supper in Anabaptism: A Study in the Theology of Balthasar Hubmaier, Pilgram Marpeck, and Dirk Philips," does a thorough investigation of Dirk's view of the Lord's supper, but since Rempel studied three Anabaptist leaders in his dissertation, he allowed only one chapter to Dirk. William's dissertation, "The Development of Dutch Anabaptist Thought and Practice from 1539–1564," deals with Dirk's theology on a variety of subjects, but it covers Menno Simons as well as Dirk in all subjects, as shown in the title of the dissertation. Therefore, in future research, it is necessary to concentrate on theological subjects in the study of Dirk. Focusing on his Christology, ecclesiology, soteriology, and anthropology in this study will be an essential contribution to the research.

Another critical point of this study is to highlight the concept of the visible church in the study of Anabaptist ecclesiology and to connect it with other theologies. As stated earlier, the main discussions in Anabaptist ecclesiology studies so far have been that Anabaptism has been misunderstood for a while, and that its ecclesiology is not essentially different from the ecclesiology of the Magisterial Reformers. This is due to the influence of the Bender School tradition. Those who claim the Polygenesis theory are also under the influence of the Bender School, at least in this matter; both groups agree on a clear distinction between those who pursued evangelical Anabaptism and those who pursued social revolt. Therefore, in this circumstance, the Anabaptist emphasis on the importance of the restoration of the pure church, which is the most important concept of Anabaptist ecclesiology, and their view of the importance of the visible church have not been dealt with in depth. Following the tradition of the Bender School, this dissertation also will argue that the theological stance of Dirk Philips's ecclesiology is not different from that of the Magisterial Reformers. In addition, this dissertation will thoroughly examine Dirk's perspective of the visible church, as well as the importance of his view, which has been overlooked.

Theologians and historians, of course, have not been entirely indifferent to the visible church in the study of the Anabaptists. This proves that there is interest in church discipline in Anabaptist research. The Anabaptists, who were interested in the visible church of this world, longed for the restoration of the holy church community, and they developed the theology of church discipline to preserve the pure church. This theology has attracted the attention of many scholars. Unfortunately, however, attempts have rarely been made to examine the connection between the Anabaptists' unique ecclesiology and their other theological perspectives; this connection is first explored in Goncharenko's dissertation, "The Importance of Church Discipline within Balthasar Hubmaier's Theology," published in 2011.[137]

Therefore, this study points out a significant need to explore the connection point of one Anabaptist leader's ecclesiology with other aspects of his theology and to find out how his view of the visible church, an essential term of Anabaptist ecclesiology, correlates with his views of other theological subjects. Moreover, while Goncharenko's dissertation focuses on Hubmaier, who has attracted much attention from many scholars, this study will make a significant contribution to concentrating on the relatively unknown field of research on Dirk Philips.

---

137. Goncharenko, "Importance of Church Discipline."

Chapter 2

DIRK PHILIPS'S VIEW OF THE VISIBLE CHURCH

Introduction

ALTHOUGH DIRK PHILIPS'S WRITINGS were systematic and organized compared to the writings of other Anabaptist leaders and the writings of Menno Simons, he never dreamed of becoming a systematic theologian. He never attempted to establish a systematic and comprehensive theology; instead, he wrote in response to specific needs.[1] *Enchiridion*, regarded as his magnum opus, was written to answer the various needs of his congregation over many years, and was written in certain situations. With the death of Menno Simons in 1561, and with the growing threat of external dangers and fragmentation within the movement, Dirk needed to publish *Enchiridion*. The reason that he is considered as more organized than other Anabaptist leaders is that *Enchiridion* is not in chronological order, but is structured as a systematic approach to Christian faith.[2]

Dirk's view of the visible church was not developed in a vacuum. He never wrote a book or article on the visible church to describe his view of the issue, nor did he discuss it specifically. However, this fact does not weaken the importance of the visible church in Dirk's theology. His life was devoted to his church and to helping his brothers remain holy saints, and he was a leader who lived his life for his organization. Thus, his view of the visible church was established throughout his life. As his thought

---

1. Keeney, *Development of Dutch Anabaptist Thought and Practice*, 22.
2. Keeney, "Editor's Introduction," 51.

developed over the years, many different arguments and persuasions affected his viewpoint on the visible church. Moreover, his ecclesiastical thought developed as he was influenced by the diversity of the Radical Reformers and others in his background—Melchior Hoffman, Jan Matthys, Obbe Philips, Menno Simons, David Joris, Adam Pastor, Leenaert Bouwens, and various mystics and humanists. He was also influenced by his Franciscan background.

The main purpose of this chapter is to describe Dirk's view of the visible church. In order to achieve this goal, this chapter includes a discussion concerning a view of the church held by those who have influenced the formation of Dirk's ecclesiology, as well as his claims concerning the visible church. In addition, this chapter will demonstrate that Dirk has a perspective on his unique visible church, unlike his predecessors.

Influences

In order to explore how Dirk Philips's view of the visible church had been formed, it is important to note that before he joined the Anabaptist movement, he was a Roman Catholic, and was educated in a Franciscan cloister. Having been educated in a Franciscan cloister in his youth, he would have been accustomed to dedicating his soul to God and practicing humility. In this environment, speculative mysticism would have become more practical. This practice emphasizes brotherhood, includes exercises on obedience, celibacy, and poverty, and pursues changes in common life.[3]

Although there is no detailed information about Dirk's childhood, it is clear that the circumstances in which he lived significantly contributed to the formation of his thought. Dirk lived in a complex, dynamic era. In the Low Countries, the sixteenth century was a period of turbulence. As is well known, the invention of mass printing practices by Gutenberg made a significant contribution to philosophical thinking and the critical study of the Scripture, and accelerated the dissemination and diffusion of knowledge. With the proliferation of travel and trade, the medieval feudalism, which was based on bartering, collapsed, and new mercantilism,

---

3. According to Cornelius Krahn, in the Low Countries area, which includes the present Dutch region, mysticism was prevalent during the Middle Ages, and the mysticism became more practical in a Franciscan manner. See Krahn, *Dutch Anabaptism*, 21–23.

which depended on money and trade, emerged.[4] Moreover, inflation was rampant, and Friesland, where Dirk lived, was suffering from flood damage due to its low altitude. In addition to these situations, the immorality of the priests was prevalent, and the facts that they had concubines and that they were allowed to have children as their legal successors show how much religion had fallen at that time.[5] Although no clear resource tells us so, it is reasonable to assume that this socially and religiously complicated situation would have stimulated Dirk's desire to leave Catholicism and accept Anabaptism.

In addition to the influences mentioned above, four additional streams of thought were even more directly influential in shaping Dirk Philips's view on the visible church: the thought of the Melchiorites (Melchior Hoffman, Jan Matthys), Obbe Philips, David Joris, and Menno Simons. However, Dirk did not agree with all of them. While Obbe Philips and Menno Simons closely cooperated with Dirk Philips and maintained a similar theology, Dirk opposed the ideas of Hoffman, Matthys, and Joris; and by disputing them, Dirk developed his own thought.

Melchiorites

Melchior Hoffman

One of the figures that should be included in the study of Dutch Anabaptism is Melchior Hoffman.[6] His thoughts and vision did not last for long, and they have never been fulfilled; in addition, his life as an Anabaptist was not long. But the beginnings of the Anabaptism movement in North Germany and the Netherlands can be traced back to him.[7] He was once a passionate follower of Luther, but in 1530, he broke with the

---

4. In the Low Countries, there were some commercially developed cities including Gent, Brugge, Louvain, Brussels, and Antwerp. Among these cities, Antwerp was the commercial center of the Low Countries, and "for almost one hundred years, from the late fifteenth century to about 1585, Antwerp was the undisputed commercial metropolis of the Western World" (Harreld, *High Germans in the Low Countries*, 2).

5. Keeney, "Dirk Philips," 20–21.

6. It is not clear whether he met Dirk Philips directly. See Krahn, *Dutch Anabaptism*, 101.

7. Most scholars agree that the origins of Dutch Anabaptism began with him. Scholars agreeing with this argument include Cornelius Krahn, William Estep, C. Arnold Snyder, and Timothy George. See Krahn, *Dutch Anabaptism*, 92–93; Snyder, *Anabaptist History and Theology*, 210; George, *Theology of the Reformers*, 271.

Lutheran camp. In 1533, he was imprisoned in Strasbourg prison. Even though his time as an Anabaptist was short, only for about three years, his influence as an Anabaptist was not small. He gave many baptisms during his ministry, and he had great success in North Germany and the Netherlands.[8]

A main characteristic of Hoffman's thought is that it is based on a sense of impending eschatology. However, it seems that he did not emphasize impending eschatology at the very beginning of his ministry. In his writing entitled *The Ordinance of God*, published early in his ministry as an Anabaptist, he sees baptism and the Lord's Supper as important issues. In this treatise, Hoffman argues that baptism should be understood as a sign of the covenant the bride has made with the bridegroom, and that the Lord's Supper signifies that the bride and bridegroom are one body, one flesh, one spirit, and one passion.[9] As for his view of the last days, Hoffman mentions the ministry of Christ and the chosen people, and insists that the chosen people are a group that is promised ultimate victory, but he makes no mention of impending eschatology.

At some point, however, Hoffman came to believe that the return of Christ was imminent, and that Strasbourg would be the New Jerusalem.[10] Hoffman's eschatological hopes emphasize the realization of the church of Christ, and he expected the actual existence of the kingdom of God on earth. His view of the visible church was distinctly different from that of the Magisterial Reformers. Krahn writes of it: "Luther emphasized the inward kingdom within the individual soul while Calvin fought for a theocratic view of the kingdom of God which is to be realized in the stress and storm of the world.... For him [Hoffman] the kingdom of God begins with the theocratically realized church of Christ growing from day to day."[11] Hoffman detested human higher education and emphasized that spiritual knowledge was superior to fleshly knowledge. He believed that God's wisdom can be perceived only by the spiritual eye, and not by

---

8. Estep, *Anabaptist Story*, 109–10. Not all scholars agree on his success. According to Pater, C. S. Neff assesses Hoffman's work as successful, while W. I. Leendertz claims that his ministry was not successful in Holland (Pater, "Study of Selected Doctrines in Melchior Hoffman's Theology," 21). Obbe Philips mentions Hoffman baptized around 300 in Emden in the Netherlands (Philips, "Confession," 208).

9. Hofmann, "Ordinance of God," 194.

10. Estep, *Anabaptist Story*, 110.

11. Krahn, *Dutch Anabaptism*, 115.

carnal effort.[12] This approach naturally led him to have apocalyptic expectations of the coming kingdom and led him to an arbitrary interpretation of the kingdom of God.

Jan Matthys

Scholars do not know whether Dirk and Matthys had a personal relationship. Matthys died soon after Dirk was baptized and joined the Anabaptist movement (between the end of 1533 and the beginning of 1534), so they probably never met or became acquainted. However, it is clear that at some point after Dirk took part in the Anabaptist movement, Matthys had a great influence on Dirk's thought, because he was baptized by Pieter Houtsagher, one of Matthys' disciples. So although Dirk was not a direct disciple of Matthys, both Dirk and Matthys began Anabaptist life as part of Melchiorite Anabaptism, since Matthys inherited the spirit of Hoffman.

Jan Matthys was a baker in Haarlem, and he was baptized by Hoffman when Hoffman stayed in the Netherlands for a while in 1531.[13] Matthys' work after the baptism is unclear, but he became active in the ministry when Hoffman was in prison in Strasbourg in 1533. His emergence was a key development and turning point of the Dutch Anabaptist movement. He became convinced that he was a prophet of the Holy Spirit, and claimed himself to be the prophet Enoch of the Last Days.[14]

The event that made Jan Matthys a well-known figure in Christian history is probably the Münster Rebellion. Matthys began collecting many supporters in Münster, which he saw as the New Jerusalem. In February, 1534, his followers, who hoped to survive the Day of Judgment, responded to his instigation, and began to gather in Münster from various regions. They hoped that unbelieving people could be saved in the visible kingdom of God, making them bolder and more courageous. Finally, Matthys attacked Münster and ruled from February 1534. As a result, most of the native leadership of Münster left, but Bernhard Knipperdolling, a former mayor, remained.[15] However, this situation did not last long. On April 4, 1534, when a Roman Catholic army besieged the

---

12. Deppermann, *Melchior Hoffman*.
13. Deppermann, *Melchior Hoffman*, 120.
14. Philips, "Confession," 214.
15. Krahn, *Dutch Anabaptism*, 139.

city, Matthys claimed to have received a revelation that he would defeat the army with a small armed force, and he rushed to disperse the army surrounding them with a few followers outside the city walls. But he died in this attack.[16]

After Jan Matthys died in April 1534, another Jan, Jan van Leyden, succeeded him in leadership. He and Matthys had first met when Matthys visited the city of Leiden. Matthys had stayed in his house for two weeks, and while he was there, he baptized him. During this stay, van Leyden would have heard about the city of Münster and soon joined Matthys' camp.[17] Once Matthys died, Jan van Leyden developed the more extreme views that he is famous for. Specifically, he attempted to change the organization of the city in accordance with the Old Testament, accepting the polygamy of the Old Testament, and having 15 concubines himself. He claimed to be "King over the New Israel," but eventually he died on January 22, 1536, as the city of Münster fell.[18]

At the center of Matthys' theology was an imminent eschatology which was the same as that of Hoffman. For Matthys, the millennial kingdom was not merely a hope for the future, but a present reality that was being made. In fulfilling this reality, both Hoffman and Matthys saw themselves as prophets whom God had called. Hoffman saw himself as Elijah, and Matthys claimed to be Enoch.[19] They saw themselves as having a special role in building the kingdom of God on earth in particular places; for Hoffman, this place was Strasbourg, and for Matthys, it was Münster.[20] Matthys, however, had a crucial difference from Hoffman: Matthys actively used violent means to realize the Millennial kingdom, while Hoffman rejected violent means.[21]

For Matthys, the visible church was an absolute means of realizing the kingdom of God. The cruel persecution of the Anabaptists led him to hope for the millennial kingdom and to believe in the necessity of establishing that kingdom himself. However, according to Krahn, most of

16. Krahn, *Dutch Anabaptism*, 140.
17. Krahn, *Dutch Anabaptism*, 134.
18. Snyder, *Anabaptist History and Theology*, 219–21.
19. Estep, *Anabaptist Story*, 110–11.
20. According to Krahn, "for all Melchiorites the corner stone of their imagery was scriptural and traditional. The 'holy city,' the 'new Jerusalem,' came 'from God out of heaven' (Revelation 21:2) and was 'not made with hands' (II Corinthians 5:1)" (Krahn, *Dutch Anabaptism*, 129).
21. Estep, *Anabaptist Story*, 111.

the Melchiorites "had no clear conception as to how the kingdom was to be established."[22] They believed that the Lord was coming soon, but they did not know what role they would play as humans in the establishment of the millennial kingdom after the Lord's coming. Matthys, on the other hand, had a clear direction on this issue. He was preparing for the Lord to come again, so he was willing to smite the Lord's enemies to hasten the day and establish a real millennial kingdom on earth.

The extreme views of Melchiorites were distinctly different from peaceful Anabaptists. Among the Melchiorite leaders, David Joris, Dirk, and Obbe Philips were opposed to revolutionary methods,[23] and Menno Simons, who joined the movement later than they did, also actively opposed the revolutionaries. In *Of the Wonderful Working of God*,[24] written in 1535 when the Münster rebellion was in progress, David Joris clearly opposes violence. He advises his readers to have meekness and long-suffering rather than violent ways.[25] It is also clear that Obbe opposed revolution, because he left the Anabaptism movement after experiencing firsthand the rebellion of revolutionary Anabaptists.[26] Dirk Philips later criticized those who had arisen with physical weapons, instead of the weapons of righteousness and the helmet of salvation, in his treatise *Concerning Spiritual Restitution*.[27] Menno Simons criticizes Jan van Leyden directly in his treatise *The Blasphemy of John of Leiden*. According to Menno, when Jan van Leyden proclaimed himself king of Israel, he committed a blasphemy against God, and the crime of elevating himself to the position of Christ. Menno argues that only Christ is the king, that he alone is our judge, and he alone is the joy of the miserable.[28]

---

22. Krahn, *Dutch Anabaptism*, 130.

23. Snyder, *Anabaptist History and Theology*, 223.

24. Unfortunately, the original version of this treatise does not exist. The current copy is the only edition available today. See Joris, "Of the Wonderful Working of God," 109–25.

25. Joris, "Of the Wonderful Working of God," 114.

26. There is no dispute among scholars that the crucial reason that Obbe left the Anabaptist movement was the Münster rebellion. However, Keeney argues that Matthys's three disciples were executed in Haarlem, which would have been the foundational causes for Obbe to leave the movement. See Keeney, "Dirk Philips," 24–25; also see Williams, *Radical Reformation*, 357.

27. Philips, "Concerning Spiritual Restitution," 346.

28. Simons, "Blasphemy of John of Leiden," 33–50.

Obbe Philips

Since Obbe was an older brother of Dirk Philips, it is natural to assume that he might influence the formation of Dirk's theology and ecclesiology.[29] Indeed, they worked together while in the movement, and Dirk was Obbe's most important co-worker at his side.[30] The two brothers also had similar beginnings as Anabaptists. Both of them began their career as Anabaptists under the influence of Jan Matthys, and they both later refused violent means when the Münster rebellion occurred. However, the positions of Obbe and Dirk in the movement were distinctly different. Obbe became one of the leaders in the movement soon after his baptism, and he later appointed Dirk as bishop.[31] Obbe's influence in the early Dutch Anabaptist movement was noticeable, and was much beyond those of his brother and of Menno Simons. Thus, George Williams labels Obbe's group as "Obbenite."[32] As Timothy George points out, if Obbe had not left the movement, the current name "Mennonite" might have been "Obbenite."[33]

Obbe's break with Matthys' movement is deeply related to the Münster rebellion. Obbe, who was from Leeuwarden and lived there until the rebellion, was blamed as an insurrectionist there, and he left Leeuwarden for Amsterdam on February 23, 1534. Not long after he arrived in Amsterdam, he saw fellow Melchiorites leaving for Münster, proclaiming that "the new city is given to the children of God" and waving swords.[34] Obbe also saw many people come and join the movement. However, Obbe disagreed with such violent ways, and he turned in revulsion from them.[35]

Obbe Phillips' ecclesiology is evident in a debate that took place between him and Jacob van Campen. During Obbe's time in Amsterdam, the atmosphere of the enthusiastic Melchiorites had not disappeared,

---

29. Obbe's birth year is not known. However, it is plausible to assume that Obbe was older than Dirk, given the earlier participation in the movement, his influence over Dirk, and the fact that Obbe's name is always mentioned before Dirk.

30. Philips, "Confession," 223.

31. Keeney, "Dirk Philips," 24.

32. Williams, *Radical Reformation*, 359.

33. George, *Theology of the Reformers*, 276.

34. In Dirk Philips's biography in this dissertation, there is a more detailed description of the cause of the incident.

35. Williams, *Radical Reformation*, 358.

and they kept up their expectations for the new city of Münster. Their leader was Jacob van Campen. Under his leadership, a strange incident occurred in Amsterdam on February 10, 1535. What happened was that seven enthusiasts walked naked through the city, proclaiming the "naked truth" of the new Eden. As a result, they were executed.[36]

In the fall of 1535, Obbe debated Jacob van Campen. The point of the debate was how to apply the Old Testament to the current time. Jacob van Campen asserted a typological interpretation of the Old Testament, arguing that the Old Testament type should be fulfilled in the present literally. He, therefore, argued that the Old Testament justified the establishment of a city of God in Münster, since such a city would be the literal accomplishment of the word of God. This view was in the same line as Hoffman's claim that hidden things of God would be revealed at the time of revelation, and that the time of the revelation had arrived.[37] Obbe, on the other hand, opposed the literal application of the Old Testament, claiming a spiritual application for these types. Obbe's view of a spiritual application of the Old Testament later influenced Dirk's ecclesiology, and it was further developed and applied in Dirk's writings.[38]

David Joris

David Joris was baptized by Obbe Philips in September, 1534, and immediately joined the Anabaptist movement.[39] Not much is known about his early works, but he seems to have played an important role in the movement.[40] There is no known evidence that he was in the city of Münster when the Münster rebellion occurred, but there is no doubt that he was well aware of the events in Münster.[41]

---

36. Williams, *Radical Reformation*, 359.
37. Pater, "Study of Selected Doctrines," 116.
38. Keeney, "Dirk Philips," 24.
39. Williams, *Radical Reformation*, 381.

40. It is not a coincidence that David Joris is the first person mentioned on Batenburg's list, and it shows his influence within the movement. See Hullu, *Bescheiden Betreffende de Hervorming in Overijssel*, 252.

41. According to Gary Waite, Joris was familiar with the Münster rebellion because he participated in the Waterland Conference in the winter of 1534–35. It is apparent that he held a lot of discussion about Münster there (Waite, *David Joris and Dutch Anabaptism*, 89).

Joris' position was close to the Obbenites rather than to the Münsterites. Perhaps Joris might have been reluctant to join the Münsterites as Obbe did, because of their recklessness and radicalism.[42] His view that no violent means could be justified is evident in his hymns. He had a variety of talents, including painting and poesy, in addition to his writing of some hymns. In a song he wrote in 1535, he encouraged all the saints to prepare for suffering and death, saying, "All the blessed [of] God must drink the clear red wine from the cup of bitterness."

However, Joris did not reject all of the Münsterites. Although he refused to use his hermeneutical framework as a means for eschatological claims and social reform, he shared many things with the ideas of Münsterites. Above all, he agreed with Hoffman that human wisdom and knowledge were insufficient in reaching the goal of the Scriptures.[43] This thought naturally encouraged him to emphasize spiritual authority in his theology, and his emphasis on spiritual authority is also similar to that of Hoffman.[44] Unfortunately, Joris' emphasis on spiritual authority causes his own interpretation to replace the Scriptures' proof-texts to support his teachings. This feature was more prominently expressed after the Münster rebellion failed. Joris devoted himself to maintaining charismatic leadership and believed it was essential to reconstructing the scattered and disunited movement.[45]

The most noteworthy aspect of Joris' ecclesiology is that he was trivial about church rites. He did not regard baptism as the external sign of salvation for children of God.[46] This indifference to the practice of baptism was distinctly different from the view of other Anabaptist leaders of his time, and he was probably influenced by Hoffman in this regard. Hoffman, in 1531, had suspended baptism to avoid persecution; he sought to escape his crisis by blurring the boundaries between the Anabaptist group and other reform groups.[47] It is understandable that Joris trivialized baptism in the same context as Hoffman did, and both Hoffman and Joris had their own grounds to trivialize baptism. Just as Hoffman used

---

42. Waite, *David Joris and Dutch Anabaptism*, 89.
43. Waite, "David Joris' Thought," 302.
44. Waite, "David Joris' Thought," 303.
45. Waite, "David Joris' Thought," 303.
46. Waite, *David Joris and Dutch Anabaptism*, 113.
47. Waite, *David Joris and Dutch Anabaptism*.

Ezra 4:24 to validate a two-year postponement of baptism,[48] Joris insisted that internal change was more important than external change.[49] Even though Joris did not allow the indulgence of believers because he emphasized perfection, he did not mean that all the church members had to live a strict church life. For him, it was not a problem to temporarily suspend the external form of church rite. He even refused to pursue martyrdom for this reason.[50]

How did Joris' thought affect the formation of Dirk Philips's ecclesiology? Obviously, Joris did not have a positive impact on Dirk. This was evident in the debate with Dirk and with Nikolaas Meyndertsz van Blesdijk, who was Joris' ardent follower. Although it is clear that Joris did not perceive himself as the Third David, he considered himself as under divine inspiration, and believed that everyone should know this.[51] This expectation was realized through Blesdijk.

Blesdijk, once a follower of Menno Simons, became the most important follower to David Joris, and was convinced that Joris was a prophet who received special revelation.[52] This conviction had led to a debate in the neighborhood of Lübeck in 1546, in which Dirk joined Menno Simons, Gillis van Aken, Leenaert Bouwens, and Adam Pastor. In the debate, Blesdijk was the only participant on Joris' side, supporting Joris' view of the church and baptism. Since Joris emphasized inner faith rather than external forms of faith, it did not matter for him to baptize children or to participate in Catholic and Reformed church service to avoid persecution. In another discussion between Blesdijk and Gillis van Aken, both agreed that Christ ordered baptisms for adults, but Blesdijk asserted that Christ had never objected to infant baptism. This was to counter the reason that most Anabaptists oppose Catholic or Reformed churches.[53] Based on this claim, Joris' followers were free to join Catholic and Reformed churches, and they avoided any persecution.

---

48. Keeney, "Dirk Philips," 23.
49. Waite, "David Joris' Thought," 311–12.
50. Zijlstra, "Menno Simons and David Joris," 250.
51. Zljlstra, "Menno Simons and David Joris," 250.
52. Keeney, "Dirk Philips," 26.
53. Zljlstra, "Menno Simons and David Joris," 254.

Menno Simons

Menno Simons was born in 1496 in Witmarsum in the province of Friesland, and he may have received a childhood education at the Franciscan monastery in Bolsward.[54] He was ordained as a Catholic priest in 1524, and for the twelve years before he was converted to Anabaptism in 1536, he worked as a Catholic priest.[55] According to Timothy George, there are three reasons that he left Catholicism. Two of the reasons were theological: his doubts over the sacramentalism of Roman Catholicism, and his doubts over their teaching on infant baptism. Another reason was the event in Münster where his brother, Peter Simons, was murdered by a Catholic army. After considering these issues, he left Catholicism.[56] Because he denied not only the baptism of the Catholic Church but also the validity of his ordinance in the Catholic Church, when he left Catholicism and joined in the movement in 1537, he was re-ordained by Obbe Philips.[57]

There is no doubt that Menno Simons and Dirk Philips had a close relationship, and it is clear that they had had a major impact on each other. Although Dirk joined the movement before Menno, Menno had more influence in the movement once he joined it.[58] He played the role of leader of the movement ahead of Dirk after Obbe Philips left the movement, and Dirk succeeded Menno immediately after his death.

Menno Simons and Dirk Philips were always at the forefront of major debates within the movement, and Dirk was a solid supporter of Menno in those debates. For instance, both Dirk and Menno debated with Nikolaas Meyndertsz van Blesdijk in the neighborhood of Lübeck in 1546, and both debated against the Unitarian view of Adam Pastor in 1547 and 1552. They were also involved in a 1547 debate in Emden about the issue of avoiding the excommunicated. In 1554, Dirk and Menno joined together at the Wismar meeting, where they mainly dealt with the issue of excommunication. After that point, the issue of excommunication caused more division within the movement, and they took the same side in the controversy. When Leenaert Bouwens argued that

---

54. Bender, *Menno Simons, Life and Writings*, 1.
55. Bender, *Menno Simons, Life and Writings*, 2.
56. George, *Theology of the Reformers*, 273–76.
57. Williams, *Radical Reformation*, 393.
58. Dirk was baptized in December 1533 or January 1534, while Menno was baptized after January 1536. See Keeney, "Dirk Philips," 23–24.

Swaen Rutgers should avoid her excommunicated husband, both Dirk and Menno supported Bouwens, and they each published a work on the excommunication in 1558. Various trips to ministry accompanied them, and Dirk was obviously familiar with Menno's writings.[59]

Although many scholars argue that the main focus of Menno's theology is not ecclesiology,[60] it is true that his life and theology are centered around the church. His theology was shaped by the needs of the church and his ministry, and many of his writings were published under discussion and debate to preserve the pure church.[61] In this respect, he was a passionate minister who emphasized practice, and his identity was not that of a mere theologian. Timothy George says, "Menno Simons is reported to have said, while on his sickbed—which was to become his deathbed—that nothing on earth was as precious to him as the church."[62] For Menno, the church is the most important organization for believers to live a holy life on this earth, and it is the institution that reflects the visible manifestation of spiritual facts.[63]

To fully understand Menno's ecclesiology, his understanding of the word of God and Christ should be examined first. Menno did not sympathize with or pursue literalism, but his view of the word of God was very strict. He was extremely alert to the mix of human tradition and scholarship with the teachings recorded in the Scriptures, and he insisted that the teachings of Jesus in the Scriptures should be followed as they are. That is why he criticized reformers for merely claiming the concept of "sola scriptura"—he argued that they themselves did not follow the Scriptures. Menno believed that the reformers did not clearly distinguish

---

59. According to Koolman, Dirk quoted Menno's two sentences when referring to Luther in his book *Concerning Baptism* (Koolman, *Dirk Philips*, 71).

60. In general, the main theme of Menno's theology is known to be Christology. George Williams says that Menno maintains his perspective on the incarnation in *The Foundation Book*, his most important work, which became the foundation of Mennonitism; but he argues that his view of the incarnation is closely related to his ecclesiology (Williams, *Radical Reformation*, 394–95). Estep also notes that Menno's view of the incarnation is the theological subject that caused the controversy among the Anabaptists (Estep, *Anabaptist Story*, 124).

61. As Keeney points out, the Dutch Anabaptists were not lacking in speculative or systematic theories, but they used them for practical purposes. See Keeney, *Development of Dutch Anabaptist Thought and Practice*, 191.

62. George, *Theology of the Reformers*, 300.

63. George, *Theology of the Reformers*.

between biblical truth and human tradition, or vain learning.[64] Menno did not advocate one way to understand the truth of Bible Scriptures, but sought to pursue the truth by pursuing a personal, dynamic way. He judged the Scriptures not as a means for rational and intellectual learning but as the basis for practice. He believed that even though physical means can not completely replace spiritual means, the truth is manifested visually through material means.[65]

Menno's view of the word of God naturally connects to his Christology, because he insisted that the Scriptures, not only the New Testament but even the Old Testament, should be interpreted according to Christ's intent.[66] In other words, Christ is the most important channel for humans to understand the word of God. According to Menno, since God himself has appeared in the flesh in Jesus Christ, one cannot only awaken true knowledge of God through Christ, but can also have a revelation or example of the existence of God through Jesus Christ. Because Jesus Christ is a true being, he is the only way to fully reveal the will of God. For this reason, all elements of the Scriptures must be subordinated to his intentions, even if there is a seeming contradiction in them.[67]

Menno's view of the humanity of Jesus was unique. To illustrate the humanity of Jesus, the Roman Catholics claimed the Immaculate Conception doctrine, while the Reformed traditions insisted that the Holy Spirit cleansed the fallen seed from Adam. Unlike these two traditions, Menno claimed that the whole being of Christ had a celestial origin. He did not want Mary to be raised to the position of goddess, but he also did not want to lower Jesus' human nature by claiming that Jesus had received the seed, although the Holy Spirit purified the seed. So he claimed that both the humanity and divinity of Jesus came from heaven, and that Jesus was born from God out of Mary.[68] To support this view, Menno used the fashionable physiological theory of the time that just as the woman was totally passive in the production of offspring, only feeding and giving birth, Mary's role was merely for the feeding and birthing of the humanity of Jesus.[69] Of course, this claim is no longer accepted

---

64. George, *Theology of the Reformers*, 288–89.
65. Keeney, *Development of Dutch Anabaptist Thought and Practice*, 44.
66. Keeney, *Development of Dutch Anabaptist Thought and Practice*, 37.
67. Keeney, *Development of Dutch Anabaptist Thought and Practice*, 42.
68. George, *Theology of the Reformers*, 297–98.
69. Keeney argues that Menno followed this physiological theory by being influenced by the Aristotelian view (Keeney, *Development of Dutch Anabaptist Thought and Practice*, 92).

today, but Menno, through this claim, wanted to explain how Jesus was not contaminated by the original sin and to emphasize the unity of the person of Christ as truly human and truly God.[70]

Menno Simons's Understanding of the Church

According to Menno Simons, the role of Jesus Christ is crucial for the word of God to be planted in the hearts of believers. Christ, having both natural birth and supernatural origin, renews all believers and gives them the ability to live a changed life. This change leads not only to spiritual and metaphysical changes but also to actual and visible changes. Through the incarnation of Jesus Christ, he became the source of the seed, and he "does not want his bride to conceive except of the incorruptible seed."[71] The Holy Spirit sprouts the seed planted by Christ, and reproduces the new life.[72] As this new life experience grows, it is nourished by Christ, and the fact that Christ nourishes it leads to the conclusion that the new life must yield good fruit.

Menno Simons, of course, did not overlook the spiritual change of the new creature. He confessed that the saved believers were the people of the kingdom of God, and that the experience of regeneration meant the beginning of the process of salvation to believers. In fact, Menno's soteriology was not different from that of the reformers. Although he had an aversion to the rigid predestination doctrine of the reformers and the antinomian tendencies included in Luther's doctrine of justification, he made it clear that salvation is by grace alone, not by good works.[73]

However, Menno's idea of bearing good fruit in Christ was distinctly different from that of the reformers. Although the reformers brought a fierce objection against the ecclesiology and soteriology of the Catholic Church, and brought the victory of soteriology through a theoretical—and sometimes direct and practical—struggle against the Catholic Church, it was not enough for Menno. For Menno, there was doubt as to whether the reformers' theoretical and speculative discussion had led to the right practice of believers. In fact, reformers' ideas of soteriology and ecclesiology were not new, since Augustine had already asserted them

---

70. George, *Theology of the Reformers*, 298.
71. Simons, "Admonition to the Amsterdam Melchiorites," 1023.
72. Keeney, *Development of Dutch Anabaptist Thought and Practice*, 44.
73. Simons, "Confession of the Distressed Christians," 506.

about a thousand years before.[74] Even though the reformers' soteriology triumphed over the corrupt ecclesiology of the Catholic Church, the proliferation of the soteriology that the reformers claimed did not guarantee an appropriate practical life among believers. Menno mentions, "The Lutherans teach and believe that faith alone saves, without any assistance by works. They emphasize this doctrine so as to make it appear as though works were not even necessary; yes, that faith is of such a nature that it cannot tolerate any works alongside of it."[75] Calvin believed that the grace of God given by the Holy Spirit could be invisible and subjective.[76] Calvin also argues for a clear distinction between the visible church and the invisible church, but he says that man cannot perceive the distinction because of his limitations.[77] This concedes, in effect, that there are major differences between the conceptual division of the church and the actual reality, which was unacceptable to Menno.

The moral and ethical behavior of believers was a very important concept for Menno. Although he did not think that moral behavior was a condition of salvation, he believed that moral and ethical behavior was essential to saved believers. In other words, new creatures in Christ are manifested in the flesh, primarily through moral and ethical behavior.[78] Moral behavior is not required to reveal one's goodness, and it is not just for the benefit of the community; it is a reaction to obedience to God. On the other hand, according to Menno, the absence of moral development is a feature of those who are not disciples of Christ, indicating that they belong to the world. Menno makes references to the importance of the moral development of believers and the lack of such a development of unbelievers in various places of his work.[79] For example, in *Reply to Gelluis Faber* in 1554, Menno makes it clear that moral improvement is linked to eternal fruit.

---

74. MacCulloch, *Reformation*, 111.
75. Simons, "True Christian Faith," 333.
76. Calvin, *Institutes*, IV.1.7.
77. Calvin, *Institutes*, IV.1.8.
78. Keeney, *Development of Dutch Anabaptist Thought and Pratcice*, 114–17.
79. See Simons, "New Birth," 87–102; Simons, "Foundation of Christian Doctrine," 111, 139, 159, 162; Simons, "Christian Baptism," 251; Simons, "Why I Do Not Cease," 299; Simons, "True Christian Faith," 359, 369–70, 380; Simons, "Clear Account of Excommunication," 528, 553, 561–62; Simons, "Reply to Gellius Faber," 663–65; Simons, "Instruction on Excommunication," 971, 976, 977, 988, 990.

> [S]ince we see with our eyes and feel with our hands that they, alas, are one and all called of such as we would wish had the Spirit of Christ; moreover that they are themselves blamable in all things, for they are of an unmerciful, tyrannical disposition, and of an earthly, carnal conduct; therefore we conclude that they pervert the Gospel and do not teach it in power and true repentance. They use the sacrament wrongly without power, spirit, and moral improvement, and dispense it to those who are no disciples of Christ. They deceive the people, do not bring forth permanent fruits, plant that which is evil, and root out that which is good; they do not really seek the honor and praise of God, but their own profit and gain, the favor of the world, and an easy, carefree life.[80]

In *The True Christian Faith*, written in 1541 by Menno, there are stages of change in the faith of those who believe.

> Whereby in turn the heart is pierced and moved through the Holy Ghost with an unusual regenerating, renewing, vivifying power, which produces first of all the fear of God, For it acknowledges the judgment and wrath of the Lord over all transgressions and sins which are committed against his will and Word. It becomes affrighted, fears, and is amazed before God and therefore dares not do, counsel, or agree to anything which it acknowledges through the Word, in Spirit, that God, the righteous Judge, hates in his soul and has forbidden in his holy Word. Next, faith also produces the love of God whereby we love him. For faith knows from the testimony of the Holy Scriptures, rightly understood in spirit, the unsearchably great riches of grace which our merciful good Father, through Christ, has so graciously granted us. Therefore it loves in return, loving God, being moved by the manifest benefit of the aforesaid grace. It is thus freely urged, through the constraining power of love issuing from such unfeigned faith, to obedience to all the commandments of God. As Christ says, If a man love[s] me, he will keep my words. John 14:23.[81]

As William Keeney points out, Menno believes that faith can be divided into three stages. The first stage is the fear of God, the second stage is loving God, and the last stage is obeying the commandments of God.[82] Be-

---

80. Simons, "Reply to Gellius Faber," 665.
81. Simons, "True Christian Faith," 329.
82. Keeney, *Development of Dutch Anabaptist Thought and Practice*, 115.

cause loving God leads to obedience to the commands of God, believers must manifest their faith in obedience to God, and this obedience is revealed in a visible form. This is to show how important for Menno the visible manifestation of spiritual reality is. Menno did not believe that the visible church was absolutely consistent with the invisible church,[83] but he did not admit that the invisible church remained invisible. In his view, the invisible church "can as little be hid as a city upon a hill, or a candle upon a candlestick," and was manifest by words and work.[84]

Menno suggested the conditions for the true church were as follows: by an unadulterated, pure doctrine; by a Scriptural use of the sacramental signs; by obedience to the Word; by unfeigned, brotherly love; by a bold confession of God and Christ; by oppression and tribulation for the sake of the Lord's Word.[85] While the above lists are both theoretical and explicit, they do not include specific practices. Although Menno did not specifically list the practical conditions for the visible church to become a true church, there are five things Menno emphasized throughout his writings in order to preserve the holy life of the church and the believers. These five things are baptism, the Lord's Supper, the relationship between the church and the state, the marriage of believers, and the discipline of the church, namely admonition and excommunication.

Of course, baptism and the Lord's Supper can be said to be the foundation of the church, since Menno, like other Reformers and Anabaptists leaders, insisted on baptism and the Lord's Supper as two crucial sign of the church. Menno details his thoughts on baptism in Part 1 of his *Foundation of Christian Doctrine, Call to a Biblical Faith*,[86] and Timothy George summarizes Menno's doctrine of baptism in three ways: (1) faith does not follow from baptism, but baptism follows from faith; (2) infants are not capable of faith and repentance and should not be baptized; (3) baptism is the public initiation of the believer into a life of radical discipleship.[87] In Part II of *Foundation of Christian Doctrine*, Menno divides his thoughts on the Lord's Supper into four parts as follows:

---

83. Menno presupposes that among those belonging to the Christian group, there is a group of true believers and those who are not (Simons, "Reply to Gellius Faber," 750–51).

84. Simons, "Reply to Gellius Faber," 747.

85. Simons, "Reply to Gellius Faber," 743.

86. Simons, "Foundation of Christian Doctrine," 120–29.

87. George, *Theology of the Reformers*, 303–5.

> In the first place, we must beware not to make the visible, perishable bread and wine the Lord's actual flesh and blood as some do. . . . In the second place, it is to be observed that there is no greater proof of love than to die for another as Christ says, Greater love hath no man than this, that a man lay down his life for his friends. . . . In the third place, we have to observe that by the Lord's Supper Christian unity, love, and peace are signified and enjoined, after which all true Christians should seek and strive. . . . In the fourth place, we have to observe that the Holy Supper is the communion of the body and blood of Christ.[88]

In the book, Menno contradicts the Catholic concept of transubstantiation by presenting his thoughts on the Lord's Supper, explaining what Christians should have for the Lord's Supper and the theological implications of the Lord's Supper. Baptism and the Lord's Supper to Menno are the most basic requirements for a visible church. The essential elements of the visible church are included in the baptism and the Lord's Supper, through which the believers learn and practice the truth, and realize how poor sinners they are.[89]

Regarding the issue of the relationship between the state and the church, Menno took a particular position on the other churches. In his writings, he discussed much of the true church, but at the same time, he dedicated a large amount of his work to criticizing the church for its close ties to the state. He often described the churches maintained by the state as "Antichrist," and he contrasted them with the true church.[90] He did not deny the state, but he maintained a dual view of the state as, first, a legitimate institution whose purpose was to maintain order, punish the wicked, and protect the good; and second, an institution that persecuted his Brotherhood by force.[91] At the heart of his thoughts about the relationship between the state and the church was the use of the sword. Menno believed "Christ has not taken his kingdom with the sword, but He entered it through much suffering,"[92] and he believed that the Christian church had been called for absolute nonresistance to evil; as a result, he rejected any church which is maintained by any sort of force. Overall,

---

88. Simons, "Foundation of Christian Doctrine," 143–46.
89. Simons, "Foundation of Christian Doctrine," 151.
90. George, *Theology of the Reformers*, 300.
91. Simons, "Foundation of Christian Doctrine," 175.
92. Simons, "Blasphemy of John of Leiden," 49.

he thought that the visible church should keep a distance from the state to maintain a holy life on earth.

To maintain the holy life of the believers in the visible church, the issue of the marriage of believers was also important to Menno. Although Menno did not directly include the proper marriage of believers as one of the signs of the visible church, Menno thought that this issue played a crucial role in maintaining the holy life of believers.[93] According to Menno, husbands and wives are the ones who can have the greatest impact on each other's faith, and if one of the two falls into apostasy, the other is likely to be exposed to the danger.[94] Therefore, Menno did not want to make any exceptions to avoiding excommunicated spouses, and he wanted to apply very conservative and strong standards. He also opposed polygamous marriages, in contrast with the Münsterites[95] and David Joris[96], and he opposed marriage for physical pleasure and selfish purposes.[97] He permitted remarriage when a spouse has committed adultery, and in his view, divorce also appears to be permissible in the case of adultery.[98]

Why was church discipline important to Menno? Keeney divides the purpose of the ban and excommunication of Dutch Anabaptists into three aspects: It is to bring the sinner to repentance, to protect believers from apostates, and to defend the reputation of the church in case of any accusations that the church is associated with extreme Radicals such as the Münsterites and the Dutch Wederdoopers.[99] Keeney's three aspects can be simplified into two categories. The first is to keep the purity of the faith of the individual, and the second is to keep the purity of the faith of the church. Menno' view of admonition is also deeply related to the purity of faith. Menno argues that admonition should be done as a means of correcting the false beliefs of brothers or sisters.[100] The admonition

---

93. Estep argues that regeneration, baptism, and discipline were the signs of the visible church to Menno (Estep, *Anabaptist Story*, 185–86).

94. Simons, "Final Instruction on Marital Avoidance," 1059.

95. Simons, "Foundation of Christian Doctrine," 197.

96. Simons, "Sharp Reply to David Joris," 1020.

97. Menno refers to Münster, Batenburg, and Davidian as examples of corrupted sects in his writing (Simons, "Foundation of Christian Doctrine," 215).

98. Simons, "Reply to False Accusations," 561. Also see Simons, "Instruction on Excommunication," 970.

99. Keeney, *Development of Dutch Anabaptist Thought and Practice*, 159.

100. Simons, "Kind Admonition on Church Discipline," 411.

is not meant to drive people out of a community by highlighting their failures, but to bring them back to the heart of the community through repentance.[101] Therefore, the main purpose of church discipline played an important role in sustaining the visible church because it was to keep the purity of the faith of individuals and churches.

Reformers' Views of the Visible Church

Of course, there is no evidence that Dirk Philips had a direct connection with the major reformers, but it is clear that Dirk knew the reformers and their arguments. Many of the Anabaptist leaders he knew were former Lutherans, and after 1560, the Reformed Church became the dominant church in the Netherlands.[102] In many places in his writings, he mentions Lutheran and Calvinists directly or at least has them in mind. Therefore, it is reasonable to assume that Dirk's familiarity with the reformers' view of the church would have influenced the formation of Dirk's own view.

As Cyril Richardson asserts, the central idea of Calvin's ecclesiology is the concept of the visible church and the invisible church.[103] Calvin's concept of the visible and invisible church is closely related to his view of predestination, and he associates the nature of the invisible church with a spiritual quality. In other words, he understands the invisible church as a group of selected people. This group can only include people chosen by God, and it is the complete and ideal group of the church. However, although Calvin thought that the invisible church was spiritually superior to the visible church, he did not reject the validity of the visible church.[104] To describe Calvin's view, the invisible church's relationship to the visible church is comparable to a subset within a Venn diagram. The visible church cannot be said to be the same as the final church, but the visible church includes the invisible church. Calvin thought that even though the visible church is mixed with chaff, the church belonged to God's eternal and mysterious plan. The saints, who are chosen by God and constitute the invisible church, are saved through the visible church,

---

101. Simons, "Kind Admonition on Church Discipline," 412–13.
102. Keeney, "Dirk Philips," 42.
103. Richardson, *Church through the Centuries*, 157.
104. Tillich, *History of Christian Thought*, 272.

and God leads them to salvation through word of God, rites, sacraments, and discipline.[105]

Before Calvin discussed these issues, Luther actually discussed the visible church and the invisible church. Luther inherited Augustine's tradition of ecclesiology, distinguishing the church of the chosen from the church of the mixed saints and sinners. However, he did not mean to claim two churches by distinguishing the two, because for Luther, the church is not a mere notion, unfounded as reality, but it actually exists on the earth; the visible church is the communion of the saints in which the gospel is preached, and the sacraments are performed correctly. Luther, however, had been criticized for neglecting the visible church by comparing the visible church and the invisible church to the flesh and the soul. According to Luther, real, true, and essential Christianity is inherent in the soul, and not in some external form. Thus, the true church is spiritual and internal Christianity, and the visible church is a material and external church.[106] However, this discussion has several weaknesses: it leads to the pursuit of only the ideal church, disregards the visible church, and makes secular authority and external conditions unnecessary. Paul Avis points out the weak points of this ecclesiology of Luther,[107] and Timothy George also points out that Luther emphasizes the invisibility and hidden state of the church.[108]

It is necessary to consider the fact that Luther set his theology against the contemporary position of the Roman Catholic Church. He opposed the fallen and selfish view of the Catholic Church regarding the visible church, and he had to argue that where the church is, by faith, communion with Christ is where the grace of God is experienced through the Holy Spirit. It is, therefore, possible that Luther's concept of the invisible church was formed in the process of asserting that the nature of the church and of faith is invisible, in opposition to the claims of the Roman Church. From this point of view, Luther's view of the invisible church was not intended to hurt the visible feature or reality of the church, but he did intend to oppose the Roman Church.

In fact, as the situation changed, there was a change in his point of view, as demonstrated in his book *On the Council and the Church*, written

---

105. Jay, *Church*, 170.
106. Luther, *Luther's Works* (hereafter *LW*), 39, 65.
107. Avis, *Church in the Theology of the Reformers*, 21–24.
108. George, *Theology of the Reformers*, 89–90.

in 1539 after the Great Peasants' Revolt from 1524 to 1525. In this book, he deals specifically with the sign of the visible church rather than with his previous writings, and he lists the lifestyles of those who have been sealed by the Holy Spirit and marked with the cross of Christ. He acknowledges the function and necessity of the visible church, and he treats the life of the believer, who is a member of the visible church, as important. This view reverses his earlier assertion that the church of the Spirit does not need to be visible and organized in this world.[109] Nevertheless, it is undeniable that he had a negative view of the visible church, whether he intended the contradictory view of the visible church or simply made a mistake in this contradiction.

What Concept Did Dirk Philips Consider as Most Important in the Visible Church?

The most important thing about Dirk's view of the visible church is whether the experience of the salvation of the people of God is justified in taking place in one's inner being without any external manifestation of godliness. Dirk rejects experiences that do not accompany any external evidence of a changed life. As will be discussed in a later chapter, for Dirk, salvation is by grace through faith, not by works.[110] Because salvation is not a result of human action, the individual has no role in or credit for their salvation. Salvation is wholly the gift of God. However, Dirk's view of salvation does not end there. Because love is the most important commandment, as the apostle Paul says, believers come to demonstrate good works. Love and good works are essential to those who have faith, and any so-called believers "who boast of their faith without love and good works, their boast is false and their faith is idle."[111] Therefore, the experience of salvation should not remain internal, but should manifest in a visible form.

The most well-known theme of Dirk Philips's theology is his Christology, because his perspective on the incarnation is unique, and the greatest part of his writing was for the purpose of explaining Jesus Christ. However, the role of the Triune God is also essential to Dirk as evidence of the salvation of believers becomes visible. Dirk distinguishes the role

---

109. Jay, *Church* 164.
110. Philips, "Our Confession," 69.
111. Philips, "Our Confession," 69.

of the Father, the Son, and the Holy Spirit on the saints in order to support his view that the saved testimony of the saints should be revealed—yet this does not mean that he believed in the essential division of the Triune God. Dirk essentially believes in one Triune God—through which believers bear good fruit in this life.

Dirk divides the discussion of God the Father into three parts.

> Three things are primarily included in the knowledge of God the Father: that one rightly confess his eternal, almighty power and wisdom (by which he created everything); his eternal divine righteousness, by which he has so severely punished sins, both of the angels and mankind, 2 Pet 2: [4–6]; and his immeasurable fatherly mercy, by which he has given Jesus Christ as a Redeemer and Savior, John 3:16.[112]

Believers learn two things from the knowledge of God. The first is that the children of God must believe only in God, and the second is that they must fear the God of justice. "This only God is a Creator of all creatures, a sustainer of all things, and a mighty King. [He is] a most high Lord, a God El Shaddai, that is, the almighty, and an all sufficient perfection of all goodness, a Lord and God Sabaoth, that is of the heavenly host."[113] Since all things come from God, he is the source and origin of all good. Thus, God, the Father, is the source of the good fruits of the lives of the saved believers, and all the good fruits are of God.

Furthermore, the God of justice is the ruler of judgment through Jesus Christ when he judges the world.[114] Dirk often contrasts those in the congregation of God and those who do not belong in it. Those who belong to the congregation of God are surely practicing the word of God. They are "with the food of the divine Word and distribute the food [to the] souls at the right time. This took place as they preached the gospel to all creatures, baptized the penitent and believers, broke the bread of the Lord with the baptized, and fed the hungry souls with the Word of Christ."[115] The opponents are those who have destroyed God's justice, and these people cannot escape the judgment of God. Dirk says that God will "with the chains of the righteous judgment of God have bound to

---

112. Philips, "True Knowledge of God," 256–57.
113. Philips, "Confession of Our Faith (Concerning) God," 62.
114. Philips, "Concerning Spiritual Restitution," 322.
115. Philips, "Concerning Spiritual Restitution," 339.

eternal destruction and punishment the disobedient, the contrary, and the obstinate."[116]

The work of Jesus as the Savior of people and as the Mediator between God and human beings is very important in Dirk's Christology. Dirk says, "we believe and confess that Jesus Christ is our Lord and Redeemer" at the beginning of his writing, *The Incarnation of our Lord Jesus Christ, the Only Begotten Son of His Eternal and Almighty Father*.[117] All believers became children of God through the work of Christ and were able to participate in the congregation of God as saved. The individual cannot be saved through his own work, and only Jesus Christ becomes the Redeemer.[118]

What Dirk emphasizes in the work of Christ in the life of Christians is that Christians have been elevated to participate in divine nature by Christ. That is, they live a Christ-like life. The work of Christ results in the salvation of believers in the spiritual, inward, and metaphysical aspects, but the evidence of the saved believers must appear in physical form in this earth and be proven through Christ-like life. For Dirk, it is not enough that believers merely confess that "Jesus Christ is the Son of the living God, conceived in Mary through the Holy Spirit, and born out of her as a true human being."[119] The believers' knowledge and faith about Christ must be proved by the living and recognizable power of God. Dirk points out that even the devil can make a merely oral confession of faith.

Dirk implies that the Holy Spirit maintains the visible church through a more direct method than that of the Father and the Son. The Holy Spirit teaches and reigns in the Christian congregation, and is leading the fellowship of the saints. Those who have true faith and understanding of the Father and the Son are led in their hearts through the enlightenment of the Holy Spirit.[120] The Holy Spirit is the channel to realize the grace of God, and the Holy Spirit also causes the inner change of man. It is by the Holy Spirit that the love of Jesus Christ is kindled in the hearts of Christians, and Christians keep the commands of Jesus Christ through the Holy Spirit.[121]

116. Philips, "Concerning Spiritual Restitution," 339.
117. Philips, "Incarnation of Our Lord Jesus Christ," 135.
118. Philips, "True Knowledge of God," 257–258.
119. Philips, "Incarnation of Our Lord Jesus Christ," 149.
120. Philips, "Confession of Our Faith (Concerning) God," 66.
121. Philips, "Our Confession," 69–70.

According to Dirk, Jesus Christ restored the creation of heaven and earth created by God. The work of Jesus Christ is done through the grace of God and the power of the Holy Spirit, and through this work, "the seed of the divine Word is sown."[122] Dirk also describes the Holy Spirit as the one who makes believers understand and enlightened to the word of God, with a good conscience and a true faith out of the word of God, by which born-again persons are granted the privilege of gathering in the congregation of God.[123]

Dirk also emphasizes the importance of Christian living. Referring to Paul's letter to the Galatians, Dirk refers to the fruit of the Christian as the fruit of the Spirit.[124] Another fruit highlighted by Dirk is the fruits of repentance. This fruit is the fruit of the divine nature and the upright new being, which the Holy Spirit has initiated in Christians, to direct the genuine development of their life.[125]

For Dirk, the fruit of the Holy Spirit is the most important concept in determining whether the visible church is true. He did not consider the organization or function of the church as a condition to distinguish whether the visible church on earth is the true church. Of course, he mentioned the signs of the true church, but the prevailing concept over all of these is the fruits of the Holy Spirit. "Thus producing the fruits of the Holy Spirit. Where that happens, there is a true faith. But where that does not happen, there is but an idle and false boasting of faith."[126]

The Continuing Issues of the Visible Church

Sending Preachers

The issue of sending preachers to maintain the organization of the visible church was a continuing problem for Dirk. He had to contend with the leaders of the false teaching in the movement and had to refute the Roman Catholic claim that the authority of the ordained ministers comes from the delegation given to Peter in Matthew 16:18. Moreover, since Dirk had not found obedience to Christ in the lives of Reformed

---

122. Philips, "Concerning Spiritual Restitution," 318.
123. Philips, "Congregation of God," 362–63.
124. Philips, "Sending of Preachers or Teachers," 209.
125. Philips, "New Birth and the New Creature," 303.
126. Philips, "Congregation of God," 365.

church ministers, it was clear to him that it was important for him to send a qualified minister. In 1559, Dirk argued in his treatise *The Sending of Preachers or Teachers* that the call of preachers came from God and his congregation. Dirk points out that when Paul and Barnabas were ordained in Acts 13, all the congregation laid their hands on them, with fasting and with united prayer.[127] Thus, the calling of preachers is not a personal call, but a community call. Dirk insists that "everyone may well see to it that he does not run by himself before he is called by the Lord or by his congregation."[128]

Teachers are not much different from preachers. Dirk lists how teachers who are called by the Holy Spirit to build up the congregation of God should be prepared: "For it is certain and undeniable that the Holy Spirit sends out no drunkards, nor adulterers, nor misers, nor servants of idols, nor hypocrites, who dissemble for the sake of the belly, and make merchandise with God's Word."[129] Dirk also connects the conditions of true teachers with fruit. To him, the fruit is for all Christians, but the fruit is also important in distinguishing whether the teacher is true or false. In quoting 1 Corinthians 4:20, he says that because "For the kingdom of God does not consist in words but in power," a teacher who obeys the gospel clearly demonstrates that the power appears as the fruit of life.[130] Dirk explains two reasons that a true teacher should bear fruit:

> The first is that whenever God's Word is spoken through the Holy Spirit it bears fruit and is not barren[,] just as the evangelical parable of the sower and his seed testifies, in which parable Christ gave us to understand that his Word is not without fruit. ... The second [is that] Christ gives us to understand, that even though the largest part remains evil, his Word is nevertheless not without fruit. There is yet perchance a good acre into which the seed of the divine Word is cast, sprouts, and brings [forth] fruit.[131]

It is clear to Dirk that the congregation of God must see a leader and minister's fruits as a condition for electing him. Because of the power of Christ Jesus, the congregation of God that exists in this earth lives to bear

---

127. Philips, "Sending of Preachers or Teachers," 202.
128. Philips, "Sending of Preachers or Teachers," 203.
129. Philips, "Sending of Preachers or Teachers," 203.
130. Philips, "Sending of Preachers or Teachers," 209.
131. Philips, "Sending of Preachers or Teachers," 207.

fruits which are commanded and taught in the Bible. For Dirk, therefore, the congregation of God is visible. He asserts that any gathering where Christ is present is always the congregation of God, and he sees that as the visible congregation of God in the earth, though there must also be the invisible congregation of God. The presence of the congregation of God on the earth requires the minister of the congregation to practice the ordinances of the visible church, to preach the gospel, and to serve for that purpose.[132]

The Reason Why the Visible Church Must Be Distinguished from the World

Dirk Philips constantly asserts that the chosen people of God must live to be distinguished from the world on this earth. In his treatise *An Apology or Reply*, Dirk claims that the reason that the people of God must live distinguished from this world is found in a command that God made to the Israelites. He says, "God commanded his people Israel that everyone should cast away the abominations which were before them and not contaminate themselves with alien gods. Yes, not to touch anything unclean, but to separate themselves and go out of the midst of the godless."[133] The Pharisees are a representative example in the Bible of people who seem to be distinguished but who are not serving God. The Pharisees seemed to practice all ceremonies and all commandments externally. However, true worship is to serve God according to the word of God. The Pharisees did not keep the commandments or ceremonies according to the word of God, but did them on the basis of their opinions and understanding.[134]

Dirk explains why the people of God must not keep human commandments and ceremonies, giving six reasons. The first is that the keeping of human commandments and ceremonies is "a diminishing of the grace of our Lord Jesus Christ."[135] The second is that "the ceremonies and institutions of humans neither serve nor further the upbuilding of the neighbor, since all the works of Christians must be directed toward them, but they are offensive, particularly to the weak."[136] The third is that

---

132. Philips, "Sending of Preachers or Teachers," 221–22.
133. Philips, "Apology or Reply," 179.
134. Philips, "Apology or Reply," 180.
135. Philips, "Apology or Reply," 180.
136. Philips, "Apology or Reply," 181.

"through the keeping of human commandments and ceremonies, false worship is established, the world is strengthened therein, and takes it as a reason of boasting against the Christians."[137] The fourth is that following human commandments and ceremonies "allows God's Word to lapse and burdens the consciences which are freed through Jesus Christ through faith, with useless and unnecessary things."[138] The fifth is that because all Christians are in fellowship with Jesus, "they must shun all false worship and the fellowship of idols and the servants of idols and the places where one serves idols."[139] The sixth is that because Christians are a temple of the living God, "they must thus separate themselves from the temple of the idols."[140]

Dirk may seem to be rejecting the institutions and organizations that human beings make in *An Apology or Reply* in a clear tone. He insists on a thorough distinction between the church and the world, and to him, the system and organization that human beings use is synonymous with the world. Thus, even if the church unites with an organization made by man to maintain an outward peace with love, that union is with the world, and can never be accepted.[141] In addition, a moderate compromise made to maintain peace cannot be true love. The true reality of love is God, and therefore, the saints must love God more than all creation.[142] It is also important to understand Christ's peace. To Dirk, Christ's peace is not the peace of this world, but the peace of conscience and the peace in the Holy Spirit through the grace and redemption and reconciliation of God.[143] However, what Dirk does emphasize in *An Apology or Reply* is a thorough separation from the world. To reveal this emphasis, it must be a priority to look at the purpose for the writing. As Dirk mentions in his treatise *Answer to Sebastian Franck*, he wrote his *An Apology or Reply* to oppose Sebastian Franck's false teaching.[144]

---

137. Philips, "Apology or Reply," 181.
138. Philips, "Apology or Reply," 183.
139. Philips, "Apology or Reply," 184.
140. Philips, "Apology or Reply," 185.
141. Philips, "Apology or Reply," 191.
142. Philips, "Apology or Reply," 191.
143. Philips, "Apology or Reply," 193–94.
144. Dirk says, "in addition have answered and developed the reasons clearly in other of my writings, especially in the 'Apology or Reply' (according to my opinion), why one should separate oneself from all false worship and hypocrisy and only maintain what the Lord has commanded [I am reluctant to answer]" (Philips, "Answer to Sebastian Franck," 447).

Sebastian Franck is well known as a spiritualist. He was born in Donauwörth in 1499 and was ordained as a priest, but he once ministered as a Lutheran preacher. As a spiritualist, Frank held that the church is entirely invisible without any external means, and therefore all attempts to establish a visible church are in vain.[145] He had a favorable view of the Anabaptists, but he held a different view of the church than the Anabaptist view.[146] In a letter to John Campanus, who was once a thorough Lutheran and became an Anabaptist under the influence of Melchior Hoffman, Frank stubbornly insists on his position:

> I believe that the outward church of Christ, including all its gifts and sacraments, because of the breaking in and laying waste by Antichrist right after the death of the apostles, went up into heaven and lies concealed in the Spirit and in truth. I am thus quite certain that for fourteen hundred years now there has existed no gathered church nor any sacrament.[147]

His main argument is that no valid church exists in this world. Moreover, he believes that because the external institutions of the church, such as the baptism and the Lord's Supper, have been misused and corrupted by the Antichrist after the apostolic period, restoration to the New Testament church is not possible, and no such effort is necessary. There is now only one church, which is spiritually among all people.

Dirk Philips emphasized that the visible church must be distinguished from the world in order to refute the spiritualist claim that only the inner changes are meaningful and that the visible church is meaningless to believers. The point that Dirk which emphasizes is that they must go back to the word of God. In order not to be like a Pharisee, the church must be built according to Bible-based teachings, not teachings that depend on their opinions or thoughts. Dirk agrees with the claims of the spiritualists that human-created institutions are not valid. However,

---

145. Williams, *Radical Reformation*, 264–65.

146. Harold S. Bender quotes Sebastian Franck in his article "Anabaptist Vision": "The Anabaptists . . . soon gained a large following, . . . drawing many sincere souls who had a zeal for God, for they taught nothing but love, faith, and the cross. They showed themselves humble, patient under much suffering; they brake bread with one another as an evidence of unity and love. They helped each other faithfully, and called each other brothers. . . . They died as martyrs, patiently and humbly enduring all persecution" (5). This article is also included in Hershberger, *Recovery of the Anabaptist Vision*.

147. Franck, "Letter to John Campanus," 149.

while the spiritualists claim that the visible church is also irreversibly contaminated by the Antichrist, Dirk argues that the visible church is valid because it is an ordained institution of God, as evidenced by word of God. Therefore, he emphasizes that the church ordained by God is necessary in this world and that the visible church should be established in accordance with God's purpose, and that it should bear fruits.

Conclusion

Dirk Philips's view of the visible church differs from the perspective of previous Anabaptist leaders and reformers. He denied the position of establishing a visible church on the earth in violent, armed forces, and denied the spiritualists' negative view of the visible church. He emphasized the balance between the two perspectives and tried to maintain that balance by acknowledging both the heavenly church and the earthly church. This can be seen in his antipathy to the Münster rebellion, through the fact that he opposed spiritualists such as David Joris and Sebastian Franck, and in his refusal to become a spiritualist, as his brother Obbe did.

Of course, Dirk is not different from his predecessors in every way. He was obviously influenced by Hoffman in the early stage of his ministry, and it is undeniable that he participated in the movement of the disciple of Jan Matthys. Dirk's unique theology of the incarnation came from Hoffman, and he developed it on that basis. However, on the question of how to establish the church of God in this world, Dirk was deeply influenced by his brother Obbe Philips. He stood on the same side as Obbe, opposing the literal interpretation of the Old Testament, which was the Melchiorites' view; their violence became the decisive reason for Dirk distinguishing himself from the Melchiorites. To Dirk, the church is visible, but it is not realized through the literal sense of the Old Testament, nor is it realized only by violent, artificial methods and human endeavors.

Unlike Joris, Dirk did not overlook the possibility of human wisdom and knowledge to fulfill the Bible's purpose. He believed that human beings play a critical role to establish the visible church of this world and that internal changes were proven in the form of external changes. Although Frank rejected the usefulness of the visible church, and Joris recognized the Saints' apostasy life because he considered the internal change of the Saints to be more important than the external change, Dirk emphasized the importance of the distinguished, holy life of the believers, arguing that this life is to be realized through the visible church.

Dirk did not attempt to distinguish intentionally between the visible church and the invisible church. He did not believe that members of the visible church were the same as members of the invisible church, but he continually asserted that members of the visible church should bear fruits as the congregation of God. This is not much different from Calvin's view, which divides the church into the visible church and the invisible church based on the doctrines of election and predestination.[148] Although Dirk and Calvin are different in emphasis on practice, this difference does not imply a difference in the concept of the church.

Unlike Dirk, although Menno did not write a book or article on the subject of the church, he speaks of Christians' fruitful life throughout his writings. He argues that the invisible church is not always the same as the visible church, but it should be revealed in visible form. This shows that Dirk and Menno have a lot in common in their view of the visible church.

---

148. Jay, *Church*, 170–71.

Chapter 3

CHRISTOLOGY

Introduction

THIS CHAPTER WILL ARGUE that Christology is at the core of the theological views of Dirk Philips, a view that several recent scholars seem to agree with. William Keeney, for example, claims that Dirk's theology has a dual focus: the words of Scripture and the incarnation. However, he argues that Dirk "generally resolved any conflicts between the two with a Christocentric interpretation of the Scripture. He gave Christ preeminence in his theological thinking."[1] Cornelius J. Dyck says that Dirk's writings in *Enchiridion* "contain pertinent Christological references and several chapters are devoted to Christology."[2]

It is in the two following treatises that Dirk focuses on Christology: *The Incarnation of Our Lord Jesus Christ, the Only Begotten Son of His Eternal and Almighty Father* and *Concerning the True Knowledge of Jesus Christ*. Christology was central for Dirk because he needed to defend himself and his congregation from charges of heresy. First, according to Dirk, many opponents questioned and mocked him and his congregation on account of their faith. Their pure enthusiasm and faith in Jesus were the targets of many people's attacks, and they were often regarded as people who did not believe in Jesus.[3]

---

1. Keeney, "Dirk Philips," 30.
2. Dyck, "Christology of Dirk Philips," 149.
3. Philips, "Incarnation of Our Lord Jesus Christ," 134–35.

The second reason Dirk treats Christology as important is that he and his congregation were treated as heretical by their opponents. Many heretical ideas were indeed prevalent at this time, and this situation led people to label Dirk and his church as heretics. Indeed, these attacks are due to the circumstances of Dirk and his church. It is true that Dirk was influenced by Melchior Hoffman's Christology, and he was baptized by Jan Matthys' disciple. Also, David Joris, a member of Dirk's movement, later claimed to have received a special revelation.[4] However, Adam Pastor was probably the one who provided the reason for the blame toward Dirk and his followers, since Pastor was a member of Dirk's group, who did not believe in the divinity of Christ and denied the Trinity.[5] The Dutch Calvinists, in particular, vehemently criticized Dirk and his followers because they believed Dirk and his congregation had the same doctrine as Adam Pastor's Christology.[6] Because of this tendency, the attack on Dirk and his church motivated him to actively defend his views as orthodox Christian thought; thereby also protecting his congregation from the prevailing heretical ideologies. According to Dirk, the heretics were those who denied the true divinity of Jesus Christ and his incarnation. Moreover, they were also corrupting the teachings of Jesus Christ.[7] As a result, Dirk believed that having the right knowledge and discernment was a very important issue for the believer, because Christ makes all grace possible with the wisdom of God, and makes all salvation possible.[8]

The core of Dirk's Christology is to confess both the eternal divinity and true humanity of Jesus Christ: he declares, "he who does not confess the eternal divinity and the true humanity of Jesus Christ is an antichrist, … for he does not believe in the testimony which God has testified about his Son."[9] Dirk argues on this issue in a clearer tone in a letter whose title is unknown: "And that is my confession about the deity and incarnation, that Jesus Christ is true God and human being, God born out of God the eternal Father and became a pure, unspotted human being in

---

4. Keeney, "Dirk Philips," 26.
5. Keeney, "Dirk Philips," 26–27.
6. Koolman, *Dirk Philips*, 41.
7. Philips, "Concerning the True Knowledge of Jesus Christ," 153.
8. Philips, "Concerning the True Knowledge of Jesus Christ."
9. Philips, "Incarnation of Our Lord Jesus Christ," 148–49.

time, conceived by the Holy Ghost and born out of Mary, the virgin, a Son of the Most High."[10]

Dirk is concerned to show his Christology involves both the divinity and humanity of Christ. He maintains the divinity of Christ, but he also argues for a balance between the perfect coexistence of Christ's divinity and humanity, thereby defending Christ's full humanity too. According to Dirk, Christ came from heaven, but was born of a human being. Keeney makes a point which is appropriate for this issue. According to Keeney, Dirk "attempted to retain the natural birth of Jesus as it would be for any other man, yet allowing for a different origin, and thereby eliminating the corrupt nature."[11] Although Christ was born on earth with human flesh like other human beings, he was able to maintain his divinity by a unique origin, which differs from that of other humans.

The main purpose of this chapter, then, is to explore in some detail Dirk's Christology. First, this chapter will explore his view of the divinity and humanity of Christ. After examining his Christology, this chapter will examine how Dirk's Christology impacts his view of the visible church. Of course, his theory of Christology and the visible church would not be directly connected. However, this chapter will show that Dirk's view of the incarnation in his Christology provides a very important motive for the holy life of the saints, and according to Dirk, the incarnation causes humans to have a divine nature in Christ.

The Humanity of Christ

In AD 451, the Council of Chalcedon formulated what has become the orthodox doctrine of the church, especially concerning the person of Christ. Chalcedon declared that he was "made known in two natures without confusion, without change, without division, without separation, the difference of the natures being by no means removed because of the union, but the property of each nature being preserved and coalescing in one *prosopon* and one *hupostasis*—not parted or divided into two *prosopa*."[12] Although this formulation did not end all the controversies between the Western and Eastern churches, it is undeniable that this declaration has been the basis of orthodox Christian Christology to this day.

10. Philips, "Unknown Letter of Dirk Philips," 633.
11. Keeney, *Development of Dutch Anabaptist Thought and Practice*, 91.
12. Kelly, *Early Christian Doctrines*, 340.

There is, of course, criticism that the results of the Council of Chalcedon are passive and that they avoid explaining many issues in detail, but this council was at least a shield to defend orthodox Christianity against heretical perspectives.[13]

Dirk's discussion of the human nature of Christ follows the traditions of the Council of Chalcedon. Although it is unclear whether Dirk was aware of the Council of Chalcedon, he follows the definition of the person of Christ formulated by the council. Dirk does not see the human nature of Christ alone constituting the person of Christ, and he also refuses to describe the human nature of Christ as impersonal. Since the impersonality of Christ's personality would assume that the human nature of Christ does not possess its own independent subsistence,[14] Dirk clearly emphasizes the human nature of Christ as an independent subsistence.[15] Dirk also makes it clear that the physical nature of the body of Christ is no different from that of other humans. Dirk says, "[Jesus] is human. Yes, he is our brother, like us in all things, except sin and all sinful nature."[16]

Perhaps logically, Dirk's thoughts on the human nature of Christ is unsettling. He describes Jesus as a normal human being except without sin and sinfulness; and at the same time, Dirk describes Jesus as the true God; yet Dirk does not discuss the nature of the relationship between Christ's humanity and his divinity. This logical weakness, however, is in line with the teaching of the church—like the tradition of the Council of Chalcedon—which neglects to explain in detail the mysteries within Christology.

The Body and Flesh of Christ

As in many places of the Scripture, Dirk does not use the word "flesh" in a value-neutral way, but instead uses it with a negative connotation. The flesh of the human body is inherently sinful, and the fact that people remain in the flesh means that humanity is sinful. Thus, the claim that Christ possesses a human body necessarily leads to a clear account of the relationship between the body of Christ and sin. Although he believed Christ was born through the seed from heaven, Dirk does not deny that

---

13. Berkhof, *Systematic Theology*, 321.
14. Berkhof, *Systematic Theology*, 322.
15. Philips, "Confession of Our Faith (Concerning) God," 64.
16. Philips, "Confession of Our Faith (Concerning) God," 64.

Christ still possesses a human body. Jesus appeared on earth in the flesh, was shown to people, and was believed in the world. He suffered on the earth with his flesh and was crucified in the flesh.[17]

According to Dirk, Christ was born in a servant-like form, possessing a servant-like flesh.[18] Thus, the flesh of every other human being and the flesh of Christ are essentially no different, except that all human beings other than Christ possessed sin. Dirk, however, also considers the various Scripture references that describe Christ, for he thinks that some descriptions in Scripture can confuse people's understanding of the humanity of Christ. He believes that although the Scripture contains many references to Christ that could seem to hint that Christ is not truly a human being—for example, references that call him a rock or a vine—this does not mean that Christ is not fully human, yet formed from supernatural seed miraculously placed into a woman's body. Christ was also named the seed of a woman and the seed of Abraham.[19]

However, according to Dirk, the body of Christ and the body of other human beings are not exactly the same. Dirk argues that the body of Christ has a crucial difference from that of other human beings. Dirk confesses that Jesus is a true human being as well as true God. He says, "[Christ] who was God became man and he who became man was God and man, and he who was God and man, he died as a man and he who died as the man rose from the dead as God."[20] The claim that the true God has become a true human being requires a logical explanation of *how* the true God could become a true human being. Without this explanation, people cannot accept that Jesus was truly God and truly human. To illustrate this, Dirk quotes John 1:14: "The Word became flesh."[21] This reference to the Word is the origin of Christ in heaven, not earth.

To support the claim that the origin of the body of Christ is in heaven, Dirk emphasizes some of the characteristics of his body. First, he points out that Christ is the second Adam. He quotes 1 Corinthians 1:47,

---

17. Philips, "Incarnation of Our Lord Jesus Christ," 147.
18. Philips, "Incarnation of Our Lord Jesus Christ," 139.
19. Philips, "Incarnation of Our Lord Jesus Christ," 141.
20. Philips, "Incarnation of Our Lord Jesus Christ," 139.
21. Perhaps Dirk seems to have regarded this verse as the most important verse to explain the incarnation. He marked John 1:14 right under the heading of his treatise, *The Incarnation of Our Lord Jesus Christ, the Only Begotten Son of His Eternal and Almighty Father.* See Philips, "Incarnation of Our Lord Jesus Christ," 134.

saying, "The first Adam is from the earth and earthy, the second Adam is the Lord himself from heaven."²²

Second, Dirk argues that if the body of Christ had come from Mary, there would be no difference between the body of Christ and that of other human beings. Again, Dirk uses Adam as an example to support the argument. He sees the first Adam as an important figure in explaining human sinfulness because the first Adam was not born out of a human body, but created by God. Adam had no father but God. Thus Christ, the second Adam, cannot come from this world because the earth was polluted by sin, and all people have been cast under a curse and have fallen in their nature. Moreover, because Christ is the living bread that comes down from heaven, the flesh of Christ is true food and true blood. If the body of Christ has the same physical characteristics as other normal human beings, or if the body comes from human beings, Christ would not exist in true food and blood. Therefore, Dirk insists that Christ has not become a man in human seed, but has become the eternal and unchanging seed of the Heavenly Father in heaven and has become human out of Mary through the power and activity of the Holy Spirit.²³

Finally, Dirk emphasizes that although the body of Christ is similar to that of other humans, his body is pure, spotless, and holy, and has not seen corruption.²⁴ For all other human beings, the human body is inherently evil and sinful, so it comes from the earth and returns to the earth; but the body of Christ has a different outcome because it has no relation to evil or sin.

The Temptations of Christ

Having argued that Christ was a true human being, Dirk uses the fact of Christ being tempted, as proof of that claim. Indeed, Christ came from heaven to this earth, but in this life of earth, he had to pass the temptations of Satan. Dirk says, "For when [Jesus Christ] was baptized of John the Baptist, he was led of the Spirit into the wilderness in order to be tempted of Satan; Satan came to him and tested him with three temptations. But the Lord Jesus Christ overcame all the temptations and cunning of Satan

---

22. Philips, "Incarnation of Our Lord Jesus Christ," 137.
23. Philips, "Incarnation of Our Lord Jesus Christ."
24. Philips, "Incarnation of Our Lord Jesus Christ," 146.

with the sword of the Spirit."[25] Dirk notes that even though Christ suffered in the temptations of Satan, he triumphed over these temptations by the power of the Holy Spirit. As a true human, Christ struggled with the temptations in the flesh, but as a sinless man, Christ overcame every temptation by the power of the Holy Spirit.

Dirk understands that the case of the temptations of Christ is in accordance with the intention of God the Father because it was the Father's will and purpose that Christ lived as a human being on this earth, just as the Father sent him to this world to reveal his name to the world.[26] In addition, Dirk believes that the temptations of Christ and his overcoming of temptations is an example to many Christians, and they also prove that Jesus was a true human being. According to Dirk, as his people resemble and follow Christ, they "will be strengthened by the Lord with his grace, and all the temptations of Satan will not harm them. Yes, Jesus Christ, our Lord, and Savior, blessed in eternity, has himself striven with Satan and overcome him."[27]

The Suffering and Death of Christ

Dirk posits that Christ has suffered, died, and resurrected according to the flesh. He believes that the physical body of Christ is not inferior to the divinity of Christ, and is not corrupted on earth: "Since then the flesh of Christ makes alive and is a food for souls, therefore, the flesh of Christ must also be the Spirit and the Word of God."[28] Because the word became flesh, Dirk believed that the body of Christ had the same status as the word of God. Dirk does not neglect the body of Christ, nor does he believe the humanity of Christ was somehow weakened in Christ's suffering and death. Dirk believes that although the body of Christ came from heaven, he suffered and died in the flesh on the cross.

Dirk's views did not go unopposed, and being aware of criticisms and attacks, Dirk seeks to contradict especially the assertion that Christ was not fully in the flesh as he suffered and died on the cross. Dirk says, "If Christ has not received his flesh and blood from Mary, how could

---

25. Philips, "Tabernacle of Moses," 280.
26. Philips, "Sending of Preachers or Teachers," 205.
27. Philips, "Tabernacle of Moses," 279–80.
28. Philips, "Incarnation of Our Lord Jesus Christ," 147.

CHRISTOLOGY 69

he then suffer and die?"[29] Two criticisms are included in this argument. First, Dirk refutes the argument that says that Christ came from Mary, not from heaven, because Christ suffered and died as the flesh; second, he refutes the argument that because Christ was from heaven, *God* suffered and died, not the flesh of Christ. Dirk refuses to accept either argument. First, he argues that because Christ came from heaven, not from Mary, he "could make eternal satisfaction and pay for our sins"[30]; he also asserts that the physical body of Christ, not the mere semblance of God, suffered and died on the cross.

Dirk gives apparent evidence of being aware of the various opinions in the history of the church concerning the suffering and death involved in Christ's crucifixion. For example, Dirk refutes Sabellianism, sometimes referred to as Modalistic Monarchianism, which defined God not on the manifestation of the essence, but on the basis of the manifestation of the mode. Sabellius asserted that God was manifested in the form of the Father in the Old Testament, in the form of the Son in the earthly ministry of Jesus Christ, and in the form of the Spirit after the resurrection.[31] In other words, the Father, the Son, and the Holy Spirit are one God manifest in different modes at different times. As a result, Sabellius' argument overlooks the essence of the Father, the Son, and the Holy Spirit, and sees the relationship between the Triune God too uniformly. In addition, this view leads to the conclusion of Patripassionism, which means that the one ultimately suffering on the cross was Father God.[32]

In responding to the heretical idea that God was dead on the cross, Dirk instead argues for the actual death of Christ's physical body: "neither the Father nor the Holy Spirit but the Son took on human form, John 1:14; 3:16, and he has taken off his divine form and has taken the form of a servant, Phil. 2:6[-7], and had died according to the flesh, but has been made alive according to the Spirit, as Peter says, 1 Pet. 3:18."[33]

Dirk also refutes Nestorius' views wherein he denies virgin Mary should be called *Theotokos*, "Mother of God."[34] According to Nestorius, it was the human nature of Jesus that was born of Mary, just as he suffered

29. Philips, "Incarnation of Our Lord Jesus Christ," 147.
30. Philips, "Incarnation of Our Lord Jesus Christ," 147.
31. For more study on Sabellianism, see Brown, *Heresies*, 102–3; González, *History of Christian Thought*, 1:148; Reymond, *New Systematic Theology*, 579, 600.
32. Sabellianism is sometimes called Patripassianism.
33. Philips, "Incarnation of Our Lord Jesus Christ," 147.
34. Nestorius, "Dogmatic Letters," 348.

and was resurrected as a human being. Thus, Nestorius argues that the virgin Mary should be called *Christokos*, "Mother of Christ, not Mother of God."[35] However, Cyril of Alexandria, who opposed Nestorius, claimed that Jesus Christ was one incarnate nature of the divine Logos, and he insisted that the two natures of Christ were organically connected.[36] Nestorianism was finally condemned for heresy in 431 at the Ephesus Council. According to Dirk, Nestorius argued that "God's Word suffered in the flesh and was crucified in the flesh."[37] Dirk points out Nestorius' view as false, contrasting with the entire Scripture, the apostles, and many bishops and teachers.

Dirk also refutes both Monarchianism and Nestorianism. While Monarchianism extremely underestimated the humanity of Christ, Nestorianism was an attempt to overly distinguish the humanity of Christ from the deity of Christ. As a result, orthodox Christianity condemned both views as heresies and sought to articulate orthodox Christian doctrine while maintaining a balance among their extreme claims. Dirk's view of the suffering and death of Christ also follows orthodox Christian theology in his attempt to keep the balance between those various theological viewpoints.

The Deity of Christ

Although Socinianism, which denies Trinitarianism and the divinity of Christ, did have a significant influence in sixteenth-century Netherlands, it is not well-known how much Dirk himself or Dutch Mennonites generally knew of the heresy.[38] Dirk does not accept any of its views. He is extremely wary of emphasizing only the human nature of Christ, as claimed by Socinianism, and this tendency leads to misconceptions as to whether Dirk acknowledges the divinity of Christ and denies the humanity of Christ. Cornelius J. Dyck points out that there are questions about Dirk's over-emphasis on the deity of Christ:

> From this theological denial of the human nature of Christ the question arises which Philips himself anticipated: "If Christ did not receive his flesh and blood from Mary, how was it possible

---

35. Nestorius, "Nestorius's Second Letter to Cyril," 137.
36. Cyril of Alexandria, "Cyril of Alexandria's Second Letter to Nestorius," 132–33.
37. Philips, "Incarnation of Our Lord Jesus Christ," 147.
38. Dyck, "Christology of Dirk Philips," 153.

for him to die?" His answer is that Christ died according to the flesh but was made alive according to the spirit. I Peter 3:18. Yet with the theological denial that Christ was "of the seed of Abraham" His redemptive activity is called into question. A complete redemption requires a human as well as a divine Christ. Christ had to become man to bring mankind to God (though it is wrong to believe that Christ did not save whatever He did not assume); "one who in every respect has been tempted as we are" (Heb. 4:15). For Philips the sinlessness of Christ is only fully guaranteed if he was free from the influence of human flesh at birth. This would, in a sense, link the efficacy of Christ's redemptive work to his physical or nonphysical attributes and not to his being the only Son of Almighty God.[39]

As Dyck points out, it is true that Dirk's attention is directed at insisting that the flesh of Christ is unrelated to sinful human nature. Because of this focus, Dirk emphasizes the deity of Christ more than the humanity of Christ and gives more space in his treatises to argue the deity of Christ.

To Dirk, the deity of Christ is the channel for reconciling sinful human beings with the Father by eternally and completely helping humans.[40] Dirk therefore asserts to his readers that human beings cannot be saved without a belief that the Son of God is the true God.[41] True faith in Jesus Christ, the Savior and Lord, is the belief that he is God.

Dirk uses various analogies to describe the deity of Christ. His favorite analogy is to describe Christ as heavenly bread. Heavenly bread shows Christ's origin. In other words, Christ is not from this earth but is a living bread that descends from heaven for the life of the world. This concept is similar to Dirk's main argument regarding the humanity of Christ: that Christ is from heaven since his flesh is not made of Mary's seed but is derived from heaven.[42]

Dirk also contrasts the perfection of Christ with the imperfection and inability of any creature in the world to express the perfection of the Creator. According to Dirk, "the God of heaven shall bring his Christ to have all power on earth and in heaven, Matt. 28:18, which honor and might and glory God the Father gives to no one except his only begotten

---

39. Dyck, "Christology of Dirk Philips," 154–155.
40. Philips, "Incarnation of Our Lord Jesus Christ," 136.
41. Philips, "Concerning the True Knowledge of Jesus Christ," 160.
42. Philips, "Incarnation of Our Lord Jesus Christ," 138.

Son, who was born of him and gone forth and is one with him."[43] Thus, Jesus Christ is the almighty only begotten Son, the Son of the almighty living God, and sufficient to show the true divinity of that one God.[44]

The text that Dirk uses to argue the divinity of Christ in Scripture is John 1. He claims that John 1:1–2 unquestionably testifies of the eternal divinity of Jesus Christ.[45] Dirk understands that the word that existed from the beginning explicitly expresses the divinity of Jesus Christ, and is Jesus Christ.

Another analogy that Dirk uses to describe the divinity of Christ is the pure fountain. Dirk says that anyone who drinks the living water of the fountain in Jesus Christ will have eternal life.[46] Dirk points out that the power of God to save everyone who believes in the gospel is proclaimed by the teachings of Jesus Christ, and there is no other gospel than the teachings of Jesus Christ and his apostles.

The Preexistence of Christ

Dirk describes Jesus as always existing with his Father. According to Dirk, Jesus is our Lord, Redeemer, the eternal being, Almighty Father, the firstborn of the living God, and one with the Father. This divinity of Christ has always existed with the Father before the world began and is eternal.[47] He was glorified with God and came down from heaven as the bread of true life.[48] Dirk uses these verses of John's Gospel as the basis of Christ's preexistence: "The only begotten Son of the living God, he who before the beginning of the world was glorified with God, John 17:5, … The Word which in the beginning was with God and was God—that

---

43. Philips, "Concerning the True Knowledge of Jesus Christ," 156.
44. Philips, "Concerning the True Knowledge of Jesus Christ," 157.
45. Dirk mentions that "In the beginning was the Word. It was in the beginning with God, etc. And the Word became flesh and we have seen his glory, glory as of the only begotten from the Father who is full of grace and truth, John 1:1 [-2, 14]. This is an incontrovertible witness of the eternal deity of Jesus Christ the only begotten Son of the Father, because he was the Word in the beginning with God and God himself was the Word, etc" (Philips, "Concerning the True Knowledge of Jesus Christ," 157).
46. Philips, "Concerning the True Knowledge of Jesus Christ," 167.
47. Philips, "Incarnation of Our Lord Jesus Christ," 134.
48. Philips, "Concerning the True Knowledge of Jesus Christ," 161.

Word has become flesh, says John, and lived among us, 'and we have beheld his glory, glory as of the only Son from the Father' [John 1:14]."[49]

Dirk's view of Christ's preexistence is likely to be misunderstood as the concept of adoptionism, since Dirk links the preexistence of Christ to the concept of *Logos* in the gospel of John.[50] Without a definition of the relationship between the *Logos* and Jesus Christ, it would be impossible to grasp Dirk's intentions fully as he does not make mention of this particular theology in any of his works. He merely makes simple claims that Jesus belongs to God's eternity; he does not try to answer the question as to whether the word became Jesus at some point in history, or whether the *Logos* was an eternal being distinct from Jesus. In other words, Dirk regards the word as being ontologically equal to Jesus and does not give any room for the possibility that they are different. Although Dirk explicitly states the preexistence of the word, the word is not different from Jesus. He discusses this issue as follows:

> John testifies to this in the beginning of his Gospel where he writes of the true divinity of Jesus Christ as follows: "In the beginning was the Word. It was in the beginning with God, etc. And the Word became flesh and we have seen his glory, glory as of the only begotten from the Father who is full of grace and truth," John 1:1[-2, 14]. This is an incontrovertible witness of the eternal deity of Jesus Christ, the only begotten Son of the Father, because he was the Word in the beginning with God and God himself was the Word, etc.[51]

As this quotation demonstrates, Dirk describes Jesus Christ as one who does not suffer the bondage of time. According to Dirk, Jesus exists beyond time; Jesus is the first and the last, as it is proclaimed in Isaiah.[52] He is the ruler of time. In addition, his discussion of the preexistence of Jesus Christ makes it possible to confess theologically that he is the creator of this world. On the other hand, the fact that Jesus has always existed indicates that he has sovereignty over this world and that he is the creator of this world. Dirk points out that "all things are created through Jesus

---

49. Philips, "Concerning the True Knowledge of Jesus Christ," 161.

50. Grenz warns that connection of the preexistence to the *Logos*, not Jesus, can lead to the conclusion that what had existed before the appearance of man in Mary was *Logos*, not Jesus. For a discussion of Jesus' preexistence, see Grenz, *Theology for the Community of God*, 311–14.

51. Philips, "Concerning the True Knowledge of Jesus Christ," 157. Cf. Isa 41:4.

52. Philips, "Concerning the True Knowledge of Jesus Christ," 157.

Christ (as is also written in the first chapter of John), that which is in heaven and upon the earth, 'visible and invisible, whether thrones or dominions or principalities or authorities—all things were created through him and in him. He is before all things, and all things exist in him,' Col. 1:16[-17]."[53]

Moreover, the fact that Jesus is the Creator of this world and the fact that all things of this world exist in him make a distinction between Jesus and angels.[54] Though angels are spiritual beings, angels are also creatures created in him, as are the creatures of this world, and only Jesus, the true God, is the Lord of this world.

Christ in the Old Testament

Dirk insists in various places in his treatise, *Concerning the True Knowledge of Jesus Christ*, that Jesus Christ is prophesied throughout the Old Testament. According to Dirk, the Old Testament passages that testify to the true divinity of Jesus Christ and the honor and glory of his eternal kingdom include the following:

> all the shadows and figures of Melchizedek, Gen. 14:[18], of Isaac, Gen. 22:[2], of Joseph and Simeon [Gen. 42:18–25], of Moses and Aaron and of their rods that bloomed in one night and bore almonds, [Num. 17:8], of the heavenly bread, Exod. 16:16, of the rock from which water had flowed, Num. 20:10, Ps. 78:15, of the serpent which Moses erected in the wilderness as a saving sign, Num. 21:9, Wisd. of Sol. 16:6, of David and Solomon, of the holy of holies both in the tabernacle of Moses and in the temple of Solomon, Exod. 36; [1 Kings 6:19–20], of the golden altar [1 Kings 6:22], of the manifold offerings, [Lev. 1–3], of the mercy seat, [Heb. 9:5], and other additional figures which all point us toward Jesus Christ.[55]

In addition to these passages, Dirk believes that Isaiah 54:5 "testifies to us, the divine and glory of Jesus Christ."[56] As God the Father is Lord and becomes a husband to his congregation, Dirk notes that Jesus Christ is the bridegroom of Jerusalem in the New Testament. He is the one who

---

53. Philips, "Concerning the True Knowledge of Jesus Christ," 158.
54. Philips, "Concerning the True Knowledge of Jesus Christ," 159.
55. Philips, "Concerning the True Knowledge of Jesus Christ," 156.
56. Philips, "Concerning the True Knowledge of Jesus Christ," 154.

will sit on the throne of David in his kingdom, he "harmonizes with that the prophet David said, 'Hear, oh daughter, consider, and incline your ear, forget your people and your father's house, and the king will desire your beauty since he is your lord, and you shall worship him,' Ps. 45:[10-]11."[57] Dirk also takes notice of the prophecies of Jeremiah. Dirk considers Jesus Christ to be the righteous plant of David who is prophesied in Jeremiah, and who will reign and execute wisely in the last day.[58] Moreover, Dirk claims that the stone in Daniel 2—which was cut from a mountain but not by human hands, which knocked the statue down, and which became a great mountain that fulfills all—would be Christ and his kingdom.[59]

Although there are several views in church tradition as to whether the Logos first appears in the Scriptures in Genesis 3:8,[60] there is no trace of Dirk's interest in the passage. However, Dirk accepts a popular Christian tradition of the relationship between Jesus and Melchizedek: namely, that Melchizedek is an Old Testament Christophany.[61] Dirk sees the book of Hebrews as linking the Lord to the Melchizedek of the Old Testament, and he calls Christ the genuine Melchizedek. He points out that Christ is "God's Son and the Son of man, one Jesus Christ, our High Priest in eternity according to the order of Melchizedek, Heb. 2:17; 5:1; 8:1, our eternal King and Prince of Peace, Isa, 9:[6]."[62]

Dirk regards Melchizedek as an important figure in the Scriptures that testify to the eternity of Christ. According to Dirk, as the writer of the book of Hebrews describes, Melchizedek "is without father or mother or genealogy, and has neither beginning of days nor end of life, but resembling the Son of God, he continues a priest forever."[63] Moreover, Dirk continues, saying, "for the apostle says of the person of Melchizedek that he had neither beginning of days nor end of life, and thereby the Son of God is compared with his person which is eternal."[64]

Moreover, Dirk argues that God's sending of his only begotten Son, Jesus Christ, to this world is closely related to the promises made to the

57. Phiips, "Concerning the True Knowledge of Jesus Christ," 155.
58. Philips, "Concerning the True Knowledge of Jesus Christ."
59. Philips, "Concerning the True Knowledge of Jesus Christ."
60. For example, Irenaeus interprets this verse as referring to Christ's advent to earth. See Holsinger-Friesen, *Irenaeus and Genesis*, 211.
61. Longman, *How to Read Genesis*, 172.
62. Philips, "Incarnation of Our Lord Jesus Christ," 141.
63. Philips, "Incarnation of Our Lord Jesus Christ," 139.
64. Philips, "Incarnation of Our Lord Jesus Christ," 140.

patriarchs of the Old Testament. Jesus Christ is not only the fulfillment of the prophecy of the Old Testament but also the fulfillment of God's promises to the patriarchs of the Old Testament. Because Christ came into the world, people should live through him, as God promised in the Old Testament. The Father showed his fatherly kindness by sending his Son to this world, and he accomplished his promise. Since God is true to his words, he wanted to keep his promises, which he made to Adam, Abraham, Isaac, Jacob, David, and the other patriarchs.[65]

Eternal Election

Dirk asserts that it is not enough to confess that "Jesus Christ is the Son of the living God, conceived in Mary through the Holy Spirit, and born out of her as a true human being."[66] Faith in Jesus Christ should include confessing that he is an eternal being. Because even the devil knows and confesses that Jesus Christ is the Son of God, it is important not only to acknowledge that Jesus is the Son of God, but also to confess that he possesses eternal life.

Dirk believes that the eternity of Christ is also supported in many places in the Scriptures. According to Dirk, "the person of the Son of God is without beginning[,] was always God, God's Word, God's wisdom[,] truly God himself[,] and essentially in divine form, glorified as God."[67] Dirk points out, however, that in some places in the Scriptures, the names that refer to Christ are not applicable to his eternal reality:

> For he is named a rock, 1 Cor. 10:4, and a vine, John 15:1, not because he essentially and naturally is a rock and a vine, but because of the significance he is so named. In like measure he is also named the seed of a woman, Gen. 3:15, and a seed of Abraham, Gen. 22: [17-] 18, not because he essentially and naturally is of the fleshly seed of the woman and Abraham, but because he was promised Adam and Eve and Abraham as a future Savior who should be born out of them according to the flesh, Gal. 3:8. But if it were really true that Christ was of a natural human seed, then humanity would be helped of God through its own seed, that is, through itself. But this be far hence, for God has helped fallen and corrupted humanity, not through fallen and

---

65. Philips, "Concerning the True Knowledge of Jesus Christ," 164.
66. Philips, "Incarnation of Our Lord Jesus Christ," 149.
67. Philips, "Incarnation of Our Lord Jesus Christ," 140.

corrupted human seed, but he willed and had to help it through his eternal Word and Son so that he was the Redeemer of humanity as well as its Creator, Ecclus. 1:4; John 1:1.[68]

Dirk admits that a rock, the seed of a woman, is not a proper name for the eternity of Christ. Such names do not express the very essence of Christ, but Dirk implies that these names do not hurt Christ's eternity because they are used in a figurative manner.[69]

In addition, Dirk sees the eternity of Christ in David. Dirk notes that even though Jesus Christ is a descendant of David, David refers to Christ as Lord in Psalm 110. Dirk believes that David calls Christ Lord through the inspiration of the Holy Spirit, and in this reference, Dirk sees the eternity of Jesus Christ.[70]

Furthermore, in the eternity of Jesus Christ, Dirk considers not only that Christ is eternal, but also that eternal life is in Christ. He acknowledges that Jesus Christ is the one who has eternal life and the one who bestows eternal life. On the other hand, Jesus Christ is the one who exists forever, and at the same time, he offers eternal life for those who believe in him. For those who believe in the Son of God will not be judged, and will have eternal life.[71]

The Incarnation of Jesus Christ

Dirk asserts there is no difference between other human beings and Christ, if the body of Christ came from Mary.[72] Of course, the body of Christ is similar to that of his brethren, but the greatest difference between Christ and his brethren is that Christ is naturally God and the Son of God.[73] Though human beings are sinful according to the flesh, the holy flesh of Christ "which is true food and makes alive, has not originally come from our flesh and blood, [and] he, Christ, is given to us from God the heavenly Father out of grace as a gift and true sign of his eternal love and fathomless mercy."[74]

68. Philips, "Incarnation of Our Lord Jesus Christ," 141.
69. Philips, "Incarnation of Our Lord Jesus Christ."
70. Philips, "Incarnation of Our Lord Jesus Christ," 144.
71. Philips, "Concerning the True Knowledge of Jesus Christ," 160.
72. Philips, "Incarnation of Our Lord Jesus Christ," 137.
73. Philips, "Incarnation of Our Lord Jesus Christ," 146.
74. Philips, "Incarnation of Our Lord Jesus Christ," 145.

According to Dirk, confessing the incarnation of Jesus Christ recognizes that he came to this world from heaven through the virgin Mary, and also that "Jesus Christ, though he has indeed appeared in the form of sinful flesh, was yet free from all sin and sinful nature, had a pure body prepared for him, by God the heavenly Father through the Holy Spirit."[75] In other words, because it is necessary to confess the divinity of Christ in order to explain that the word of God took on a body, Dirk confesses Christ as living bread from heaven.[76]

In fact, on the concept of the incarnation, Dirk's position is not much different from that of Menno Simons. While Menno says that "[Jesus] did not become flesh of Mary, but in Mary . . . He did not simply assume flesh in Mary but of Mary,"[77] Dirk insists that "because Christ the eternal Word became flesh, John 1:14, was conceived of the Holy Spirit in the virgin Mary, Matt. 1:20; Luke [1:35], and was born out of her, therefore, his flesh is also pure, spotless, and holy, and has not seen corruption, Acts 2:31; but is the living bread which gives life to the world, John 6:51."[78]

These concepts within Menno and Dirk's view of Christ's incarnation can be traced back to Hoffman. Hoffman used several analogies to illustrate how Christ was born through Mary. In the most well-known of these, he described Christ as a pearl. Hoffman says that the dew of heaven falls on mussel and becomes a pearl, but the pearl in the mussel does not have any characteristics of the mussel.[79] In the same way, according to this view, Jesus Christ came from heaven and was born through Mary, but no character of a human being was taken from Mary. Hoffman insisted that the body of Christ came from heaven and that his body was the visible word of God.[80] To Hoffman, "Christ was not half earthly and half heavenly but was flesh, bones, spirit, and blood, the true God."[81] Although Menno and Dirk did not use this analogy, their view of incarnation is very similar to that of Hoffman.

Dirk finds the cause of the incarnation to be God's fathomless grace and mercy. God gave his only begotten Son in love for human beings

---

75. Philips, "Concerning the True Knowledge of Jesus Christ," 160.
76. Philips, "Incarnation of Our Lord Jesus Christ," 138.
77. Simons, "Brief Confession on the Incarnation," 432.
78. Philips, "Incarnation of Our Lord Jesus Christ," 146.
79. Pater, "Study of Selected Doctrines," 50.
80. Hofmann, "Ordinance of God," 194–97.
81. Pater, "Study of Selected Doctrines," 44.

and made them have eternal life.[82] The incarnation is the most crucial channel of God's fulfillment of his love for humanity, and the righteousness and love of God have been revealed in Christ. As a sacrifice for all humankind, Christ reconciled people with God forever, and has forgiven humanity's sins "through his death and blood triumph against the devil, sin, death, and hell."[83] Christ is also the only alternative to fallen humanity. Dirk says, "Further, it is here to be observed and reflected upon that humanity, once it had fallen, could in no way be helped except by the one by and through whom it had been created."[84]

Existence of Christ in the World

As already mentioned above, Dirk stresses that Jesus was born with a human body on earth to emphasize the humanity of Christ. Moreover, in referring to the birth of Jesus, which he testifies is found in the New Testament, Dirk has no doubt about the birth of Jesus. He assumes that this article of the faith is true.

Dirk clearly asserts that the birth of Jesus is a divine event in which the word has become flesh. However, he also sees this birth as a phenomenon that was visible and concrete in the world, and not merely an illusion. Dirk is well aware of the events regarding Joseph and Mary before the birth of Jesus, events which are introduced by the Gospels. Dirk quotes the Gospel of John and the First Epistle of John to give the theological implication of the events of the birth of Jesus, also citing Jesus' birth story in the book of Matthew and Luke.[85]

In his treatise *The Incarnation of Our Lord Jesus Christ, the Only Begotten Son of His Eternal and Almighty Father*, Dirk, in reference to the birth of Christ, generally emphasizes the fact that Christ came to earth with a human body. However, Dirk never overlooks the divinity of Christ as he discusses the birth of Jesus Christ. He points out that Jesus was born to the virgin Mary in the flesh, but also as the holy Son of the Most High. Thus it would be appropriate to assume that both the humanity and divinity of Christ are of great importance to Dirk in reference to the birth of

---

82. Philips, "Concerning the True Knowledge of Jesus Christ," 165.
83. Philips, "Concerning the True Knowledge of Jesus Christ," 162.
84. Philips, "Incarnation of Our Lord Jesus Christ," 138.
85. Dirk specifically refers to Matt 1:20; Luke 1:35; John 1:1–3, 1:14, quoting 1 John 1:1. See Philips, "Incarnation of Our Lord Jesus Christ," 136.

Christ. Dirk sees the Holy Spirit and Mary as the most important aspects of the birth of Christ; he says that Christ was conceived in Mary through the Holy Spirit, and that Christ came from the virgin Mary because he is the Holy Son of the Most High, the second Adam, the Lord in heaven, and the living bread that descends from heaven.[86]

Although Dirk does not have a particular interest in any specific miracles or signs that Jesus Christ did during his public life, he acknowledges that Jesus Christ performed many signs and miracles. The miracles and signs of wonder that Jesus performed are a testimony to the gospel and also serve to testify of his divinity. According to Dirk, "since Christ is the end of the law and a mediator of the New Testament, therefore his teaching had to be confirmed with strong signs and wonderful works, just as the Old Testament was confirmed with signs and miracles, Rom. 10:4; Heb. 7:11; Gal. 3:20; Heb. 12:24."[87]

However, while Dirk acknowledges the signs and miracles of Jesus Christ, he is extremely alert to some Christians' problematic pursuit of signs and miracles. For Dirk, signs and miracles can sometimes be tricks of false prophets, and they can interfere with believers' acquiring of true beliefs.[88] Dirk notes that Jesus said in John 4:48, "Whenever you do not see signs and wonders do not believe."[89] Dirk points out that, as seen in Jesus' words, even some of those who saw the signs of Jesus did not possess true faith, and they continually demanded signs and miracles.

Dirk's view of signs and miracles is based on his view of the ministry of church leaders. In his treatise *The Sending of Preachers*, he asserts that preachers and teachers do not need to perform signs and miracles as did Jesus Christ, because there is no longer any reason for the preachers and teachers to do them. Dirk says, "now that the teaching of Christ has once been established, and no other teaching is taught or maybe taught, yes, cursed is the one who preaches another gospel than that which Christ and his apostles have preached to us, Gal. 1:9."[90] Moreover, for Dirk, signs and miracles do not help strengthen believers' faith; proper teaching is more important for the improvement of their faith. In places where the word of God is taught correctly, and where the glory of God is revealed, people

---

86. Philips, "Incarnation of Our Lord Jesus Christ," 143.
87. Philips, "Sending of Preachers or Teachers," 224.
88. Philips, "Sending of Preachers or Teachers," 199.
89. Philips, "Sending of Preachers or Teachers," 223.
90. Philips, "Sending of Preachers or Teachers," 224.

will receive salvation.⁹¹ In other words, for Dirk, what people see—signs and miracles—is not as important as what leads people's lives—the word of God.

In fact, for Dirk, a more important miracle than any signs and miracles that Jesus Christ performed is the miracle that Jesus came to this earth himself and died on the cross for the people. Therefore, Dirk considers that it is sinful to seek other signs and miracles. He says,

> Because the gospel has now been confirmed with such glorious miracles (the like of which had never taken place) [and] in addition was empowered with the innocent death and precious blood of the spotless Lamb, Jesus Christ, Heb. 9:13[-14], and was for a long time obscured, but now through the grace of God [has] again come to light, so all devout Christians must allow themselves to be satisfied therewith. So that whoever requires a sign beyond this must hear "an evil and adulterous nature seeks for a sign," etc. Matt. 12:39.⁹²

Dirk does not discuss the transfiguration of Jesus, but he considers the transfigured Jesus on Mount Tabor to be the same as he will be when believers encounter him in the last days.⁹³ That is, when believers will meet Jesus in the final new heaven and the new earth, he will have the same the appearance that he had on Mount Tabor during his public life.

Because of his particular purpose in writing, Dirk does not have an interest in the events of the transfiguration other than the connection between his eschatological interest and the transfiguration. Among Dirk's entire writings, references to the transfiguration of Jesus appear in only in one letter. This letter was written by Dirk to a brother's wife, whose husband was imprisoned in Antwerp. Although it was not known whether the brother was eventually martyred,⁹⁴ Dirk encouraged his brother's wife to devote herself to the end for the truth. In this situation, Dirk encourages all those who believe in Jesus that they will meet Jesus, who was transfigured in Mount Tabor, in the future.⁹⁵

The sacrifice and crucifixion of Christ is the key element in the Christian faith and the proclamation of faith, for Christ died and completed

---

91. Philips, "Sending of Preachers or Teachers," 204.
92. Philips, "Sending of Preachers or Teachers," 224.
93. Philips, "Epistle to the Wife of I. the S.," 627.
94. Philips, "Epistle to the Wife of I. the S.," 618.
95. Philips, "Epistle to the Wife of I. the S.," 627.

the work of the atonement on the cross. Dirk understands that Christ was crucified on the cross because he died for the human race and that he became a sacrifice to solve the problem of human sin.[96] Jesus Christ, for the human race, suffered pain in a pure and holy body, allowed others to put a crown of thorn on his head, and finally submitted to a shameful death on the cross.[97] Because of Christ's death on the cross, everything in heaven and on earth could be reconciled, and the whole world was given the opportunity to receive the Lord and obtain eternal life. The cross also demonstrates the love of God in that Christ died for humanity.[98]

Dirk argues that the cross of Christ is closely related to the Old Testament. He argues that David's words that "I am a worm, and no man; scorned by men, and despised by the people, All who see me mock at me, they make mouths at me, they wag their heads" prophesied the suffering of Christ,[99] and he also believes that the suffering of the cross of Christ is prophesied in Isaiah 53: 6.[100]

While Dirk refers directly to the crucifixion of Christ, he also uses other phrases to refer to the crucifixion. Dirk uses "the blood of Christ" primarily in the discussion of the Lord's Supper,[101] and as a phrase to support the true humanity of Christ.[102] However, Dirk also uses "the blood of Christ" as a phrase that implicitly portrays the work of Christ. According to Dirk, "the blood of Christ" is for the redemption and reconciliation of his people,[103] and "the blood of Christ" just as the figurative Paschal Lamb of God was called the "Passover of God."[104]

Dirk believes that the resurrection and ascension of Jesus Christ are important factors in the knowledge of the grace of Jesus Christ:

> The knowledge of the grace of our Lord Jesus Christ teaches us that we shall not be saved through our works, neither through any other means than through the merit of Jesus Christ alone, Eph. 2:4. For he is our righteousness, holiness, and eternal life, 1 Cor. 1:[30]. He is our redeemer, 1 Tim. 2:5, Advocate, 1 John

96. Philips, "Concerning the True Knowledge of Jesus Christ," 162.
97. Philips, "Concerning the True Knowledge of Jesus Christ," 162–63.
98. Philips, "Concerning the True Knowledge of Jesus Christ," 163–64.
99. Philips, "Concerning the True Knowledge of Jesus Christ," 162.
100. Philips, "Supper of Our Lord Jesus Christ," 124.
101. Philips, "Supper of Our Lord Jesus Christ," 113–14.
102. Philips, "Baptism of Our Lord Jesus Christ," 80.
103. Philips, "Supper of Our Lord Jesus Christ," 118.
104. Philips, "Supper of Our Lord Jesus Christ," 123.

2:1, Reconciler, Savior, and throne of grace, through faith in his blood, Rom. 3:25. His suffering is our joy; his cross is our triumph, Col. 2:14; and boasting, his death is our life; his resurrection from the dead is our rising to eternal glory, 1 Cor. 15:21; his ascension is our way to the Father; his union with us is our union with God, John 17:21; and makes us partakers in the divine nature and immortality, 2 Pet 1:4.[105]

Dirk discusses the resurrection and ascension of Christ in line with his divine attributes—righteousness, holiness, and eternal life—and his ministry—redeemer, advocate, reconciler, savior. Dirk does not raise any doubt about the resurrection and the ascension in his discussion of the life of Jesus Christ, but he does focuses on discussing their meaning.

Dirk sees an example of the resurrection of Jesus Christ in connection with the story of Abraham in the Old Testament. Dirk argues that Abraham's willingness to give Isaac to God because he was afraid of God is a good example of how God accomplishes what he wants, and that God's restoration of Isaac to Abraham is a good example of resurrection.[106]

According to Dirk, the resurrection of Jesus Christ is the means by which God's mercy renews believers.[107] God's promise to his people was fulfilled through the resurrection of Jesus Christ, and the resurrection makes it possible to bind and unite God to all true believers.[108]

Dirk prefers to understand the resurrection from the eschatological point of view. He claims that true believers will be resurrected at the end of time, just as Jesus Christ was resurrected. This resurrection is the reward of the eternal life of true believers.[109] The resurrection of Christ is the ultimate triumph of the kingdom of God,[110] and this ultimate victory is sufficient reason for true believers who face persecution and suffering to endure during their temporal life.[111] Dirk insists that since the righteous will be resurrected and will meet again in the will of God, there is no need to fear enemies, but only to fight for the truth of the gospel.[112]

---

105. Philips, "True Knowledge of God," 258.
106. Philips, "Answer to Sebastian Franck," 454.
107. Philips, "Three Admonitions: No. III," 421–22.
108. Philips, "Frisian-Flemish Division," 501.
109. Philips, "Congregation of God," 382.
110. Philips, "Three Admonitions: No. I," 386.
111. Philips, "Three Admonitions: No. I," 387.
112. Philips, "Three Admonitions: No. III," 425.

The Relationship of Christ to the Trinity

Dirk focuses on the name of the Triune God in the Scriptures as evidence that the Father, the Son, and the Holy Spirit are one. Dirk says that God "has, in accordance with his character, nature, and activity, many names in the Old Testament with which he was called. But, in the New Testament God is actually called the Father, Son, and Holy Spirit by Jesus Christ himself. With these three names, the whole divine being (insofar as it is humanly possible to comprehend it) was expressed by the Lord himself."[113] Dirk clearly believes that the almighty and living God is one and is expressed in the name of the Father, the Son, and the Holy Spirit in the diversity of God's divine presence.

In the relationship between the Father God and Jesus Christ, Dirk emphasizes that the Father and the Son are one substance. Jesus Christ is the Son of God, but he "is one substance, identical in character and nature with the Father."[114] Although the Son of God is named the Word, "the Son is not a spoken but a speaking Word."[115] Dirk argues that the Son is not a subordinate being derived from God, but the same being as God. Dirk's claim is based on the testimony of many prophets and apostles of the Bible, claiming that the Scriptures have shown the relationship between Jesus Christ and the Father in many places.[116] Thus, Jesus Christ, like the Father, is the object of worship and respect, and the object of the faith of all believers. However, the fact that Jesus Christ and God the Father are one substance does not imply that the Father and the Son have the same

---

113. Philips, "Confession of Our Faith (Concerning) God," 62.

114. Philips, "Incarnation of Our Lord Jesus Christ," 136.

115. Philips, "Incarnation of Our Lord Jesus Christ," 136.

116. Dirk says that "The prophets and apostles also express and bear him witness that he is the 'mighty God, the everlasting Father,' Isa. 9:[6], the omnipotent Lord, Isa 40:25, the Lord of hosts, the Holy One of Israel, Isa. 54:5, the righteous branch of David, Jer. 23:5, the Lord our righteousness, Jer. 33:15, the only begotten Son of the most high and living God, Matt. 16:16, through whom all grace and truth have come into existence, John 6:69; 1:17, in whom are hidden all the treasures of the wisdom and knowledge of God, Col. 2:[3], the Word of God in whom the whole fullness of God dwells bodily, Col. 2:9, yes, the same is the wisdom of God, the Word of God, 1 Cor. 1:[21]; Rev. 19:[13], the truth and eternal life. Col. 2:3; Prov. 8:22; John 1:1, God whose throne shall endure for ever and for ever, Ps. 45: [6]. He is the Creator of heaven and earth for all that is was created through him, and without him nothing that is was created, Heb. 1:[10]; John 1:3; Col. 1:16. All things exist in him, [Col. 1:17], and he does all that he sees the Father doing, Heb. 1:2; John 5:[36]" (Philips, "Concerning the True Knowledge of Jesus Christ," 159).

role. Dirk understands that the Son of God has become the savior of this world by God the Father for the sins of human beings, and that the Son represents the Father's mercy on earth.[117]

In his discussion of the relationship between the Son and the Holy Spirit, Dirk emphasizes that the Spirit is the one who works to enable the ministry of the Son. According to Dirk, the Son and Holy Spirit are equal in essence, but different in their roles just as the roles of the Father and the Son are different.[118] The role of the Holy Spirit is understood as the role of the intermediary. Jesus Christ came through the Holy Spirit when he came to this earth as the Eternal and Almighty Word, and his ministry could be possible only in the Holy Spirit. Dirk argues that the work of the Holy Spirit comes from the Father and proceeds through the Son. Sometimes the Son is also described as having a close relationship with the Holy Spirit in revealing God's eternal truths: "Therefore everything that the Holy Spirit has declared and spoken through the prophets and apostles, 2 Pet [1]:21, yes, through Jesus Christ himself, that is the eternal and trustworthy truth, and the testimony of God."[119]

Functional Christology

Christ's ministry is traditionally categorized into three offices—a prophet, a priest, and a king.[120] Dirk also refers to these three ministries of Christ. Generally, in Dirk's account of the three offices of Christ, the ministry of Christ is not limited to any specific time and situation. Dirk does not hold the view that Jesus Christ performed the office of the prophet only before the resurrection, since he had a human appearance, and that he was unable to carry out the office of the priest and king during his public ministry in the world. Dirk sees Jesus Christ as fulfilling human needs through various functions in any circumstance, and as satisfying God's righteousness. Christ performs the office of a prophet, delivering the

---

117. Philips, "True Knowledge of God," 257.
118. Philips, "True Knowledge of God," 258–59.
119. Philips, "True Knowledge of God," 259.
120. Although not everyone agreed historically on this distinction, Calvin was the man who led the division of the ministry of Christ into three offices. For a discussion of Christ's offices, see Berkhof, *Systematic Theology*, 356–66, 406–12; Reymond, *New Systematic Theology of the Christian Faith*, 623–24; Grudem, *Systematic Theology*, 624–29. Erickson uses the terms "revealing," "ruling," and "reconciling" to describe the three offices of Christ (Erickson, *Christian Theology*, 697–703).

message of the Father and resolving the ignorance of humans. As a priest, Christ offered himself to God as a sacrifice to reconcile the church and God, and he solved the problem of human sin. In carrying out the office of king, Christ invites his elected people to become his people, to rule over them, and to give them power and protection.[121]

However, it is a misjudgment to assume that Dirk's view of Christ's function is limited to the three aspects above. In fact, Dirk is not interested in presenting the function of Christ in an official form using a specific concept. He is not interested in artificial distinctions; he is just presenting the work of Christ in the Scripture. Thus, in addition to the above three offices, Dirk expresses the function of Christ by using christological terms that correspond to one or more of these additional offices of Christ's ministry: the Mediator, the Lamb, the Shepherd, and the bridegroom.

According to Dirk, Christ carries the message of the Father as he performs the office of prophet.[122] This prophet declares the message of God to the people of God, prophesies the future, and performs his duties by revealing God's will for salvation by the Holy Spirit. To support this idea, Dirk presents the text of the prophet prophesied in Deuteronomy 18 as crucial evidence. Specifically, Dirk believes that in Deuteronomy 18:15, the prophet who will be raised in the future is Jesus Christ.[123] The prophet who appears in Deuteronomy is to proclaim the word of God—which brings death if people do not follow it, but Dirk says they will be saved if they believe the words of this prophet.[124]

Christ fulfilled the righteousness of God as he performed the office of the priest and sacrificed himself to God for the salvation of his people. As a basis for the priesthood of Christ in the Scripture, Dirk mentions that Christ was designated by God as being of the order of Melchizedek. Dirk recognizes Jesus Christ as holding an eternal priesthood like Melchizedek's, as mentioned in Hebrews 7. Dirk says that "[t]hese words actually may not be taken to indicate the figurative Melchizedek but one must understand them to apply to Jesus Christ, the Son of the most high

---

121. Reymond, *New Systematic Theology of the Christian Faith*, 624.

122. Philips, "Concerning the True Knowledge of Jesus Christ," 172.

123. Dirk says, "This Moses had certainly seen in the Spirit; namely that one should now hear Christ Jesus alone and that the punishment of God shall come upon all despisers and transgressors of the saving teaching of Jesus Christ. (Philips, "Concerning the True Knowledge of Jesus Christ," 171–72).

124. Philips, "Concerning the True Knowledge of Jesus Christ," 172.

God, our only High Priest according to the order of Melchizedek, [Heb. 5:5–7]."[125]

As the one who holds the office of the king, Christ calls his chosen people and rules among them, rebuking, reproving, and ruling. Dirk argues that because Jesus Christ is the eternal King, David called Jesus Christ Lord. Although Jesus was a descendant of David in the flesh, David was able to call Jesus the Lord because Jesus did not come from the seed of David.[126] According to Dirk, although Jesus Christ has not sat on the throne of David physically, he will "will sit upon the throne of David in his kingdom, to prepare and establish it with fairness and justice to eternity."[127]

Another office of Christ that Dirk refers to in this context is the office of the Mediator. Dirk sees Jesus Christ as the only true Mediator between God and man. Dirk understands the Mediator office of Christ by directly connecting his divinity and humanity. In other words, Jesus had to be the true God and a true man in order to mediate between God and humankind as the Savior of humanity. He says as follows:

> According to his divinity, he was able to help us eternally and completely reconcile us to the Father, Heb. 10:14, and accomplish his will, John 10:17; yes, the will of the Father is also the will of Christ, John 17:20[-21]. But according to his humanity, he was able to offer himself for us as a pure, holy, and well-pleasing offering and fragrant sacrifice to the Father, Eph. 5:2, for the forgiveness and cleansing of our sins, Eph. 1:7; 2:4 [-5]; Rev. l:[5-]6, because he died innocently in our behalf, and human nature in him was unblemished and without sin, [1] Pet 1:18 [-19];Isa.53:8[-9];1 Pet 3:18.[128]

As the Lamb of God, Jesus Christ, according to the command of his Father in heaven, forsook his life and took charge of the sins of the world.[129] The office of the Lamb of Jesus Christ is closely related to the office of the Mediator and the priest. Jesus Christ was crucified on the cross as the Lamb of the Passover, performing the office of the Mediator

---

125. Philips, "Confession of Our Faith (Concerning) God," 65.
126. Philips, "Incarnation of Our Lord Jesus Christ," 143.
127. Philips, "Concerning the True Knowledge of Jesus Christ," 154.
128. Philips, "Incarnation of Our Lord Jesus Christ," 136.
129. Philips, "Incarnation of Our Lord Jesus Christ," 148.

to reconcile the dying humans with God the Father, and the sacrifice of himself has served the priesthood.[130]

Dirk describes Jesus Christ not only as the Lamb but also as the only Good Shepherd.[131] The meaning of the office of the Lamb, which gives its life for humankind, is similar to that of the office of the Good Shepherd. Dirk understands that the character of the Good Shepherd is to seek for his lost sheep and to lay down his life for his sheep. This role is similar to the sacrifice of the lamb of the Passover.[132]

Finally, Dirk also refers to the office of the bridegroom of Christ. Christ is the bridegroom of God's church. He loves his bride and will protect it to the end. As a pure bride, the church should be left for only one husband, and only the bridegroom should be honored and worshiped.[133]

Summary

Dirk does not subdivide the themes of Christology, but his discussion of Christology involves a variety of topics, including the humanity, divinity, incarnation, and work of Christ. Dirk strives not to lose balance in understanding Jesus Christ, and he seems to know that it is possible to recognize both the divinity and humanity of Christ. In addition, he knows how heresies misused the divinity and humanity of Christ, and he constantly seeks to stay away from them.[134]

The way Dirk balances the divinity and humanity of Christ is by maintaining logical ambiguity, in the same way that the Council of Chalcedon did.[135] In his discussion of the humanity of Christ, he says that Christ possesses human flesh, but he also claims that he is from heaven.[136] Although Dirk is silent about the scientific and logical reasons for how Christ in human flesh could come from heaven, he affirms the claim

---

130. Philips, "Incarnation of Our Lord Jesus Christ."
131. Philips, "Concerning the True Knowledge of Jesus Christ," 154.
132. Philips, "Concerning the True Knowledge of Jesus Christ."
133. Philips, "Concerning the True Knowledge of Jesus Christ," 155.
134. Philips, "Incarnation of Our Lord Jesus Christ," 134–35; Philips, "Concerning the True Knowledge of Jesus Christ," 153.
135. See "The Humanity of Christ" of this chapter for the discussion of Dirk's view on the humanity of Christ.
136. Philips, "Incarnation of Our Lord Jesus Christ," 137–38.

that Christ had flesh but came from heaven, not human seed.[137] He does not consider any other possibility at all.

Regarding the humanity of Christ, Dirk understands that Christ, through his human body in this world, overcame Satan's temptation, and that he suffered and died on the cross.[138] In particular, his claims that Christ suffered and died physically on the cross deny the heresies of Docetism and Patripassionism.[139]

Regarding the divinity of Christ, Dirk shows that many parables and explanations of the Scripture support the divinity of Christ. According to Dirk, Christ preexisted before this world; he is timeless and different from angels. The divinity of Christ is proved by several prophecies in the Old Testament, and the New Testament also testifies of his divinity in many places. Moreover, Christ is not only the living God but the bestower of everlasting life.

Dirk claims that the Father, Son, and Holy Spirit are one, and that the Triune God exists as one substance. Dirk, however, clearly distinguishes the role of the Triune God and understands Christ's work in the relationship between the Father and the Holy Spirit. Regarding the function of Christ, Dirk recognizes the three offices of prophet, priest, and king; but in addition, he describes the work of Christ in various ways, such as his work as the Mediator, the Lamb, the Shepherd, and the bridegroom.

Although Dirk's Christology covers a variety of topics, it is true that he does not discuss each theory in detail. Dirk insists that Christ has both divinity and humanity, but does not take an in-depth approach to discussing the christological controversy in church history—the question of the exact nature of the relationship between deity and humanity in the person of Jesus Christ. He asserts that Jesus Christ possesses both divinity and humanity, but does not provide a logical explanation of how that is possible. Keeney points out, Dirk developed most of his theology from his personal experience than from a contemplative or reflective examination.[140]

A notable disadvantage of Dirk's Christology is that while he discusses much about the birth of Christ, his discussion of the work and life of Christ is relatively poor. In other words, his discussion includes

137. Philips, "Incarnation of Our Lord Jesus Christ."

138. Philips, "Tabernacle of Moses," 279–80.

139. For Dirk's view of Christ's physical suffering see Philips, "Incarnation of Our Lord Jesus Christ," 147.

140. Keeney, *Development of Dutch Anabaptist Thought and Practice*, 22.

relatively little about Jesus' work on earth, its meaning, the cross, the resurrection, and the ascension. The reason for this is the fact that his main argument in Christology is regarding the incarnation; as a result, other subjects probably received relatively little attention.

The Correlation of Dirk Philips's View of the Visible Church with His Christology

The relationship between Dirk's Christology and his view of the visible church is both indirect and direct. The relationship between the two is indirect in that Dirk does not mention the visible church in his discussion of Christology. On the other hand, the relationship between the two is direct because Dirk's discussion of Christology provides a close lesson on the lives of believers in the visible church. Dirk deals with the direction and nature of the life of regenerated believers in Jesus Christ. Dirk does not appear to allow any possibility of truly knowing about Jesus Christ without faith in Jesus Christ. Thus, Dirk's Christology is closely related to the lives and practices of believers in the visible church. The relevance can be understood in three ways as follows.

First, the meaning of the believers in the visible church knowing Jesus Christ is that they follow Jesus Christ. One of two treatises in which Dirk mainly deals with Christ is "Concerning the True Knowledge of Jesus Christ."[141] As the title of this treatise suggests, Dirk was well aware of the detriment of having a false knowledge of Jesus Christ, and he knew how important it was to have a true knowledge of Christ. However, Dirk makes no distinction between knowing Jesus Christ, loving Jesus Christ, and keeping the commandments of Jesus Christ. To Dirk, knowing that Jesus Christ is eternal life is true knowledge of Jesus Christ, but this is different from simply knowing the theoretical, historical knowledge of Christ. The true knowledge of Christ causes God to do a living and powerful work through those who confess Christ, and he transforms those who are determined to confess and follow Christ. It is they who are lovers of Jesus Christ, and loving Jesus Christ means keeping his commandments.[142]

Second, Dirk's Christology is closely linked to the work of the Holy Spirit, which affects the life of believers. The true knowledge of Jesus

---

141. Philips, "Concerning the True Knowledge of Jesus Christ."
142. Philips, "Concerning the True Knowledge of Jesus Christ," 165.

Christ is what the Holy Spirit brings to Christians. The Holy Spirit enlightens people, gives them true knowledge, and helps them keep the commands of Jesus Christ. Therefore, to have the true knowledge of Jesus Christ is to live with the help of the Holy Spirit. According to Dirk, the Holy Spirit not only active in Christ's conception, but also helped Jesus in his life and ministry in the world; at the same time, the Holy Spirit provides people with a constant knowledge of the Lord Jesus Christ.[143] By the Holy Spirit people come to believe that Jesus Christ is Redeemer and come to peace with God. Such faith transforms and renews people within, making them partakers of eternal life as Christians.[144]

Third, Jesus' work affects those who believe in him. Dirk recognizes Jesus Christ as the only true Mediator between God and humankind, so he understands that one of Jesus' important ministries is to mediate between people and God. The result, then, is that people live as the people of God. Eventually, the victorious Lord will cause the congregations of Christ to win victory and to overcome, so that those who are in Jesus Christ will be affected his work.[145] Believers will become children of the Most High through participation and fellowship in the divine nature of Jesus Christ, gaining everlasting life, and declaring glory and purity. In his discussion of Christ's incarnation, which is the core of his Christology, Dirk claims that believers are elevated through Jesus Christ: "Just as the believers are now elevated through Christ and transposed into God, participants of the divine nature, 2 Pet 1:4, and become like Christ in glory, so Christ has also humbled himself for the sake of his brothers, Phil. 2:5 [-8]."[146] For Dirk, the ministry of Jesus brings about a change in the status of those who believe in Jesus, and this changed status causes believers to live a new life.

In conclusion, Dirk Philips deals with Jesus Christ in his discussion but does not intend to introduce Jesus Christ to everyone. Dirk's readers already seem to be clearly limited. In other words, Dirk does not intend to introduce Jesus Christ to those who have no information about him, nor to communicate accurate theological knowledge of Jesus Christ to those who have faith in him. The most important thing for Dirk seems to be practice. According to Dirk, knowledge of Jesus Christ is the pledge

---

143. Philips, "Confession of Our Faith (Concerning) God," 66.
144. Philips, "Our Confession," 69.
145. Philips, "Incarnation of Our Lord Jesus Christ," 142.
146. Philips, "Incarnation of Our Lord Jesus Christ," 146.

of the believers' practice. Dirk, of course, intends the believers to avoid falling into heresy by coming into the true knowledge of Jesus Christ, but he insists that the true knowledge of Jesus Christ is evidenced not from knowing him but from loving him and keeping his commandments. In addition, as the Holy Spirit worked in the incarnation of Jesus Christ and in his life on the earth, the Spirit also works in the lives of believers. Finally, through Jesus' ministry, believers live new lives.

Chapter 4

ECCLESIOLOGY

Introduction

As DISCUSSED IN PREVIOUS chapters of this dissertation, scholars have argued that ecclesiology is central to Anabaptist theology.¹ Although the Dirk scholar Keeney argues that the center of Dirk's theology is the word of God and the incarnation, it is also being argued here that Dirk's theology is directed toward the congregation of God and their lives. After all, Dirk's discussion of the word of God and incarnation is to promote the pure life of the congregation of God. John Rempel would be one scholar who supports this claim. Rempel, for example, argues that Dirk's belief in the incarnation logically leads to his view of the sacraments.² In other words, Dirk's view of the sacraments that were to be practiced by the congregation of God was based on his theology of incarnation.

Rempel, however, did not extend his arguments to ecclesiastical subjects other than the sacraments, whereas it will be argued here that Dirk's Christology was the decisive theoretical basis for shaping his ecclesiology in general. Rempel's focus was quite narrow, looking particularly at Dirk's views on baptism, admonition, excommunication, avoidance, and the Lord's Supper. In each of these areas, the incarnation and divinity of Jesus Christ are at the core of the subjects, and above all, Jesus Christ is the fundamental reason for the lives and changes of believers who

---

1. Bender, "Anabaptist Theology of Discipleship," 26; Friedmann, *Theology of Anabaptism*, 116; Price, "Anabaptist View of the Church," 190–96; Krahn, "Prolegomena to an Anabaptist Theology," 10–11; Davids, "Anabaptist View of the Church," 81–93.

2. Rempel, *Lord's Supper in Anabaptism*, 169.

practice church ordinances and church discipline. The various themes of Dirk's theology all point to the pure life of the congregation of God.

The purpose of this chapter is to explore Dirk's ecclesiology and how it relates to Dirk's view of the visible church. This chapter will deal with Dirk's views on baptism and the Lord's Supper, as well as his views on church discipline, which involve admonition, excommunication, and avoidance. This chapter will also examine how Dirk's theological writings deal with the life of God's congregation that constitutes the visible church in Dirk's thought.

Dirk's View of Baptism

Two concepts are essential to understanding Dirk's view of baptism: "validity of baptism" and "faith in baptism." He believes that baptism is a biblically based ordinance instituted by Christ and is an essential ordinance of the Christian community. He also believes that it functions to distinguish believers from unbelievers through the confession of believers. In addition, Dirk sees faith as the most important condition for baptism. For Dirk, hearing, understanding, and believing the gospel of Christ are prerequisites for baptism. Those who do not have faith for themselves are not eligible to be baptized. This is the key reason for Dirk's refusal of infant baptism.

In Dirk's treatise *The Baptism of Our Lord Jesus Christ*, which deals specifically with baptism, Dirk uses a different form from his other writings. Specifically, this treatise is dialectical. In this treatise, Dirk brings up arguments against him and his community in relation to baptism, and he provides a theological basis for the effective defense of his community. In most of his writings, Dirk presents an analysis of the subject through biblical knowledge with theological power.[3] But in the treatise, Dirk introduces the arguments of others he disagrees with and provides grounds for refuting them.

---

3. See introduction of chapter 1 of this dissertation for the discussion of Dirk's biblical knowledge and theological abilities.

Internal and External Christian Baptism

Dirk promotes both internal baptism with the Holy Spirit and external baptism with the water.[4] According to Dirk, the internal baptism takes place with the Holy Spirit and fire. He believes that the first baptism of the Holy Spirit occurred on the day of Pentecost, as the Lord promised his apostles.[5] Although Dirk generally uses John's gospel and letters a great deal to support his various claims throughout his writings, on the subject of the baptism of the Holy Spirit, he deals with Luke's record of the event of the receiving of the Holy Spirit more than that of John.[6] In other words, Dirk does not expound upon the event in which Jesus told his disciples, "receive the Holy Spirit" in John 20:22, nor does he see this instance as the coming of the Holy Spirit to people generally. Dirk believes that Jesus Christ proclaimed the day of the coming Spirit during his earthly ministry. He spoke of the day when the Spirit of God would be gloriously poured out upon his people, and this occurred on Pentecost, as testified in Acts.[7]

External baptism, on the other hand, is baptism with water in the name of the Father, Son, and Holy Spirit. Dirk believes that "the external baptism with water is a witness to spiritual baptism, a proof of true sorrow, and a sign of faith in Jesus Christ."[8] The reason that baptism is important to Dirk is the fact that Jesus Christ instituted the ordinance. Dirk points out that in Matthew 28, Jesus' commandment when he left his disciples was to baptize people. Dirk also stresses in Mark 16 that believers who have been baptized will be saved.[9]

The Meaning of Water Baptism

What does it mean for believers to be baptized? Why should believers be baptized? Dirk provides a clear answer to this question. Baptism proves

---

4. Philips, "Baptism of Our Lord Jesus Christ," 72.
5. Philips, "Baptism of Our Lord Jesus Christ."
6. Dirk generally presents a variety of biblical passages as evidence to support his claim, but he deals with the Gospel of John more than the other Gospels, especially in John 1, which he quotes the most.
7. Philips, "Baptism of Our Lord Jesus Christ," 73–74.
8. Philips, "Baptism of Our Lord Jesus Christ," 72.
9. Philips, "Baptism of Our Lord Jesus Christ," 73.

that the person being baptized has heard the gospel, has sorrow for his sins, and manifests his faith to the public.[10]

The most important meaning of baptism for Dirk is that it is the official confession of faith of those who are baptized.[11] Dirk refuses to give a spiritual meaning to the ordinance of baptism, saying that baptism itself has no spiritual efficiency with regard to salvation; but he does not think that external baptism with water is without spiritual meaning.[12] He does not believe that baptism is an absolute means of salvation, but he believes that the baptism commanded by Jesus Christ is a confession of faith for believers.[13] Dirk, therefore, is interested in explaining the meaning of the baptized person's confession in explaining the meaning of water baptism.

Dirk summarizes the confession of faith in baptism as follows:

> With these words the apostle gives us to understand what Christian baptism means to the believer, namely, the dying of the flesh or putting to death the old Adam, the burial of sins, the putting off of the sinful body, and a resurrection to a new life, Col. 2:[11]-12. For this reason and with this instruction, since Christ has died, was buried on behalf of our sins, and was raised from the dead for our justification, Rom. 4:25, we through faith are first incorporated into him and then become partakers of his death, his righteousness, his holiness, yes, of all that is his. To this his fellowship we have been called by God out of grace and become established in and through baptism. Therefore, we must also for his sake die to sin, bury it, and live in righteousness in the Spirit so that we may be his true members.[14]

As Dirk mentions, baptism means that the old sinful body dies and is resurrected to a new life. Because Christ died, buried, and rose from the dead for human sin, believers live a new life through faith in him. Therefore, the most noteworthy point of Dirk's argument is the new life. The concept of a new life is key to understanding Dirk baptism. Dirk believes "no external sign alone is of any value without true faith, without the new birth, and without a sincere Christlike being."[15] Overall, Dirk constantly

---

10. Philips, "Baptism of Our Lord Jesus Christ."

11. Philips, "Baptism of Our Lord Jesus Christ," 74–75; Philips, "New Birth and the New Creature," 300; Keeney, "Dirk Philips," 31.

12. Philips, "Baptism of Our Lord Jesus Christ," 76.

13. Philips, "Baptism of Our Lord Jesus Christ," 74.

14. Philips, "Baptism of Our Lord Jesus Christ," 75.

15. Philips, "Baptism of Our Lord Jesus Christ," 76.

insists that a new, Christlike life is the life of the baptized, and that the most important meaning of baptism is to testify and declare a new life.

As mentioned earlier, Dirk does not believe that baptism has any spiritual efficiency that leads to salvation. In addition, he does not acknowledge baptism as valid if it does not accompany true faith and new life. In order to stress true faith and new life, Dirk explains the connection between believers' baptism and the putting on of Christ. Dirk argues that being baptized is to put on Christ, and "to put on Christ is actually to become partakers of Christ and his being, his character and nature, his spirit, and all that is his."[16] In other words, being baptized is not only a confession of true faith in Jesus Christ, but also evidence of living a new life, and an expression of a willingness to live a new life. Also, those who are baptized do not only receive washing with water, but they receive their righteousness and the inheritance of eternal life through the renewing work of the Holy Spirit poured out in abundance through Jesus Christ. Therefore, "Baptism is not a simple washing but rather is attached to the gospel and faith with the promise that whoever believes and is baptized will be saved."[17]

Baptism in the Scriptures

Dirk constantly argues that the various texts of the Scripture support the practice of baptism.[18] During the New Testament and early church period, Baptism was a widespread ordinance, not performed in a temporary or restricted practice. As mentioned earlier, the Scripture proves that baptism is a direct command of Jesus Christ to his disciples. But in Scripture, it is not just a command; the practice is carried out regularly and continuously by the apostles. Dirk briefly introduces five instances in which the apostles baptized people. Philip baptized the Ethiopian eunuch for his confession of faith when he came to faith (Acts 8:38). When Peter proclaimed Jesus Christ and the word of life at Cornelius' house, Peter commanded them to be baptized in the name of Jesus Christ (Acts 10:48). Paul and Silas preached the gospel to the jailer and all his family, baptizing them and rejoicing that they believed in God (Acts 16:33). Paul also met some disciples in Ephesus, preaching the gospel and baptizing

16. Philips, "Baptism of Our Lord Jesus Christ," 78.
17. Philips, "Baptism of Our Lord Jesus Christ," 79.
18. Philips, "Baptism of Our Lord Jesus Christ," 73–75.

those who did not know the Holy Spirit (Acts 19:5). Paul himself lost his sight, but when Ananias, who had received orders from the Lord in Damascus, laid his hands on Paul, Paul regained his sight, got up, and was baptized (Acts 9:18).[19]

In addition to the specific examples of baptism performed by the apostles, Dirk presents the circumcision of Christ that Paul mentioned in Colossians 2 as a biblical image to illustrate baptism. In the Old Testament, God made a covenant with Abraham that involved circumcision. This covenant, given to Abraham and his descendants, included a promise to give them the land of Canaan forever; all men were commanded to make this covenant eternal by removing the foreskin.[20] In New Testament times, this external sign was in danger of being replaced by baptism, but Paul said that the circumcision practiced by the Israelites in Old Testament times is no longer used as a sign of the covenant in New Testament times, and the (spiritual) circumcision of Christ is now valid. Dirk follows Paul's position, making this concept clear. he mentions that "external circumcision was not a symbol of external baptism (as the perverted scribes say and the blind world thinks) but of the circumcision of Christ, which does not take place on the foreskin of the flesh but in the heart, not with hands nor with a stone, but without hands through God's Word and Spirit."[21]

Dirk seems to be reluctant to give spiritual effects to any external symbol. Rather, Dirk argues that in the Old Testament, circumcision was used as a sign of the covenant, but after the New Testament, the function of the Old Testament circumcision was replaced by faith in Christ through the Holy Spirit, not external baptism. Therefore, the ordinance of baptism alone cannot reveal the grace of Christ, but it can be gained through faith in Christ.[22]

Furthermore, Dirk connects baptism with the reference to Noah's ark in 1 Peter 3 to explain baptism. According to Dirk, baptism symbolizes salvation amid all death, just as in the days of Noah's ark, only the people who stayed in the ark could be saved in the midst of the flood.[23] Just as Noah was a preacher of righteousness in his day, Jesus Christ is

---

19. Philips, "Baptism of Our Lord Jesus Christ," 74.
20. Philips, "Baptism of Our Lord Jesus Christ," 101.
21. Philips, "Baptism of Our Lord Jesus Christ," 76–77.
22. Philips, "Baptism of Our Lord Jesus Christ," 102–3.
23. Philips, "Baptism of Our Lord Jesus Christ," 80.

a righteous, true preacher, a true teacher, and a messenger from God. Thus those who hear his command will be saved in the same way that some were preserved in the ark, and those who do not hear his word will perish.[24]

Dirk uses the medium of water to connect the ark and baptism. Water is a sign of salvation through the resurrection of Jesus Christ from the dead. As no one could survive the ark and perish through the water in the days of Noah's ark, those who are not in the ark of Jesus Christ cannot survive, be saved, or have eternal life. Dirk, however, does not regard the water of Noah's ark and water of baptism as the same image. In Noah's ark, water was an instrument of judgment and destruction; in contrast, the water of baptism is a means for salvation and preservation.[25] Dirk argues that baptism is not simply a means of washing away sin, but a covenant of a good conscience with God through the resurrection of Christ. Therefore, "in baptism the washing or pouring with external water does not accomplish the matter but [only] the covenant of a good conscience with God through the resurrection of Christ."[26]

Qualifications for Baptism

The Appropriate Time for Baptism

Dirk's understanding of baptism has an impact on defining the appropriate time for baptism. Dirk believes that since baptism has nothing to do with the spiritual efficiency that brings salvation, a person who is baptized must make a confession of faith before he or she is baptized.[27] Although Dirk does not identify the experience of salvation with the confession of faith, he agrees that those who do not repent or confess will not be saved. Dirk does not distinguish between saved people and those who repent and confess, often using the terms interchangeably. Logically, though baptism does not lead to salvation, those who are baptized must have already experienced salvation, so they have also repented and confessed their faith. For this argument, Dirk notes that the apostles taught people and preached the gospel before they baptized. When people heard the

24. Philips, "Baptism of Our Lord Jesus Christ," 81.
25. Philips, "Baptism of Our Lord Jesus Christ," 82.
26. Philips, "Baptism of Our Lord Jesus Christ," 82.
27. Philips, "Baptism of Our Lord Jesus Christ," 76.

gospel, repented, and had faith, they were baptized by the apostles following their confession of faith.[28] Therefore, the preaching of the gospel should be given priority over baptism, and those who hear the gospel and truly repent should confess and express their faith through Christian baptism. Dirk also speaks about life after baptism, saying that "after Christian baptism a steadfast, good, and pious life must follow. This is the correct order of the Lord Jesus Christ and the practice of the apostles."[29]

Dirk's claim that the appropriate time to be baptized is after hearing the Gospel, repenting of sins, and having faith in Christ demonstrates that he has a premise for the appropriate time for baptism. In other words, the appropriate time to be baptized is when the believer can hear, understand, and confess the faith in his or her language. In addition, it should be a time when he or she can walk according to a good conscience in God's covenant.[30] Naturally, this discussion leads to the issue of infant baptism, so Dirk's view of infant baptism will be addressed later in this chapter.

Life of the Baptized

One of the features of Dirk's writings on baptism is that he refers to the life of the baptized.[31] Dirk mentions faith as a precondition for baptism but insists that belief or confession is closely related to life. Baptism demonstrates that the person being baptized is saved by God's grace, eternal love, and endless mercy, but it is also an expression of his or her commitment to serve him throughout his or her life.

For Dirk, there is no difference to believers before and after baptism. Because baptism is a public confession of faith, the experience of baptism does not affect the believer's life; what is more important is whether believers have faith and live their life in faith. Dirk thinks that because baptism is received by those who have already heard the gospel and truly repented, baptism is not for the purpose of causing some effect; instead, the person who is baptized should be motivated to live a life worthy of it.[32]

28. Philips, "Baptism of Our Lord Jesus Christ," 74.
29. Philips, "Baptism of Our Lord Jesus Christ," 75.
30. Philips, "Baptism of Our Lord Jesus Christ," 82.
31. Philips, "Baptism of Our Lord Jesus Christ," 78.
32. Philips, "Baptism of Our Lord Jesus Christ."

Dirk connects the lives of those who are baptized with Christ and the Holy Spirit. According to Dirk, those who are baptized are those who have put on Christ. He says, "to put on Christ is through faith to become partakers of Christ and his being, to be united with Christ and be incorporated into him, yes, to be transplanted out of the fleshly nature of Adam and transformed into the spiritual heavenly divine nature of Christ."[33] In addition, those who are baptized are united in faith by Jesus Christ and share in his death, his righteousness, and his holiness. Dirk emphasizes the role of the Holy Spirit in this life, for those who are baptized should live righteously with the Holy Spirit.[34]

Dirk's most important concept in the lives of those who are baptized is a rebirth. Because those who are baptized have experienced new life, and express their willingness to live a new life in the future, they are "with the law of God . . . heartily admonished to penitence so that they amend themselves, lament their sins before God, confess, and bear remorse over them."[35] In other words, after they believe the gospel, they confess faith and live a new life, created and renewed in the image of the Father in heaven. They are following Christ Jesus, forsaking the old human nature, and living a new spiritual life.[36]

Baptism is not about washing with water, but about inheriting God's eternal life through Jesus Christ, who saves us. Thus, for Dirk, baptism does not directly lead to salvation; but baptism and salvation are closely related. Dirk says, "baptism is not a simple washing but rather is attached to the gospel and faith with the promise that whoever believes and is baptized will be saved."[37]

Dirk's View of Infant Baptism

The most substantial part of Dirk's discussion of baptism is his discussion of infant baptism. Dirk's constant criticism of infant baptism shows that this was a sharp issue at the time. In addition, Dirk directly mentions his

---

33. Philips, "Baptism of Our Lord Jesus Christ," 76.
34. Philips, "Baptism of Our Lord Jesus Christ," 75.
35. Philips, "Baptism of Our Lord Jesus Christ," 77.
36. Philips, "Baptism of Our Lord Jesus Christ," 78.
37. Philips, "Baptism of Our Lord Jesus Christ," 79.

opponents in his writings on this subject. These opponents include the Pope, Luther, and Erasmus.[38]

Dirk criticizes the Pope not only for baptizing children but also for involving them in the Lord's Supper. In this criticism, Dirk relies on Erasmus' words. Little is known about Erasmus' influence on Dirk, but Dirk was clearly familiar with Erasmus' writings. According to Dirk, Erasmus mentions in a treatise he wrote to the bishop of Spain that the Pope involved children in the sacrament of the altar.[39] Erasmus never rejected infant baptism in his writings, but his concept of pre-baptismal affirmation influenced Anabaptists' views of baptism, and Hubmaier, who had a direct relationship with Erasmus, considered pre-baptismal affirmation to imply rejection of infant baptism.[40] Moreover, it is clear that Erasmus' interpretation of the Great Commission has influenced various groups of Anabaptists, including Menno Simons.[41]

Dirk is also familiar with Luther's writings because he expresses his opinion on Luther's views several times.[42] Although Dirk does not debate Luther's claims in detail, it is clear that he did not agree with Luther's support for infant baptism. Dirk seems to agree with Luther's claim that no one can be baptized without faith, but he disagrees with Luther and his followers that infants can believe and be baptized by their faith.[43] Luther appears to have properly pointed out that personal faith, not the faith of the church or parents, is an important qualification for baptism. Nonetheless, he believed that no single Scripture verse proves that a child cannot believe in baptism—although it is not known how the faith is created—and unlike adults, the child cannot deceive, so children can come to Christ and be baptized, just as John came to Christ.[44]

There are three main reasons why Dirk rejects infant baptism. The first is that children lack understanding. Children do not have the right faith because they do not know or understand it even when they hear the gospel, so they do not possess the essence of faith.[45] Dirk regards this lack

---

38. Philips, "Baptism of Our Lord Jesus Christ," 101.
39. Philips, "Baptism of Our Lord Jesus Christ."
40. Williamson, "Erasmus of Rotterdam's Influence upon Anabaptism" 60.
41. Friesen, *Erasmus, the Anabaptists, and the Great Commission*, 43–75.
42. Dirk refers directly to Martin Luther in "Baptism of Our Lord Jesus Christ," 84–85, and "Apology or Reply," 174.
43. Philips, "Baptism of Our Lord Jesus Christ," 85.
44. *LW* 40, 242–46.
45. Philips, "Baptism of Our Lord Jesus Christ," 76.

of understanding as the same concept as the lack of faith. Thus, children who do not have faith do not experience rebirth and do not reach new birth. Dirk says, "For baptism belongs to no one and may not be given rightly to anyone except the born again children of God, that is, to believers who have been inwardly renewed after the image and likeness of God."[46]

Dirk's second reason for opposing infant baptism is that baptism requires a confession of faith. According to Dirk, the Bible teaches that baptism is a testimony and a sign of sincere penitent faith. Those who are baptized must be men of firm faith, understanding their confession, holding it in their hearts, and confessing it with their mouths.[47] However, Dirk believes that children are not only unable to understand faith, but are also deficient in holding and confessing it.

Dirk's last and most obvious reason for opposing infant baptism is that there is no Biblical evidence for infant baptism.[48] Dirk insists that this ordinance was created and established by Christ himself, and maintained by the apostolic church; but in the case of infant baptism, Dirk argues that the Bible proves nothing. Therefore, he contends that infant baptism does not appear in the New Testament, and Christ did not make infant baptism known to his people.[49] Dirk thus argues that infant baptism cannot be accepted as God's command. Adding or subtracting from God's word is ungodly, and worshiping on the basis of human reason without God's command is idolatry. Since God teaches and shows how humans serve God, infant baptism is idolatry and an idol that is not based on his Word.[50]

Dirk seems to be well aware of the criticisms directed at him on the issue of infant baptism because he suggests that there were various attacks on the subject, and he refutes seven other arguments against his own position. First, Dirk disagrees with the claim that someone could be baptized based on the faith of the church or his father. According to Dirk, the claimant notes those who brought the paralytic to the Lord, as well as the centurion and the Canaanite woman helping and comforting

---

46. Philips, "Baptism of Our Lord Jesus Christ," 80.
47. Philips, "Baptism of Our Lord Jesus Christ," 83.
48. Dirk uses "infant baptism" and "child baptism" interchangeably.
49. Philips, "Baptism of Our Lord Jesus Christ," 83.
50. Philips, "Baptism of Our Lord Jesus Christ," 84.

others by Jesus Christ because of their faith.[51] Dirk acknowledges that these characters in the Scriptures performed in faith for others, and he says that the Scriptures teach believers to pray for one another and to pray when they see a brother's sin. However, he insists that the Scriptures never direct children to be baptized in the faith of the church or their parents, and that in one example similar to these, Christ did not order anyone to baptize a child. Dirk says, "we do have in the Scripture another example of how one should pray for the children, namely, that believing parents brought their children to Christ and desired of him that they might be blessed through the laying on of his hands."[52]

Second, Dirk counters the claim that Almighty God can give faith to infants through baptism. Dirk denies linking infants' lack of the ability to comprehend faith with the omnipotence of God. For God has made infants unable to speak or understand according to his power. Because God is almighty, he made all things of this world obedient according to his pleasing will, and it was by his will that he created infants without the ability to comprehend faith until a certain age.[53]

Third, Dirk opposes the argument that a child can be baptized on the basis of the references to Jeremiah being sanctified in his mother's womb and to John the Baptist rejoicing in Christ in his mother's womb.[54] Dirk points out that Jeremiah and John the Baptist were exceptional figures with marvelous work of God.[55] Each of them was filled with the Holy Spirit from his mother's womb, and God wanted to accomplish his work with them. Nevertheless, Dirk points out that Jeremiah's and John the Baptist's cases are special and not generally applicable. Dirk insists that "all children may not be compared in the gift and power of the Spirit with Jeremiah and John,"[56] and that none of those born of women are greater than John the Baptist.

Moreover, Dirk explains why Jeremiah and John the Baptist's case are not generally applicable in connection with life after baptism. Dirk claims that the spiritual powers of Jeremiah and John the Baptist in the

---

51. Philips, "Baptism of Our Lord Jesus Christ," 86.

52. Philips, "Baptism of Our Lord Jesus Christ," 86.

53. Philips, "Baptism of Our Lord Jesus Christ," 88.

54. Although not mentioned directly by Dirk, Luther and Calvin supported infant baptism on the basis that John received the Holy Spirit in his mother's womb (*LW* 40, 242; *Institutes* IV, xvi, 17).

55. Philips, "Baptism of Our Lord Jesus Christ," 88.

56. Philips, "Baptism of Our Lord Jesus Christ," 89.

mother's womb were not hidden or lost after their birth.[57] They became spiritually strong after birth and walked with God, unlike those who were baptized as infants and who then lived contrary to their faith. Dirk also points out that the argument for infant baptism based on Jeremiah and John the Baptist was in contradiction. Jeremiah and John the Baptist were not baptized in infants, and if the children received the Holy Spirit in the mother's womb, it is to be assumed that in infant baptism the unclean spirit should be expelled from them, and they would not need ordinances such as infant baptism for salvation.[58]

Fourth, Dirk rejects the insistence that infant baptism must be done on the basis of Jesus' statement "let the children come to me, for to such belongs the kingdom of heaven."[59] Dirk notes that the concept that children are given the kingdom of heaven does not mean that their salvation depends on baptism. Dirk mentions, "For Christ accepted the children and promised them the kingdom of heaven on the basis of grace and mercy, and not an account of baptism. For he neither baptized them nor commanded that they be baptized but blessed them through the laying on of his hands"[60]

Fifth, Dirk refutes the need to baptize infants because of these words of Jesus to Nicodemus: "Unless someone is born out of water and the Spirit, he may not enter the kingdom of God."[61] Dirk is convinced that this statement is for adults only, because it is about a new birth, and a new birth cannot happen without the word of God, faith, and the Holy Spirit. According to Dirk, infants cannot have these things, so if the words Jesus spoke to Nicodemus were also applicable to infants, the Scriptures would be in contradiction. Likewise, Dirk argues that the statement "For by one Spirit we were all baptized into one body and are all refreshed with one Spirit" in 1 Corinthians 12 is not for children but for adults.[62]

Sixth, Dirk does not see 1 Corinthians 10 as a justification for infant baptism. This passage says that "all were baptized under Moses."[63] In this case, Dirk demonstrates his tendency to reject literal interpretation in

---

57. Philips, "Baptism of Our Lord Jesus Christ."
58. Philips, "Baptism of Our Lord Jesus Christ," 90.
59. Philips, "Baptism of Our Lord Jesus Christ," 91.
60. Philips, "Baptism of Our Lord Jesus Christ," 91.
61. Philips, "Baptism of Our Lord Jesus Christ," 94.
62. Philips, "Baptism of Our Lord Jesus Christ," 100.
63. Philips, "Baptism of Our Lord Jesus Christ," 96.

biblical interpretation.[64] He says that interpreting this statement of the apostle Paul as literal is a misunderstanding of what the apostle intended. Dirk believes that the apostle used the above expression to describe the salvation of mankind through Jesus Christ, not to assert that everyone, including infants, should be baptized.[65]

Seventh, Dirk does not think infant baptism should be supported by God's covenant with Abraham. Dirk has a firm theological interpretation of circumcision. He thinks that "God made a covenant with Abraham and his seed, that is, with all believers, had accepted them with all their children out of grace, as heirs of his eternal kingdom, and surrendered Jesus Christ, his only Son, into death for us, John 3:16, as a sure sign of divine grace."[66] However, circumcision does not hold this theological meaning, according to Dirk, after the coming of Jesus Christ, and all believing Christians are not bound to such an external symbol anymore. Circumcision is no longer necessary for believers, and there is no reason to compare circumcision with baptism. Therefore, child circumcision is not the basis of infant baptism; instead, Dirk believes that the New Testament people are dependent on the mercy, love, and goodness of God for salvation, not infant baptism, just as the Old Testament Israelites depended on grace and mercy of God, not on flesh circumcision.[67]

Dirk's View of the Lord's Supper

In Dirk's time, people were divided in their opinions on the Lord's Supper. Catholicism insisted on transubstantiation, Luther believed in consubstantiation, and Calvin believed in Spiritual Presence.[68] With these various opinions about the Lord's Supper, Dirk needed to clearly present his congregation his teachings about the Lord's Supper, desiring them to learn the correct teaching of the Scriptures on this issue. Thus, Dirk published *The Supper of Our Lord Jesus Christ* in 1557.[69] In this treatise, although Dirk does not elaborate on Luther's or Calvin's views of the

64. Shantz, "Ecclesiological Focus," 118.
65. Philips, "Baptism of Our Lord Jesus Christ," 97.
66. Philips, "Baptism of Our Lord Jesus Christ," 103.
67. Philips, "Baptism of Our Lord Jesus Christ," 105.
68. Mathison has written a recent, well-arranged study of the Lord's Supper debate (Mathison, "Lord's Supper," 643–73).
69. There is also an opinion that *Enchiridion* became the first publication in 1544 (Keeney, "Editors' Introduction," 51).

Lord's Supper, but he sharply criticizes the Catholic view of the subject and provides a detailed biblical basis for and interpretation of the Lord's Supper.

Dirk demonstrates that the Lord's Supper was instituted by Jesus Christ and is supported by the Scriptures.[70] Dirk, however, is wary of giving meaning or theological interpretation beyond what the Scriptures teach about the Lord's Supper. He claims that the Lord's Supper is to be understood spiritually and is a commemoration of the Lord's suffering and death.[71]

The Lord's Supper as Spiritual Food

The main argument in Dirk's discussion of the Lord's Supper is the spiritual interpretation of Christ's words "this is my body" and "this is my blood." The argument contradicts the Catholic view that the bread and wine are physically changed in the sacrament.[72] It also contradicts Luther's view that Christ is present as a reality rather than as a symbol.[73] Dirk takes the greatest part of *The Supper of Our Lord Jesus Christ* to provide a basis for a spiritual understanding of the Lord's Supper. To this end, Dirk offers five arguments, which will be introduced in this section.

Dirk's first argument for a spiritual understanding of the Lord's Supper is that "in the Scripture, eating is so often used as believing and

---

70. Dirk introduces four principles on the biblical basis of the Lord's Supper: "Thus, the Holy Scripture now teaches us to believe and take to heart about the Lord's Supper four principal parts or points: In the first place, Christ broke the bread and gave it to his apostles and said, 'Take, and eat; this is my body that is broken for you,' etc., Matt. 26:26; 1 Cor. 11:[24]. In the second place, Paul said to the Corinthians, 'The cup of thanksgiving which we say thanks for, is it not the fellowship of the blood of Christ? The bread which we break, is it not the fellowship of the body of Christ?,' 1 Cor. 10:16. In the third place, the bread and wine in the Supper are a memorial sign of the death and blood of Christ. For he himself said, 'As often as you do this, do it to my remembrance of me.' Again Paul said, 'As many times as you eat from this bread and drink from this cup, thus you proclaim the Lord's death until he comes,' Luke 22:19; 1 Cor. 11:[26]. In the fourth place, the Lord thus said of the cup, 'This cup is the New Testament in my blood,' Luke 22:20. Matthew and Mark thus add, 'This is my blood of the new covenant which is poured out for many for the forgiveness of sins,' 1 Cor. 11: [25]; Matt. 26: [28]; Mark 14:24" (Philips, "Supper of Our Lord Jesus Christ," 113).

71. Philips, "Supper of Our Lord Jesus Christ," 114.

72. Berkhof, *Systematic Theology*, 645, 652.

73. For Luther's view of the sacraments, see Luther, "Babylonish Captivity of the Church," 208–329. Also see Althaus, *Theology of Martin Luther*, 375–77.

drinking as trusting."[74] In other words, Dirk points out that in Scripture there are many passages that use eating and drinking as a metaphor, including the passages of the Lord's Supper. Sometimes the Scripture refers to believing as eating—especially the example of eating the bread of heaven and the word of God as referring to gaining life. "Therefore, whoever believes in the crucified Jesus Christ, his soul will be nourished with the bread of heaven, with the Word of God, yes, with the flesh and blood of Christ."[75]

Dirk also notes Christ's words that "the flesh is of no avail, the spirit makes alive" in John 6:63. For Dirk, believers are not meant to eat and drink in the flesh, but to be nourished by the Spirit; spiritual food such as the flesh and blood of Christ must be received spiritually.[76]

The second reason for the spiritual interpretation of the body and blood of Christ is that "Christ himself explained his words in the Supper."[77] To explain this, Dirk notes the situation of the first Lord's Supper. When the Lord said "this is my body," the apostles did not eat Jesus' natural body, conceived by the Holy Spirit and born out of the virgin Mary. What they ate was bread, and what they drank was wine. However, because the Lord said that his body would be given or broken for his apostles, Dirk notes that Lord's body is given for the redemption of believers. In other words, the bread refers to the body of Christ, which was broken for the salvation of human beings; but the bread itself is not a physical body.

The third reason for Dirk's claim that the Lord's Supper is a spiritual remembrance is that "Judas also ate of the bread and drank of the wine, but nevertheless he did not receive the flesh and blood of Christ."[78] If the bread itself were the body of Christ and had any efficiency, those who received the flesh and blood of Christ could not betray the Lord. Jesus says in John 6:56, "whoever eats from my flesh and drinks my blood abides in me and I in him."[79] However, Dirk believes that participation in the sacrament without faith does not mean participation in the Lord and his gifts; Judas' participation during the Last Supper proves this fact. Judas took part in the Lord's Supper without faith. He ate bread and drank

74. Philips, "Supper of Our Lord Jesus Christ," 114.
75. Philips, "Supper of Our Lord Jesus Christ," 114.
76. Philips, "Supper of Our Lord Jesus Christ," 115.
77. Philips, "Supper of Our Lord Jesus Christ," 116.
78. Philips, "Supper of Our Lord Jesus Christ," 116.
79. Philips, "Supper of Our Lord Jesus Christ," 116.

wine, but these elements did not change his faith. Thus, an unbeliever or an evil one's participation in the sacrament, eating bread and drinking wine, does not mean participation in the flesh and blood of Christ. Dirk emphasizes that only by faith can one be a spiritual participant in Christ, his body, and his blood.

The fourth reason is that "the Scripture often speaks in a figurative manner."[80] Dirk gives various examples of Scriptures that must be spiritually understood and interpreted. He says, "the Scripture calls Christ the door to the sheepfold, John 10:7, a true vine, John 15:1, a rock, 1 Cor. 10:4, and additional other names which one must all understand and interpret spiritually."[81] Just as we interpret these verses figuratively, Dirk believes that the words of Jesus at the Lord's Supper should be interpreted in the same way. In addition, Dirk notes that John refers to "eating his flesh and drinking his blood" many times outside of the Lord's Supper and interprets these references as spiritual eating. Thus, Dirk believes that these examples provide the basis for the Lord's Supper to be interpreted spiritually.

Dirk's fifth reason is that the Scripture testifies that Christ remains in heaven at the right hand of God until the last days.[82] In other words, Dirk believes that Christ's omnipresence is realized spiritually, not physically. The actual flesh of Christ is not present in all creation, or in the bread and wine of the supper. His flesh died, rose, and ascended to heaven. He went to the Father and no longer exists in this world. Dirk believes that this biblical testimony proves that Jesus Christ is not physically present in the bread and cup of the Supper.[83]

The Lord's Supper as a Memorial of Christ's Suffering and Death

The difference between Dirk's view of the Lord's Supper and that of Catholics or other reformers is that Dirk interprets the Lord's Supper as a commemoration of the suffering and death of Jesus Christ, rather than describing it as Christ's actual or spiritual presence. This was a view that began with Zwingli and was supported by other Anabaptist groups.[84]

80. Philips, "Supper of Our Lord Jesus Christ," 118.
81. Philips, "Supper of Our Lord Jesus Christ," 118.
82. Philips, "Supper of Our Lord Jesus Christ," 119.
83. Philips, "Supper of Our Lord Jesus Christ," 120.
84. For the view of Swiss Breden, see Williams, *Radical Reformation*, 85–101.

Dirk presents his commemorative view of the Lord's Supper clearly, rather than vaguely or arbitrarily. He says, "The Lord Jesus Christ out of great love ordained it primarily as a memorial of his death for the believers, as an admonition, promotion, and establishment of Christian love and unity."[85] According to Dirk, the bread and wine of the supper are the monumental signs of Christ's death and his blood. To support this, Dirk suggests, on the basis of the verses of Luke 22:19 and 1 Corinthians 11:26, that the act of eating the bread and drinking the cup at the Lord's Supper proclaims the death of the Lord.[86]

Dirk sees the bread and wine of the Lord's Supper as a sign of commemoration of Christ's suffering and death, and he compares this to seeing Christ as the Lamb of Passover. Just as Israel commemorates, in accordance with God's command, God's deliverance from Egypt each year by eating the Paschal lamb, a sign of grace, the Lord's Supper commemorates Christ's suffering and death. This memorial reminds participants that Jesus Christ experienced a bitter death and that his death took place because of human sin.[87]

In the debate over the Lord's Supper, the reformed tradition criticizes memorialism as limited to a belief in the Lord's name and a reliance on his death. According to Calvin, memorialism is related only to Christ's past work—that is, his death. However, Calvin argues that the sacrament is related to Christ's present spiritual work—that is, the living Christ in glory.[88] According to Calvin, Christ is not physically and locally present at the sacrament, but he is present as an entire person, including his body and blood. This view emphasizes the whole person and the mystical union of believers and the Lord.[89]

According to Calvin, the sacrament is both a symbol and a guarantee of our participation in the body of Christ. The sacrament not only indicates that the believers became one with Christ, but also that the flesh of the Lord is the food of the believers and that the blood of the

---

Rempel compared Hubmaier, Marpeck, and Dirk's view of the Lord's Supper. According to Rempel, their common view is that there is no automatic effect or reality without the presence of faith and love in the Lord's Supper (Rempel, *Lord's Supper in Anabaptism*, 22).

85. Philips, "Supper of Our Lord Jesus Christ," 112.
86. Philips, "Supper of Our Lord Jesus Christ," 113.
87. Philips, "Supper of Our Lord Jesus Christ," 123–24.
88. Calvin, *Institutes* IV, xvii, 3–4.
89. Berkhof, *Systematic Theology*, 653.

believers is the drink of the believers.[90] Calvin criticizes Zwingli and the Anabaptists—memorialism—in this regard. Calvin argued that some people believe that eating Christ's flesh and drinking blood simply demonstrates faith in Christ. "But there is this difference between their mode of speaking and mine. According to them, to eat is merely to believe; while I maintain that the flesh of Christ is eaten by believing, because it is made ours by faith and that that eating is the effect and fruit of faith."[91]

The answer to the question of whether Dirk's view of memorialism merely commemorates Christ's past work, the suffering and dying Christ, and overlooks the glorious living Christ is given in the next section. Of course, because Calvin is not directly attacking Dirk, understanding Dirk's point of view is not a proper answer to Calvin's argument. However, if Calvin's arguments against memorialism do not correspond to Dirk's views, then at least Calvin's arguments could not be used as criticisms of Dirk. Furthermore, it will be a mistake to criticize the views of the Lord's Supper for the entire Anabaptist movement based on Calvin's arguments.

The Lord's Supper as Unity

Dirk argues that the Lord's Supper is not meant only as a memory of Christ's death, but has another important meaning—love and unity among believers. He argues that the misinterpretation of the Lord's Supper damages the Lord's Supper in its function of signifying the love and union of believers, a function which was established by the Lord.[92] According to Dirk, the Lord's Supper, ordained by the Lord with his great love, was instituted to establish Christian love and unity.

The unity of the Lord's Supper, mentioned by Dirk, holds two meanings. The first unity is the union of the divine mystery.[93] The Lord's Supper establishes the communion and fellowship between believers and Christ. Christians experience this true unity through the Holy Spirit and through faith, breaking bread and drinking wine in that unity.[94] For this reason, those who participate in the Lord's Supper must be those who

90. Calvin, *Institutes* IV, xvii, 4.
91. Calvin, *Institutes* IV, xvii, 5.
92. Philips, "Supper of Our Lord Jesus Christ," 112.
93. Philips, "Supper of Our Lord Jesus Christ," 123.
94. Philips, "Supper of Our Lord Jesus Christ," 121.

have true faith in Jesus Christ. These are people who want to die and live with Christ, and who rightly love Christ and their neighbor. Those who are not one with Christ cannot participate in the supper. Thus, the mysterious unity that Dirk refers to is possible by the Holy Spirit, but only those who reveal the reality of the unity externally demonstrate this unity and can participate in the supper.[95]

The second unity which Dirk refers to in the Lord's Supper is the unity of believers. Dirk says, "through the bread and through the wine of the Supper, the unity and the agreeableness and fellowship of believers is portrayed and testified."[96] The Lord motivated believers to fellowship and to unite with one another in the supper. Dirk, however, does not overlook union with Christ in referring to the unity of believers. He says, "all Christians must be united with Christ and with each other."[97]

The Function of the Lord's Supper

According to Dirk, communion and fellowship with Christ are established and renewed through the Lord's Supper. Dirk believes that fellowship with Christ means partaking in one bread. It is as though the Israelites participated in the fellowship of the altar in the Old Testament, but now with Jesus Christ, the only true high priest. As the believers break bread and drink wine at the Lord's Supper, they demonstrate that they are in this fellowship and that they are participating out of God's grace and election through faith. Thus, the most important function of the Lord's Supper is the believers' public confession of faith; and the development of faith is accomplished through unity with Christ.

For Dirk, the idea that believers are united with Christ through the Lord's Supper is important for the following reasons: First, Dirk emphasizes that unity with Christ is made possible by faith.[98] True Christians unite with Jesus Christ in full faith in him, being transformed and changed in their nature and character into his nature and character. The unity with Christ does not mean being physically united by eating bread and drinking wine, but being spiritually united with Christ, changing in nature and character. Secondly, Dirk stresses that this unity does not

---

95. Philips, "Supper of Our Lord Jesus Christ," 129.
96. Philips, "Supper of Our Lord Jesus Christ," 122.
97. Philips, "Supper of Our Lord Jesus Christ," 122.
98. Philips, "Supper of Our Lord Jesus Christ," 122.

lead to personal change only. Those who participate in this unity must be enkindled in love, sharing the burdens of others, and fulfilling the law of Christ.[99] Dirk says that as the Apostle Paul said that Christ and his congregation are one flesh and bone, it is a wonderful unity of blessings for all Christians to be one body and bread in Christ Jesus. Dirk also says, "according to the example of the natural body, be of one heart and soul and serve each other, be helpful and comforting, just as the members of the natural body do."[100]

Another function of the Lord's Supper, insisted upon by Dirk, is related to his perspective of memorialism, and that is the didactic function that the Lord's Supper has to believers. He believes, "the bread and the wine in the Supper are thus a memorial sign of the bitter suffering."[101] To commemorate Christ's suffering and death is to remember Christ's body and blood, and to remember that sin was cleansed by Christ's suffering and death. Dirk thinks that the greatest benefit of this memory is that believers are taught to fear God and hate sin. Believers in the Lord's Supper remember that Jesus Christ suffered and died because of their sins, and the Lord's Supper reminds believers that this happened because God hates sin. Thus believers come to "self-knowledge, to the true humility, to the pure fear of God, to the true remembrance of the suffering of Christ, and to the hatred of sin."[102]

The Correct Practice of the Lord's Supper

Dirk suggests correct practice on the basis of his views of the Lord's Supper. There are four requirements that he suggests, three of which relate to the qualifications of those who participate in the supper, and one about the form of the supper.

The first method is that those who attend the supper must be true believers in Christ and participants within congregations of Christ gathered in the name of Christ. Dirk points out the relationship between the congregation of Christ and the acts of eating bread and drinking wine: all believers have been eternally saved by the body and blood of Christ,

---

99. Philips, "Supper of Our Lord Jesus Christ," 123.
100. Philips, "Supper of Our Lord Jesus Christ," 123.
101. Philips, "Supper of Our Lord Jesus Christ," 123.
102. Philips, "Supper of Our Lord Jesus Christ," 124.

so those who eat bread and drink wine at the Lord's Supper are qualified only in the congregation of Christ.[103]

In the second requirement, Dirk specifies the exclusivity of the Lord's Supper. He says, "this Supper shall not be held except only with the friends of God, the true Christians."[104] The friends of God, the true Christians, is synonymous with the congregation of Christ mentioned above. Dirk's emphasis in this requirement is not only that the congregation of Christ participates in the Lord's Supper, but that those who are not God's friends or who are not true Christians cannot participate in the Lord's Supper. According to Dirk, true Christians are those who accept the gospel and are being transformed by it, have been baptized because of their confession of faith, and walk in their faith as Christians. "In Summary, [those] who are one body with Christ and all the saints—these and no others are according to the evidence of the gospel to be renewed, admonished, and established with this Supper in the fellowship of Christ and all the saints."[105]

In a third requirement, Dirk emphasizes the Lord's Supper as a community event. Dirk argues, "the Supper shall be harmoniously kept with all believers (as many as are together), not with one person alone as commonly takes place."[106] According to Dirk, the Lord's Supper is an ordinance where the Lord wants all Christians to participate together, not alone, and it is right for as many Christians to participate as the Lord intends.

Finally, Dirk argues that those who attend the Lord's Supper must test themselves. Dirk recalls Paul's teaching: "Paul admonishes us that a man must first test himself before he eats the bread of the Supper and drinks from the cup."[107] Dirk's emphasis in this requirement corresponds to the first and the second requirements. In other words, the person who participates in the supper must be part of the true congregation of Christ, must have true faith in Christ, and must walk in Christ.

Dirk gives six tips for self-testing. First, the believer must remember that the Paschal lamb was unblemished. Because the pure Paschal lamb refers to Christ, those who eat spiritually and physically through faith

---

103. Philips, "Supper of Our Lord Jesus Christ," 128.
104. Philips, "Supper of Our Lord Jesus Christ," 128.
105. Philips, "Supper of Our Lord Jesus Christ," 128.
106. Philips, "Supper of Our Lord Jesus Christ," 128.
107. Philips, "Supper of Our Lord Jesus Christ," 129.

will escape God's punishment and come out of Egypt. Second, believers should observe the Passover with the sweet bread of sincerity and truth, as the Israelites were not allowed any leaven at Passover. Third, the fact that the Israelites ate the Passover Lamb with bitter herbs indicates the suffering of Jesus Christ. Fourth, believers must gird up the loins of their hearts, just as the Israelites ate the Passover Lamb hurriedly with belts on their waists, sandals on their feet, and canes in their hands. Fifth, one who is uncircumcised in heart cannot participate in the Lord's Supper, as strangers and the uncircumcised were not allowed to eat the Paschal lamb. Finally, believers should receive all of the words of Jesus Christ, just as the Israelites had to eat all of Paschal lamb and burn the rest. That is, all the words and teachings of Christ are to be kept, and partial adoption or rejection of his words is to be excluded.[108]

Dirk's View of Church Discipline

It is necessary to point out that in order for his congregation to have successful Christian lives, Dirk advised them in the faith in several ways. For Dirk, the process of church discipline consists of three steps. The first step is admonition, which is delineated in *Three Admonitions*.[109] The second step is the ban or excommunication, which is outlined in *The Ban*[110] and *Evangelical Excommunication*.[111] The third step is avoidance, which is closely related to the ban and is related to Christian marriage. This third step is represented well in *A Confession about Separation* [112]and *About the Marriage of Christians*.[113] In addition, *Omitted Writing about the Ban and Avoidance* deals with both the topics of excommunication and avoidance.[114]

---

108. Philips, "Supper of Our Lord Jesus Christ," 129–31.
109. Philips, "Three Admonitions: No. I"; Philips, "Three Admonitions: No. II"; Philips, "Three Admonitions: No. III."
110. Philips, "Ban."
111. Philips, "Evangelical Excommunication."
112. Philips, "Confession about Separation."
113. Philips, "About the Marriage of Christians."
114. Philips, "Omitted Writing about the Ban and Avoidance."

Admonition

Reasons for Admonition

Dirk thinks of himself as receiving a small gift from God that through admonition he can help the believers' faith.[115] In this conviction, Dirk admonishes his congregations. For Dirk, not just anyone can perform the work of admonition; it is only for those who have the correct teaching of the Scripture and who have Christian love and an affectionate mind.[116] According to Dirk, admonition is of great benefit for every believer. First given in brotherly love to the congregation of God, admonition provides the strength and peace of their souls. So they walk with God with genuine faith, and because of these benefits, Dirk believes that admonition cannot be stopped.[117] Dirk finds another benefit of admonition in believers' relationship with God. Because of God's chastisement, God's beloved children are shown to be his. If there is no such chastisement, they are not true children of God, but bastards.[118] Moreover, admonition is the demonstration of the love of Christ among the believers,[119] emphasizing the believers' walking in Jesus, whom they have accepted as their Savior.[120]

Dirk seems to come to his view of admonition by focusing on the admonition of the apostles to their readers in Scripture. Dirk's admonition has an atmosphere similar to that of Paul's epistles in that it gives the reader advice for the development of faith. Also, it is clear that the letters of the apostles motivated Dirk's admonition since he begins with "I, with the apostle Paul" at the first part of his *Admonitions: No. III*.[121] Dirk quotes not only the admonition of the apostle Paul, but also the admonitions of the apostles Peter, John, and James, using them as a basis for his own admonition.[122]

Dirk also tells his congregation why his admonitions are needed, giving five specific and practical reasons for them. One reason for his admonitions is to prevent his congregation from being influenced by spiritual

---

115. Philips, "Three Admonitions: No. III," 413.
116. Philips, "Three Admonitions: No. III," 412.
117. Philips, "Three Admonitions: No. I," 383.
118. Philips, "Three Admonitions: No. I," 388.
119. Philips, "Three Admonitions: No. II," 399.
120. Philips, "Three Admonitions: No. II," 408.
121. Philips, "Three Admonitions: No. III," 412.
122. Philips, "Three Admonitions: No. III," 421.

charlatanry.[123] Dirk is wary of many false prophets and antichrists and recognizes that they have a direct impact on his congregation.[124] Dirk, therefore, insists on the importance of preaching and teaching the word of God, admonishing his congregation for that purpose. The second purpose of Dirk's admonition is to help his congregations be enlightened by God and to live lives worthy of his calling. According to Dirk, it is natural for believers to produce good fruit on earth because of God's grace and the gift of the Holy Spirit, because God is the one who sends rain to produce good fruit on earth.[125] The third purpose of Dirk's admonition is to strengthen his congregation in the Holy Spirit. To this end, Dirk introduces his congregation to stories from the Scriptures of God's people overcoming persecution. According to Dirk, tyrants have persecuted Christians for a long time, and as the Scriptures show, God is the one who, along with his Spirit, gives believers the strength and faith to overcome suffering.[126] The fourth purpose of admonition is Christian thanksgiving. Dirk believes that Christians must thank God for giving them new life, and Dirk emphasizes that the Lord gave eternal life and allowed the crown of righteousness.[127] The purpose of the final admonition is for all believers to be at peace in Jesus Christ. Dirk emphasizes that believers are people who have a new birth, so they must live up to that new birth. He says, "let this new birth be powerful in you, and be eager to keep the unity of the Spirit through the bond of peace."[128] Dirk offers wisdom as a way to be at peace with each other. He means not only that wisdom is needed to be at peace with each other, but that since true wisdom comes from fearing God and asking him for it, Christian peace with brotherly love and unity comes from being with God.[129]

Dirk's Admonition

Dirk's admonition to his congregation can be divided into three sections. First, Dirk admonishes those who are suffering. This reflects the fact that

123. Philips, "Three Admonitions: No. II," 400.
124. Philips, "Three Admonitions: No. III," 412.
125. Philips, "Three Admonitions: No. II," 402.
126. Philips, "Three Admonitions: No. II," 404.
127. Philips, "Three Admonitions: No. II," 407.
128. Philips, "Three Admonitions: No. II," 408.
129. Philips, "Three Admonitions: No. II," 409.

Dirk and his congregations were in various persecutions and sufferings to defend their faith. Indeed, Dirks says, "My work in the congregations is not unknown to you. Pressure and suffering, anxiety and need are also with me."[130] However, Dirk confesses that God graciously looks upon believers and makes them strong and comfortable with the Holy Spirit.

In the thought of Dirk, the most important function of suffering is to distinguish between genuine and false saints. Genuine saints rejoice in the Holy Spirit when they suffer from persecution and slander, and after overcoming all this persecution for righteousness, they reveal that they are chosen of God, and they are purged as gold is in fire.[131]

Dirk also argues that following Jesus means not only believing in Jesus Christ, but also suffering on his behalf.[132] Christians therefore do not need to fear persecution by tyrants and persecutors, nor do they have to question the loss of temporary goods in order to possess something eternal in heaven.[133] In Dirk's thinking, these things simply demonstrate God's omnipotence. He advises his congregation not to love what is temporary because God is superior to anything else in the world.[134] He also says that man can be freed from temporary suffering, but no one can escape from God's eternal omnipotence. God is the only one that believers should fear, not the persecutor or anyone else. Moreover, Dirk emphasizes that Christians remember that one reason for overcoming is that there is everlasting happiness after life in this world.[135] However, when the trumpet of God blasts in the end times, enemies who hear the trumpet of God will be afraid, and they will come to shame.[136]

Second, Dirk admonishes those under the influence of false teachings. As mentioned earlier, Dirk says his admonition is to prevent the ungodliness of spiritual charlatanry. This false teaching comes from Satan, Dirk believes. Satan "sends his prophets out in sheep's clothing, but inwardly they are ravenous wolves."[137] Dirk says it would have been better if these people did not know about the way of the Lord. For Dirk, these

---

130. Philips, "Three Admonitions: No. II," 409.
131. Philips, "Three Admonitions: No. I," 385.
132. Philips, "Three Admonitions: No. I," 386.
133. Philips, "Three Admonitions: No. I," 386.
134. Philips, "Three Admonitions: No. I," 389.
135. Philips, "Three Admonitions: No. I," 391.
136. Philips, "Three Admonitions: No. II," 406.
137. Philips, "Three Admonitions: No. II," 400.

people are like the demon-possessed man who seven other evil spirits reenter, and who try to deceive God.[138] In his *Admonitions*, Dirk focuses on discussing the causes and origins of these wrong teachings, rather than affirming the right Christian faith or arguing against the claims of the wrong teaching.

Finally, Dirk admonishes his congregation on life as believers. Dirk's discussion of the believer's life is closely related to the purpose of his admonition. Dirk's various admonitions have a direction for the believer's appropriate life. The fruitful life, the strong life in the Holy Spirit, the thanksgiving of Christians, and the peace of Christians relate to the attitude of life that people of Christ who have experienced the new birth must hold, without trying to escape from God's holiness.

Excommunication

Dirk wrote two treatises related to excommunication. His first treatise, *The Ban*, was included in the *Enchiridion* of 1564, and the second, *Evangelical Excommunication*, appears to had been written about a year before Dirk's death in 1568. Another work by Dirk, *A Confession about Separation*, addresses the issue of separation, the result of excommunication; but since separation is also related to Christian marriage, these topics will be discussed in the next section.

In order to properly understand Dirk's view of excommunication, it is necessary to clarify his understanding of God. Dirk understands God as one who seeks to punish evil from the beginning; he also desires to separate those who commit public sins and despise his word from his congregation. This view of God comes from Dirk's understanding of the attributes of God. First, Dirk claims that Holy Scripture proves that God is righteous, loves righteousness, and hates injustice. God is also "gracious and merciful toward the penitent and pious, but severe and wrathful toward the evil [ones]."[139] Dirk reminds his readers that because God is light, there is no darkness in him. Furthermore, since the true God, Jesus Christ, has nothing to do with sin, anyone in him is without sin, and those who do sin against God by doing fleshly things are enemies of God; darkness and sin are far away from God.

---

138. Philips, "Three Admonitions: No. II," 401–2.
139. Philips, "Ban," 242.

Second, Dirk argues that God distinguishes between error and ignorant sin from willful sin. He says, "God has testified and confirmed that in his law he has instituted sacrifices for the sins of ignorance and error, but willful sinners and evildoers, such as murderers, adulterers, servants of idols, God blasphemers, magicians, and similar transgressors, he has commanded to be punished with death, and thus to root them out of Israel."[140] Dirk believes that this understanding of God's attributes should be applied to the lives of believers. God wants purity for spiritual Israel, Christians, just as Israel remained pure before God and had unclean people dwell outside their camp in order to keep the camp pure and holy.[141]

So Dirk explains the excommunication of physical and spiritual Israel in two separate categories: excommunication of the law and excommunication of the gospel. "There is a difference between the excommunication of the law and that of the gospel: to wit, that by the excommunication of the law, several sins and transgressions were judged and punished by death. But by that of the gospel, the transgressors and sinners are segregated from the Christian church, 1 Cor. 5:13, in the name and power of our Lord Jesus Christ."[142] Thus, evangelical excommunication is instituted by the Lord in order to keep the church of God pure, belonging only to the Lord, and not having unfruitful works of darkness.[143]

Reason for Excommunication

Dirk discusses why the Christian church should practice excommunication in both his treatises related to excommunication. William Keeney argues in the introduction of *Evangelical Excommunication* that the reason for excommunication shifts between Dirk's two treatises.[144] *The Ban* focuses on individual salvation issues, while the second treatise, *Evangelical Excommunication*, is concerned about the church being influenced by people who have fallen out of faith. Keeney's argument is correct in that the second treatise deals much more with false teachings and doctrines that despise the word of God than the first treatise does. However,

---

140. Philips, "Ban," 254.
141. Philips, "Evangelical Excommunication," 597.
142. Philips, "Evangelical Excommunication," 597.
143. Philips, "Evangelical Excommunication," 598.
144. Philips, "Evangelical Excommunication," 592–93.

a comparison of the reasons for excommunication presented by Dirk's treatises confirms that the argument that Dirk's reason for excommunication shifts is excessive.

First, there are three reasons for excommunication presented by Dirk in *The Ban*.

> The first is so that the congregation not become participant of the estranged ones' sins, 2 John 1:11, and that a little leaven not ferment the whole lump, 1 Cor. 5:[6]; Gal. 5:9. The second reason is so that those who have sinned be shamed and disciplined in their flesh, and that their spirit be saved in the day of the Lord Jesus, 1 Cor. 5:[5]. The third reason is so that the congregation of God not be blasphemed because of evil and bear no guilt before the Lord on account of them, 2 Thess. 3:14; Ezek. 36:20; Rom. 2:24; Josh. 7:20[-26]; 1 John 1.3; Deut 13:[6–10]; 17:7; 19:19.[145]

In *Evangelical Excommunication*, Dirk, on the other hand, gives two reasons for excommunication.

> The first is in order that the church be not entirely polluted by the evil ones, 1 Cor. 5:5. That has been sufficiently enough recited and declared above. The second is in order that the transgressor be ashamed and become able to recognize himself in genuine repentance, as Paul testified to the Corinthians and Thessalonians.[146]

Although there is no significant difference in the reasons for the excommunication presented by Dirk's two treatises, Dirk presents conditions of excommunication that are not mentioned in *The Ban* in *Evangelical Excommunication*. The first condition of excommunication is when someone has sinned against his brother but refuses to reconcile with him. The second is when someone accepts false doctrine and turns from the word of God. The third is when one seeks a disordered and evil life. The fourth and final condition is when someone disobeys and despises the doctrines of the apostles.[147] In the second treatise, Dirk demonstrates more alertness to false doctrines, evident in the conditions of excommunication he proposes. However, as Dirk presents the conditions of excommunication, it is right to see a shift in emphasis in the practice of excommunication according to his church's changing situation. Dirk's

---

145. Philips, "Ban," 246.
146. Philips, "Evangelical Excommunication," 600.
147. Philips, "Evangelical Excommunication," 599–600.

idea of why the church should perform excommunication developed in the situation.

Dissent to Dirk's View of Excommunication

Dirk recognizes that there are many objections to his view of excommunication. He introduces these claims and presents his own arguments against them. Dirk points out that some people insist that if God forgives before the church's excommunication, the church should forbid punishment and judgment.[148] However, Dirk points out that the key to excommunication is the fruit of repentance. Since "the kingdom of God does not consist in words but in power, just as the apostle says, 1 Cor. 4:20,"[149] God's forgiveness must be visible in the life of the transgressor, and without this evidence, he must be separated with the congregation.

Another objection is that, in the Scripture, David and Peter sinned, but they were not subjected to excommunication or punishment. It seems that Dirk avoids direct answers for this argument. Yet he notices that both David and Peter demonstrated repentance. The implication is that God forgives those who repent by his grace. David and Peter produced fruit of repentance, which is a sign of complete repentance and of God's forgiveness.[150] Those who repent should bear this fruit, and those who bear this fruit should not be excommunicated.

Dirk also says in his dissenting argument that it is possible for believers to share food and drink with excommunicated people before their restoration. Dirk, however, argues that dialogue with them is allowed only for the purpose of admonishing them with the word of God, and that eating and drinking with them is not an experience of the kingdom of God.[151]

Avoidance

It is well known that Dirk was very rigid not only about excommunication, but also about avoidance. He insisted on excommunication without exception to those who did not show the fruit of repentance, and he

---

148. Philips, "Ban," 247.
149. Philips, "Ban," 247.
150. Philips, "Ban," 248.
151. Philips, "Evangelical Excommunication," 603.

forbade any fellowship with those who were excommunicated from the congregation. In the end, his strong position led to great disruption in the movement, but Dirk did not allow any possibility of compromise from this firm stance.[152]

Dirk's view of avoidance was formed for two different situations. The first was how the excommunicated ones should be treated by brothers and sisters who still remain faithful in the church. The second was a more complex question: how to treat excommunicated spouses in a family who was still faithful in their faith.

Dirk uses several examples to address how believers in the congregation were to deal with excommunicated people. First, Dirk claims that the Scripture opposes eating with the excommunicated. He says, "the Scripture commands and teaches us not to eat with them."[153] To avoid eating with these people is to walk in certain safety and not to be accused on this account. Dirk also prohibits daily business with the excommunicated one. This seems to block the possibility of any influence in everyday life; and Dirk claims that by participating in daily business with the excommunicated, the souls of believers can be lost through ignorance. Finally, Dirk is also against greeting. Since John clarifies in the second letter that "one shall not receive the apostate in his house nor greet him, for whoever greets him has fellowship with his evil works," Dirk argues that believers should follow this command of the word of God by not greeting the excommunicated ones.[154]

Although Dirk has a strict stance on avoidance, he has a generous stance on the issue of what to do if an excommunicated brother or sister needs help. In this case, Dirk insists that believers should have mercy on them. Dirk clearly states that the purpose of excommunication and separation is to improve, not destroy, brothers.[155] That is, excommunication takes place to help anyone in need. Showing God's mercy and giving welfare to the poor should not be forbidden.

As is mentioned above, avoidance of an excommunicated spouse was never an easy issue to solve. Within the Mennonite movement, there were voices against separation of excommunicated spouses and against dividing God's instituted marriage. However, even in these arguments,

---

152. The first agenda of the conference, held in Harlingen in 1557, was about shunning in the family (Koolman, *Dirk Philips*, 81–87; Keeney, "Dirk Philips," 28–29).

153. Philips, "Confession about Separation," 612.

154. Philips, "Confession about Separation," 613.

155. Philips, "Omitted Writing about the Ban and Avoidance," 583.

Dirk insisted constantly that the spouse of an excommunicated person should avoid him or her, and it is right to avoid the spouse following the command of God since the word of God has authority.[156] However, Dirk's position did not mean that he neglected or lightly considered marriage. Although Dirk did not consider marriage to include the mystery found in other sacraments, he still took it seriously.[157] He saw marriage as commanded by God, believing it should be practiced by believers.[158]

Although marriage is an institution established by God, Dirk did not see it as a superordinate concept over other institutions established by God. He preferred to think of the community in connection with marriage. In other words, marriage was possible only within the community, and the church's decision could disrupt a marriage both mentally and physically; but keeping faith was more important than maintaining a marriage. Dirk was wary of Christian marriage harming community purity, and as a result he opposed mixed marriages, where believers marry unbelievers. According to Dirk, marriages instituted by God are confined to a man and a woman among believers, and marriages between believers and unbelievers are according to human desires.[159]

Dirk criticizes those who oppose the practice of separating from an excommunicated spouse saying that God created a man and a woman and said that man leaves his father and mother and adheres to his wife, which two shall be one flesh; Dirk argues that the act of disdain for God cannot be considered under any circumstances.[160] He also does not accept the claim that believer can live in peace with his unbelieving spouse and yet preach the gospel to his or her unbelieving spouse.[161]

Summary

This chapter explores Dirk's ecclesiology in three categories: baptism, the Lord's Supper, and church discipline. These three categories were the subjects that Dirk covered in detail in his ecclesiastical arguments. This chapter examines that Dirk's long treatises dealing with baptism and the

---

156. Philips, "Confession about Separation," 613.
157. Conant, "Marriage Views," 64.
158. Philips, "About the Marriage of Christians," 554.
159. Philips, "About the Marriage of Christians," 558.
160. Philips, "About the Marriage of Christians," 568.
161. Philips, "About the Marriage of Christians," 570.

Lord's Supper, as well as other treatises in relation to church discipline, including admonition, excommunication, and avoidance.

The point of Dirk's view of baptism is that baptism has no effect on salvation but serves as a public confession of faith, and only believers should be baptized. Dirk's primary argument was against infant baptism, which led to his assertion of the significance of water baptism. Yet he never mentions the mode of baptism in his works. Dirk acknowledges both internal and external Christian baptism, and says that those who are baptized confess their faith and express their willingness to live a new life in Jesus Christ. In addition to supporting baptism in the New Testament, Dirk argues that there are typologies in the Old Testament that support baptism. Dirk argues that only those who confess their faith are eligible for baptism, but this qualification is not conferred by verbal confession and is not granted unless it is witnessed by living the word of God. Those who are baptized are to be devoted to the word of God before and after their baptism, and to live out one's rebirth is the life of the baptized. Thus, Dirk believes he cannot accept the practice of baptizing infants, who cannot confess their faith.

The key to Dirk's view of Lord's Supper is that he owns a memorialist view. He clearly opposes the views of transubstantiation, consubstantiation, and Spiritual Presence. He understands that bread and wine at the Lord's Supper are spiritual foods, and also considers the Lord's Supper to commemorate the suffering and death of Jesus Christ. In addition, Dirk sees the Lord's Supper as demonstrating the love and the union established by the Lord. The union with the Lord is the union of the Lord and the believers by divine mystery, which also leads the believers to unite with one another. In practicing the Lord's Supper, Dirk believes that only believers can participate in the Lord's Supper. Those who are not in the congregation of God are excluded from the Lord's Supper, and those who participate in the Lord's Supper are in harmony with each other and keep their faith properly.

Dirk discusses three aspects of church discipline: admonition, excommunication, and avoidance. Since church discipline is directly related to the life of the congregation of God in the visible church, Dirk's view on church discipline closely reflects his view on the visible church. Regarding admonition, Dirk claims that it benefits the lives of believers. Admonition provides the strength and peace of the soul of God's congregation; it also reflects God's love for children, and helps believers walk in Jesus Christ. Dirk admonishes his congregations to rely on the Lord, who is victorious in persecution and suffering, to escape from false teachings, and to live the life of the believer. On the second aspect of church discipline, excommunication, Dirk reminds his congregation of the God who punishes evil. According to Dirk, the benefit of excommunication is that it prevents the congregation of God from being affected by evil; the guilty believer will be ashamed of sin, realize his or her sin, and make true repentance. The third aspect, avoidance, is closely related to excommunication. This aspect refers to how believers deal with those who have been excommunicated from the congregation of God. Dirk had a very strict view on the issue, allowing no fellowship with excommunicated ones—even families—except to help in needs such as extreme poverty.

The Correlation of Dirk Philips's View of the Visible Church with His Ecclesiology

The relationship between Dirk's ecclesiology and the visible church is very direct and closely intertwined. Above all, his views are related to his purpose in writing with respect to ecclesiology and his own life. Dirk wrote to his congregations about baptism, the Lord's Supper, and church discipline, in order to adequately provide them with theoretical knowledge. His most important purpose in writing was for his congregations to correctly practice baptism, the Lord's Supper, and church discipline.

As already mentioned in this chapter, Dirk clearly points out the qualifications of the person being baptized to assist in the practice of baptism in his congregation and points out the inadequacies of infant baptism. He also emphasizes the importance of internal baptism as well as external baptism, thereby preventing his congregation from falling into formalism. The reason Dirk wrote a treatise on the Lord's Supper is to help his congregation understand the biblical meaning of the Lord's Supper, ordained by Christ. He urges his congregation to interpret the blood and flesh of Christ in the Lord's Supper spiritually. He also claims that only the true children of Christ who have accepted the gospel and have experienced inner transformation can participate in the Lord's Supper. Dirk clarifies the guidelines for church discipline, suggesting a way of life that his congregations should have as part of the visible church. Through his perspective on church discipline, he also teaches his congregation the conditions and its justification for the Christian community to be distinguished from the world.

Dirk also had to defend his congregation from many false accusations and attacks against himself and his congregation, and to prevent the entry of false doctrines and ideas into his congregation; so his writing was both educational and practical. Thus, naturally, the discussion of the subjects related to his ecclesiology was not only theoretical and theological, but also presented and introduced as the norms of the visible church in this world.

Dirk also tends to discuss ecclesiastical subjects not only in terms of the biblical meaning and spiritual significance of those themes, but also in terms of the qualifications and attitudes of the believers who practice them. Dirk's ecclesiology does not consist merely of metaphysical and abstract argument, but of debate that is meaningful to those who deal with these issues in the church. Although Dirk does not make a direct reference to the visible church, his ecclesiology discussion is more meaningful for the visible church on earth than for the invisible universal church. At the heart of his ecclesiastical discussion is the life of believers on earth.

In his discussion of baptism, the concept that Dirk uses to emphasize the importance of the believer's life as a member of the visible church on earth is new life. Since Dirk insists that only believers can be baptized, one condition for baptism is living the new life, which proves a believer is genuine; also, being baptized is an expression of a willingness to live a new life in the future. For Dirk, baptism does not have any spiritual effect on members of the invisible church. Baptism is a public confession of faith among the members of the visible church and serves as a proof of a believer's spiritual life. Although Dirk mentions the theological meaning and spiritual benefits of baptism, he is more interested in discussing the life of the baptized and the life after the baptism, and his interest explains why he opposes infant baptism, where the faithful life of the baptized one is not guaranteed. Dirk argues that infants should not be baptized because they cannot confess faith; the infant's inability to confess faith means that there is no guarantee that he or she will live in faith in the future. Dirk points out that some infants who have been baptized live without faith, and he is well aware that if life in faith is excluded, the ordinance has no benefit and meaning.

In Dirk's discussion of the Lord's Supper, what is important to the visible church is the believer's unity. Dirk mentions two different concepts of unity. The first is unity with Christ. Dirk argues that the Lord's Supper leads believers to spiritual unity with the Lord, not simply metaphysical unity, but a unity that involves concrete and practical changes and transformations in life. The second unity is of believers: unity with Christ leads to unity of believers. According to Dirk, the Lord motivates, encourages, and leads believers to unite with each other. Therefore, believers who participate in the Lord's Supper are united with the Lord and united with one another, and therefore they should be worthy of this, and they should always test themselves and live a life worthy of this.

Dirk's discussion of church discipline clearly shows his view of the visible church. The basic reason for Dirk's writing on church discipline is to discuss the way in which the visible church exists in this world. In other words, even though the visible church exists in this world, Dirk was reluctant to be influenced by any false theology, thoughts, or corrupt ways of life in the world, and he made constant efforts to protect his congregation from them. In fact, Dirk's attitude can be seen as the pursuit of a totally flawless Christian community in the world. Indeed, Dirk clearly says that people born of God cannot sin,[162] and this argument has much room for the criticism that he pursued an unrealizable utopian world on earth. However, even if he pursued a thorough and pure life of believers, he should not be condemned as an idealist. He did not identify a completely invisible church with a visible church; but he wanted the congregation of the visible church to live with pure faith. He was well aware of the reality of believers who were wrestling with sin, and he did not let the wrongdoers be driven out of his community—to protect his congregation—and to go to ruin. He admonished them to return to true repentance, pointing out that one of the reasons for excommunication and avoidance was to lead true repentance. Dirk refused to cover the wrongs of the guilty believers in order to maintain the purity of the church, and he tried to bring them to the surface so that hidden sins would not exist in the congregation of God.

In conclusion, the greatest feature of Dirk's ecclesiology is that in his discussion of the subjects such as baptism, Lord's Supper, and church discipline, he deals with how the congregation of God in the visible church must live. Dirk provides his theological interpretation and biblical grounds on each subject, but his ecclesiology functions as a guidebook for the visible church because he always deals with the practice of believers' lives. Thus, it is no exaggeration to say that as a pure faith community, the visible church not only motivates his ecclesiology, but also is at the heart of his ecclesiology.

162. Philips, "Three Admonitions: No. II," 403.

Chapter 5

SOTERIOLOGY

Introduction

WHILE THERE ARE A variety of words that characterize Anabaptist soteriology, a noteworthy viewpoint in twentieth-century Anabaptist soteriology research is that of Robert Friedmann, who argues that "brotherhood," which is essential to salvation, is the central idea of Anabaptism:

> Now then, the Central idea of Anabaptism, the real dynamite in the age of Reformation, as I see it, was this, that one cannot find salvation without caring for his brother, that this "brother" actually matters in the personal life. This is the teaching of Christ and of the Apostles (particularly of John). This interdependence of men gives life and salvation a new meaning. It is not "faith alone" which matters (for which faith no church organization would be needed) but it is brotherhood, this intimate caring for each other, as it was commanded to the disciples of Christ as the way to God's kingdom.[1]

What is noteworthy in Friedmann's argument is that he sees brotherhood not only as an important principle of the Christian community, but also as a sign of salvation. According to him, for the Anabaptists, brotherhood was not merely a virtue to be possessed and practiced by the people of God who had been saved; it was a necessity to judge salvation. He believes that through brotherhood, also called "essential fellowship,"

---

1. Friedmann, "On Mennonite Historiography," 121.

members of the church qualify as saved and discover a true model of Christian discipleship.[2]

Harold S. Bender, on the other hand, defines the central idea of Anabaptist soteriology as regeneration and discipleship. According to Bender, "the Anabaptist doctrine of regeneration and discipleship was expressed in the context of Reformation theology and practice, and in conscious opposition to it."[3] Bender points out that the Reformation emphasized doctrines such as the sole authority of the Scriptures, grace, and justification by faith, but the Anabaptists emphasized "walking in the resurrection."[4] He believes that the Anabaptists did not deny the doctrines that the Reformers emphasized or orthodox Christian doctrines, but they emphasized that believers learn to live on the resurrection side of the cross.[5] Bender argued that Anabaptists were more interested in pragmatic life as a saved people than in discussing theoretical and metaphysical soteriology.

This opinion of Bender's is evidenced in Dirk's soteriology. Dirk and his congregation, of course, valued brotherhood, which Friedmann emphasized as the core of Anabaptist soteriology. Contrary to Friedmann's argument, however, it is difficult to find an emphasis on brotherhood in Dirk's discussion of salvation. Dirk, instead, as Bender points out, concentrates mostly on regeneration in his discussion of salvation, and he deals with the life of regenerated believers.

This chapter will look at Dirk's view of each aspect in the order of salvation and its relation to the visible church. As Bavinck points out, salvation is explained in several orders through theoretical divisions, but in fact all of these explanations of each order describe one change, the immediate work of the Holy Spirit, in humans.[6] In this respect, the limitation of this chapter is that Dirk does not intend this distinction. Dirk, rather than being concerned over the order of salvation, had a very simple soteriology: he believed that salvation comes from God and that those who are saved must live accordingly. Therefore, this chapter will analyze Dirk's soteriology, not to understand salvation as a sequential

2. Friedmann, "On Mennonite Historiography," 122.
3. Bender, "'Walking in the Resurrection,'" 102.
4. Bender, "'Walking in the Resurrection,'" 104.
5. Robert Kreider also believes that "the Anabaptists accepted the Lutheran formula of justification by faith, but they insisted that this faith must be evidenced (Bussfertigkeit) by newness of character." Kreider, "Anabaptism and Humanism," 138.
6. Bavinck, *Reformed Dogmatics*, 491.

procedure or order—although this chapter describes Dirk's soteriology in the order of salvation—but to discover what Dirk claims about various aspects of salvation and what he intends to emphasize.

Dirk's View of Predestination

Summarizing the views of predestination in the sixteenth-century Protestant movement in which Dirk lived is not an easy task. Since it was a period of occurrence, coexistence, and competition among various groups, analyzing and making conclusions regarding their particular theology has the challenge of considering many variables. Therefore, in order to deepen understanding of the period's views of predestination, it is necessary to clarify each Anabaptist group's perspective on predestination. Similarly, comparing the views of specific groups in the Anabaptist movement with the Magisterial Reformers is not an easy task and requires careful analysis. In particular, it is challenging to compare the views of Anabaptist and Magisterial Reformers because it is almost impossible to specify a view that is representative of Anabaptists as a whole. For this reason, a description of Anabaptist perspectives on predestination has the limitation of generalizing the perspective of some groups within the Anabaptist movement.

Despite the above limitations, A.J. Beachy published an important study on Anabaptists' views of predestination in which he presented a compact analysis of perspectives of predestination in the sixteenth century. Basically, Beachy says, "At no other point did the Radical Reformers differ so strongly with the Magisterial Reformers as on the question of the bondage of the will."[7] However, Beachy also defined the differences between the Anabaptists and the Magisterial Reformers. He began by arguing that both Luther and Calvin mostly agree on a view called the forensic view of grace. They both see God's grace as a divine act of eternal election, and they both believe in "God's act of forensic justification where the righteousness of the Christian becomes the imputed righteousness of Christ."[8] Based on this grace, Christians are promised eternal life; in reality, however, Christians live their lives both as justified saints and as sinners. As an analogy, the believer is like a person who is promised health; he will eventually be well, but receiving that promise

---

7. Beachy, *Concept of Grace*, 173.
8. Beachy, *Concept of Grace*, 4.

does not mean present health. Thus, according to Beachy, this view does not require Christian ontological or metaphysical changes.[9]

Beachy, on the other hand, argues that the key phrase regarding salvation from the perspective of the Radical Reformation is the "divinization of man."[10] From this viewpoint, the grace of God is manifested through the act of God working in humankind. God renews a person, puts a divine image in the person, and invites him or her to participate in his divine nature through the Holy Spirit.[11] Beachy notes that the Radical Reformers did not believe that God's saving grace could be obtained through the work of human beings. Nevertheless, he pointed out that the Magisterial Reformers' forensic view of grace probably led to the Radical Reformers' turning of the grace of God into cheap grace.[12]

Although Beachy did not analyze Dirk Phillips, his views provide one possible way to understand Dirk's view of predestination. It is true that Dirk, unlike Calvin, does not deal with predestination directly in his treatises. He was not interested in introducing or refuting particular theories of predestination, but that does not mean Dirk denied the doctrine of predestination. In Dirk's writings, he suggests God's grace and election as the only way of salvation for human beings.

The Grace of God

The most important and most frequently mentioned concept that Dirk uses in his discussion of salvation is probably that of the grace of God. Dirk acknowledges that all the aspects of salvation are made possible by the grace of God. It is by grace that God chooses his people, gives his people faith, and eventually brings his people to salvation.[13] According to Dirk, God's grace to save his people can be found in God's covenant with Abraham. Through God's covenant, all believers are accepted by God and become heirs of his eternal kingdom.[14] Dirk also demonstrates clearly that salvation comes from God's grace when he discusses the concept of circumcision:

9. Beachy, *Concept of Grace*.
10. Beachy, *Concept of Grace*, 4–5.
11. Beachy, *Concept of Grace*, 4–5.
12. Beachy, *Concept of Grace*, 5.
13. Philips, "Baptism of Our Lord Jesus Christ," 88.
14. Philips, "Baptism of Our Lord Jesus Christ," 102.

> just as in the Old Testament salvation rested primarily in the grace of God and not in circumcision, Rom. 3:1 [-2], nevertheless, circumcision as an ordinance of God was profitable to those who observed the law, so now in the New Testament, salvation rests primarily upon the mercy and grace of God, the heavenly Father, and in the merits of Jesus Christ, Rom. 3:24; 5:1; 8:1; 11:22.[15]

Dirk argues that in the process of saving humanity, the grace of God for the human is actually accomplished through the sending of the Holy Spirit. Dirk believes that the grace of God is realized through the working of the Holy Spirit within believers:

> But the pledge and true seal of this grace of God and Jesus Christ is the Holy Spirit, who is poured into the hearts of believers from the heavenly Father and through Christ as a witness to the divine covenant, as a sealing of their salvation, 2 Cor. 5: 5; John 14:16; 15:26; 16:7, and as a renewing of [human] thoughts and emotions, [Heb. 4:12; Eph. 1:13; 4:30.[16]

Dirk also reveals that it was the grace of God to save humans that God sent Jesus Christ to the earth. The grace of God was revealed to humanity through Jesus Christ, and it is through Jesus Christ that true righteousness, holiness, and salvation appeared to humans. As humankind's Savior and Redeemer, Jesus Christ bestowed all heavenly blessings upon believers; through him, believers obtain peace with God and possess the privilege of being children and heirs of God.[17] Of course, believers cannot be exactly like Jesus Christ because they are substantially different from Christ—Christ is naturally God. Dirk, however, claims that believers will partake of God's nature and become children of God through Jesus Christ, a status which is due to the "grace of God through election, adoption, and impartation of the divine nature and gifts."[18]

Election

Although he does not discuss theologically the subject of election, Dirk thinks God's election began from the beginning of eternity. In his treatise

---

15. Philips, "Baptism of Our Lord Jesus Christ," 107.
16. Philips, "Baptism of Our Lord Jesus Christ," 102.
17. Philips, "Our Confession," 69.
18. Philips, "Incarnation of Our Lord Jesus Christ," 146.

Concerning the True Knowledge of Jesus Christ, he refers to his congregations as "all brothers and sisters whom God from the beginning chose for salvation."[19] Dirk agrees that God planned his salvation work from the beginning and elected his chosen people.[20]

According to Dirk, the characteristics of his chosen people are that they have faith and that God works in them through his Spirit. Thus, for Dirk, God's election is inseparable from his people's faith. It is impossible to partake of Jesus Christ and his gifts without possessing faith, nor is it possible that the unbelieving and evil ones who are not chosen by God will have faith.[21]

It is also an essential issue for Dirk to proclaim the true word of God because God creates faith through the Holy Spirit in his elected ones by their hearing of his Word.[22] Thus, since the children of evil create their faithless children through false doctrine, it is crucial that the true doctrine and the true word of God be proclaimed in this world.[23] Those who have true doctrine and the word of God become attentive to the true knowledge of God; they have firm faith, they love God, and they love the brothers and sisters of Jesus Christ.[24]

Dirk does not believe that God's reprobation began from the beginning although he asserts that God's election started from the beginning. In his discussion of the order of salvation, Dirk has a clear concept that God chose his people by grace; but he does not discuss the concept of God abandoning the unchosen or reprobation based on some concept of God's mysterious agenda such as limited atonement. Rather than focusing on reprobation, Dirk focuses on God's judgment against unbelievers,[25] and he teaches his congregation not to be part of the judged group by possessing the characteristics of those who are judged by God.[26]

Dirk is undoubtedly one who tried to bridge the gap between the visible and invisible church. He believed theologically that those whom

---

19. Phiips, "Concerning the True Knowledge of Jesus Christ," 152.

20. In Dirk's thinking, God's election in the beginning means that his work began before the beginning of the world. However, Dirk does not provide information on whether he has surpralapsarian or infralapsarian perspectives.

21. Philips, "Supper of Our Lord Jesus Christ," 116.

22. Philips, "Sending of Preachers or Teachers," 217.

23. Philips, "Sending of Preachers or Teachers."

24. Philips, "True Knowledge of God," 263.

25. Philips, "Short but Fundamental Account," 518.

26. Philips, "Sending of Preachers or Teachers," 232.

God chose were no longer accused, but sought to live as children of God who would confess to believing in God. Unbelievers, of course, will face God's judgment, but he does not accept the claim that God has predestined unbelievers to reprobation.

Dirk's View on Justification

Throughout Luther's life, he devoted more time and energy to the doctrine of justification than to any other doctrines.[27] For Luther, the doctrine of justification is not just one of the doctrines, but the basic and main doctrine of faith with which the church stands or falls, and upon which the entire doctrine of the church depends; this doctrine is the heart and soul of Luther's Reformation theology.[28]

Luther's doctrine of justification relates to the study of the Anabaptist's understanding of justification. Indeed, Luther believed that Anabaptists and other Radicals rejected justification by faith in favor of justification by works, a belief that led him to attack Anabaptists in some of his writings.[29] Anabaptists, on the other hand, accused Luther of treating good works as unimportant in the lives of believers. Of course, because the center of Anabaptist theology cannot be easily defined, it is true that not all Anabaptists have the same view of Luther's doctrine of justification. However, according to Egil Grislis, "the most precise analysis of the origin and role of good works, . . . is found in the writings of Menno Simons. With conviction and clarity Menno Simons taught that salvation is not by our own merits and works, but by grace through Christ Jesus."[30]

Although Grislis does not mention Dirk, it is certain that Dirk agrees with his colleague Menno Simons. Dirk mentions Luther directly three times in his writings.[31] All three instances appear in *The Baptism of Our Lord Jesus Christ*, and each time Dirk mentions Luther, he does

---

27. Althaus, *Theology of Martin Luther*, 225.

28. Lohse, *Martin Luther's Theology*, 258.

29. Luther's specific criticism of Anabaptism is well described in Finn, "Curb Your Enthusiasm," 168–72.

30. Grislis, "Meaning of Good Works," 175–77.

31. Koolman argues that Dirk's first mention of Luther comes from Menno's *A Basic Confession of the Poor and Miserable Christians* (1552), that the second mention is baded on Dirk's literal translation of Luther's *Preface to the Prophets*, and that the third mention is borrowed from Sebastian Franck's quote from the Chronicle (Koolman, *Dirk Philips*, 71–72).

so to criticize Luther and his followers, who favored infant baptism. One thing to note is that it is Luther's own argument that Dirk provides as a reason for criticizing Luther and his followers. Specifically, Dirk says that it is inappropriate to baptize infants based on Luther's argument that no one will be saved or justified through the faith or justification of another but only through his own. Dirk, therefore, argues that Lutherans should prohibit the baptism of infants according to Luther's doctrine of justification. Dirk not only knows Luther's doctrine of justification but accepts it and claims that infant baptism is not appropriate based on the doctrine.[32]

In the thought of Dirk, justification is the event of God's calling a person to salvation in Jesus Christ from the beginning through his eternal love. God called his chosen people by grace without merits and placed them in the place of mercy through the blood of Jesus Christ. Dirk said that God's justification is for the elect who were under sin and for all who have faith in Jesus Christ.[33] The old person was crucified with Jesus Christ, and their sinful body might cease and no longer serve sin because anyone who died is justified from sin.[34]

For Dirk, God's justification is not only one time in the beginning but also definitive. Dirk argues that those whom God has justified cannot be accused or condemned. It is God who justifies people, and for those whom God has justified, their righteous status is definite. Dirk quotes Romans 8 for this argument:

> Therefore no one may accuse or condemn them, just as Paul says, "If God is with us, who will be against us? He who did not spare his own Son but gave him up for us all, how should he not give us all things with him? Who will accuse the elect of God? God is here, who justifies; who will condemn? Christ is here, who has died, yes, much more, who was also awakened, who also is at the right hand of God, and prays for us," Rom. 8:31[-34]?[35]

Moreover, Dirk believes that justification takes place through the imputation and sharing of God's righteousness out of grace. Dirk understands justification as an event at the beginning, but also as a present event that causes believers to live a new life and to be renewed in the

---

32. Philips, "Baptism of Our Lord Jesus Christ," 85.
33. Philips, "Our Confession," 68.
34. Philips, "Baptism of Our Lord Jesus Christ," 75.
35. Philips, "New Birth and the New Creature," 313–14.

image of the Father in Heaven. That is, those who are born anew through Jesus Christ are those who are justified and who walk in new spiritual life away from the old self.[36]

Dirk's View of Conversion

Dirk indicates that the Christian life represents something different from the way believers lived before because of its true nature and righteousness. Christians now live new lives against the past, which was dead in sin and transgression. Conversion, which is an act of turning from our sins through repentance and toward Christ in faith, is the first step in this new life.[37]

Conversion can be logically divided into two categories: repentance and faith. But at the same time, it is a single reality with indivisible aspects. Since repentance is a return from the unbelief of sin, and faith can be understood as a return to Christ, the two aspects are incomplete without each other, and each is motivated by the other.[38]

Dirk also has a distinct conception of repentance and of faith, but he understands that repentance and faith are tied to one event. Dirk insists that both repentance and faith come after unbelievers hear the gospel, but prior to baptism.[39] He understands that repentance, confession of their sins, and faith in Jesus Christ are the decisive factor in the conversion from unbelievers to believers.[40] Most of Dirk's discussion of repentance is in his account for baptism. This may be the case because he wrote about baptism while not writing about conversion and repentance. However, since repentance is closely related to baptism, Dirk does cover a great deal about repentance in his discussion of baptism.

Although Dirk does not discuss the details of the order of salvation and conversion within the order, what is found in Dirk's claims about baptism is the place of conversion in the order of salvation. He argues that only after sinners have faith after hearing the gospel can they be baptized. To be baptized means that someone already has faith and has repented of

36. Philips, "Baptism of Our Lord Jesus Christ," 78.

37. Philips, "Baptism of Our Lord Jesus Christ," 76, 83, 98; Philips, "Congregation of God," 359.

38. Erickson, *Christian Theology*, 865.

39. Philips, "Baptism of Our Lord Jesus Christ," 75.

40. Philips, "Baptism of Our Lord Jesus Christ," 98.

their sins and has openly confessed.[41] Baptism, therefore, is meant as an open confession for believers, but repentance is meaningful in that unbelievers receive new life and become believers through repentance.[42] Dirk also recognizes that repentance is the channel through which people are freed from the law of God's wrath and the severe judgment of God upon sin. This is why Dirk has no choice but to emphasize the proclamation of the Gospel, because for him the proclamation of the Gospel is a means by which people can hear the Gospel and those who hear it can repent and be saved by hearing and repenting. Thus, hearing and repenting are crucial requirements in the order of salvation.[43]

Dirk also makes a clear argument about the subject of repentance. Dirk says "[b]ut we shall learn therefrom that God is gracious and merciful, longsuffering and of great goodness, and takes away the misdeeds and transgressions and forgives the guilt of all those who amend themselves from their hearts and make sincere repentance, Num. 14:18; Ps. 103:3."[44] Dirk insists that aspects of God's character, such as grace and mercy, make it possible for humans to repent; he also insists that God is sovereign in forgiveness of sins through human repentance. Indeed, in Dirk's writing, there is no specific reference to the degree of human will in repentance, but according to Dirk, it is inevitable that the whole process of repentance is due to Christ's choosing and sending of individuals. He expressly and implicitly acknowledges that God is sovereign in the process of repentance.[45]

Dirk mentions both repentance and faith, but he does not always make a distinction between repentance and faith. He logically distinguishes repentance from the faith, as mentioned above, but sometimes he mentions only repentance and does not mention faith. This proves that Dirk does not appear to have substantially made a distinction between the two. However, in his treatise, *The Congregation of God*, Dirk clarifies the relationship between repentance and faith.

> Since no one can be born or made alive, and no one can believe the gospel unless he first genuinely repents, just as the Lord Jesus Christ himself testifies, for he taught the people repentance first,

---

41. Philips, "Baptism of Our Lord Jesus Christ," 73.
42. Philips, "Concerning the True Knowledge of Jesus Christ," 169.
43. Philips, "Sending of Preachers or Teachers," 207–8.
44. Philips, "Ban," 248.
45. Philips, "Congregation of God," 365.

Matt. 3:2, and after that faith, and he has also thus commanded his apostles so to do, Luke 24:46[f.].[46]

Despite Dirk's general tendency to treat repentance and faith as one event in his discussion of conversion, he insists in *The Congregation of God* that repentance comes before faith. As a basis for this, Dirk suggests that John the Baptist proclaimed repentance in Matthew 3, and he mentions that "repentance and forgiveness of sins will be preached" in Luke 24.

Dirk also argues not only for repentance in an internal and theological sense but also for repentance accompanied by substantial changes. Dirk considers it important in his discussion of repentance that repentance leads to the renewal of believers, and that repentance requires evidence of a changed attitude in one's behavior.[47] True repentance and a life worthy of repentance are indistinguishable, and true repentance is followed by abandoning the old man and living free from sin.[48]

Dirk emphasizes in his treatise "Our Confession Concerning the Creation, Redemption, and Salvation of Humanity" that humans cannot be saved by their faith alone; the grace of God saves them through faith. "For by grace you have been saved through faith; and this is not your own doing, it is the gift of God, not because of works, lest anyone man should boast."[49] For Dirk, faith has a very active aspect. Faith causes believers to turn to Christ and hold on to Christ more. Faith is God's work in believers, and it is through faith that believers participate in the divine nature. Faith is also meaningful when accompanied by love and good works. Dirk argues that faith causes humans to love God and to do God's work through the Holy Spirit. "Therefore, those who boast of their faith without love and good works, their boast is false and their faith is idle."[50]

Dirk's View of Regeneration

Among the themes of soteriology, regeneration is the only aspect of Soteriology that Dirk deals directly with in his writings. In his treatise, *The New Birth and the New Creature*, he deals with the lives of the newly born believers. Dirk's main argument in this treatise is regarding the meaning

46. Philips, "Congregation of God," 359.
47. Philips, "About the Marriage of Christians," 553.
48. Philips, "About the Marriage of Christians," 565.
49. Philips, "Our Confession," 69.
50. Philips, "Our Confession," 70.

of experiencing regeneration and its effect on the lives of believers who have experienced it.

Dirk argues, first of all, that the true new birth and the nature of the new creature is found in only a few people. He criticizes those who claim to be living in but who are living a life that is not truly in Christ. He believes he lives in a time of false godliness, and claims this tendency to be one of Satan's cunning tricks, "who can transform himself into an angel of light, exhibits himself with great power in his ministers."[51] Therefore, those who have experienced a new birth must be partakers of the divine character because they are born of God, and are to be led to Jesus Christ and the Holy Spirit.[52]

The theological concept that Dirk considers essential to explain the life of regenerated believers is the image of God, and he reminds his readers that God created the first person in his image and likeness. Dirk also does not overlook Jesus Christ in his understanding of God's image. He says, "God in the beginning created human beings for eternal life, as an upright, immortal, and divine being, yes, in the image and likeness of his only born Son, Jesus Christ."[53] Jesus Christ is the Son of God, the perfect model of God's image, the image of eternal light and the divine glory of God. Although Jesus is the image of God, since Adam was created from God, humans have sinned and come to death and corruption instead of staying in the first created state. However, because of his mercy, God, according to his promise, sent his only begotten Son to the earth to save those who sinned. Thus, "Through this gracious gospel of Christ Jesus, the person was again comforted, renewed, after the image of God and born again to eternal life."[54]

Here, Dirk takes the same form of the structure of creation, fall, and redemption that forms the backbone of the Reformed worldview.[55]

> Since the person was created by God the Father after his image and likeness, that is, after the image and likeness of Christ, and after his fall was by grace again restored through the obedience and righteousness of the Son of God, Rom. 5:18, therefore also every person must (as he comes to maturity and is able to

51. Philips, "New Birth and the New Creature," 293.
52. Philips, "New Birth and the New Creature," 294.
53. Philips, "New Birth and the New Creature," 294.
54. Philips, "New Birth and the New Creature," 295.
55. To study the reformed worldview of creation, fall, and redemption, see Wolters, *Creation Regained*.

distinguish good from evil) be born again through the enlightenment, activity, and illumination of the Holy Spirit to a new divine being.[56]

The most significant feature of Dirk's argument mentioned above is that after he briefly mentions creation, fall, and redemption, he emphasizes that those who are reborn are new beings who partake of God's nature. Dirk does not provide the theological meaning and explanation of creation, fall, and redemption, but rather states that this world was created in the image of God, and that people were fallen and are restored through the obedience and righteousness of the Son of God. Dirk's explanation, however, leads to one conclusion. It is for believers to live as new beings. Here, as with Dirk's description of other subjects, Dirk uses his theological knowledge to teach believers how to live their lives, and he mentions rebirth not only for a theoretical and doctrinal explanation but also to teach believers.

Dirk cites two of Jesus' references to the new birth recorded in the Gospel of John. The first is what Christ said to Nicodemus: "Truly, truly, I say to you, unless one is born anew, he may not see the kingdom of God," John 3:3; the other is John 3:5: "Truly, truly, I say to you, unless one is born of water and the Spirit, he may not enter the kingdom of God." Dirk, as the Lord said, understands the new birth as a precondition for entering the kingdom of God, and in other words, no one who denies the kingdom of God is born anew.[57] Also, Dirk argues that in addition to John's testimony, there are pieces of evidence and teachings about the new birth in many other parts of the New Testament. Dirk quotes from 1 Peter, James, and Titus:

> But how this new birth and renewal takes place, that the apostle Peter testifies to with these words: "You have been born again, not of perishable seed but of imperishable, that is, through the Word of the living God," 1 Pet 1:23. James is in accord with this and says, "Every good and every perfect gift comes down from above, from the Father of lights with whom there is no variation or changing of light and darkness. Of his own will, he brought us forth through the Word of truth so that we should be the first fruits of his creatures," James 1:17[-18]. And Paul writes to Titus that God has saved us through the washing of regeneration and renewal of the Holy Spirit which he has poured out richly upon

---

56. Philips, "New Birth and the New Creature," 295.
57. Philips, "New Birth and the New Creature," 295.

us through Christ Jesus, so that we should be justified through his grace and according to this hope become heirs of eternal life, Titus 3:5[-7].[58]

Dirk argues that, based on the biblical teachings above, believers who have been born anew hear the word of truth and live a new life after being transformed by the Holy Spirit. Those who believe in Jesus Christ are born out of God, and "all that is born out of God overcomes the world."[59] Thus, the new birth is the work of God in people according to his will. God is the origin of new creations, and the word of the heavenly Father is the seed of new creation.[60] Even though the new creation by God is maintained and renewed by the Holy Spirit, Dirk emphasizes that the new birth is the work of God because the origin of the new creation is in God.

The word Dirk uses to define those who have regeneration is "firstlings."[61] He uses firstlings as an eschatological image: the same status that all believers will have in the last days. Of course, there are various images of Christians that Dirk uses: he says "all Christians are a separate people of God, chosen out of all peoples, bought with the precious blood of the Lamb, Jesus Christ, and sanctified through the Holy Spirit, to God as a sweet-smelling savor and well-pleasing sacrifice."[62] Dirk argues that these Christians will later stand as firstlings. Dirk says that firstlings of the creatures of God, and will "stand on Mount Zion with Christ Jesus the Lamb of God, that is, who are in his congregation, signed in their foreheads with the name of the heavenly Father, whom they confess in true faith, whose name they bear, whom they praise without ceasing, and sing a new song."[63]

According to Dirk, newborn believers are firstlings born out of God because of God's powerful and active work and are children of God who will stand before God and praise God's glory as a saved people in the last days.[64] Dirk thus has an eschatological understanding of regeneration. As mentioned many times, Dirk tends to emphasize the practice of the faith of believers who have experienced a new birth. He is constantly telling

---

58. Philips, "New Birth and the New Creature," 295–96.
59. Philips, "New Birth and the New Creature," 296.
60. Philips, "New Birth and the New Creature," 296.
61. Philips, "New Birth and the New Creature," 297–98.
62. Philips, "New Birth and the New Creature," 297.
63. Philips, "New Birth and the New Creature," 297.
64. Philips, "New Birth and the New Creature," 304–5.

his readers to live as the people of God, and he encourages them to live a life that demonstrates evidence of rebirth. His theology of regeneration, however, does not remain at the practical level. According to Dirk, believers who have experienced regeneration will live forever with God as people in the kingdom of God after the judgment of God in the last days.

Dirk portrays Jesus Christ as the model for newborn believers. Dirk argues that Jesus Christ is the model for regenerated believers because he has accomplished the righteousness of both the Old and New Testaments perfectly. He says, "we must observe and reflect upon the whole life and practice of Christ, how obedient he was to his Father, how faithfully he did his Father's will, and spoke his word, yes, that he perfectly fulfilled all righteousness of both the Old and the New Testaments."[65] Dirk notes that Christ never failed to follow his Father's will, and he fulfilled the Old Testament law rather than breaking it.

Dirk teaches that Jesus Christ prepared the way for believers because he was the true mediator of the New Testament. Just as Jesus Christ was baptized by John the Baptist, believers should be baptized by Christ. The baptism of Christ means being baptized with the Holy Spirit and fire, and simultaneously outwardly with the same water baptism that Jesus received.[66] Thus, Dirk criticizes the despising of external baptism by emphasizing only internal baptism; and he criticizes the overlooking of the change of a true inner being by emphasizing only external baptism. Dirk's balanced view of both outward and inward baptism may make his claims unclear, but he understands that emphasizing both inward and outward baptism follows the example of Jesus Christ.

Dirk confesses that it is God's genuine grace that Jesus Christ is an example for believers and that they can follow Jesus Christ.[67] However, not all are given the privilege of enjoying this grace. Those who do not realize God's secret wisdom are those who disdain the teachings and ordinances of Jesus Christ.[68] Dirk criticizes them for thinking they need nothing because they are blind to their wickedness. They regard themselves as wise virgins or maidens with enough oil, but in reality, they are like foolish virgins or maidens who have no oil when the groom comes. Dirk's mention of a person who does not follow Jesus' example leads to

---

65. Philips, "New Birth and the New Creature," 299.
66. Philips, "New Birth and the New Creature," 300.
67. Philips, "New Birth and the New Creature," 301.
68. Philips, "New Birth and the New Creature," 302.

criticism of believers who do not live out the practice of regenerated people. In other words, those born of God should not despise the water of rebirth, and those who have been baptized outwardly should glorify Christ through the Holy Spirit in their lives.[69]

Although Dirk emphasizes external ordinances and the transformation of regenerated believers, he does not neglect an emphasis on believers' internal change. Dirk supports Paul's claim that both circumcised and uncircumcised persons should be transformed through spiritual circumcision of the heart. After all, the external form, such as circumcision, is not decisive for the rebirth of believers, but as the apostle Paul says, faith working through love is important in Christ, and it does not matter whether a believer is circumcised or uncircumcised.[70]

The issue of Dirk's views on sin will be discussed in the next chapter, but it is appropriate to deal with some aspects of Dirk's view of sin in this section because the issue of sin is a real problem for regenerated people. As has already been noted, Dirk concludes regarding new birth and new creation that born-again children of God and new creatures are born again in Christ Jesus, so they become participants of the divine nature in the heavenly Father and Christ Jesus; and through the Holy Spirit, they are renewed and sanctified.[71] Thus, as Dirk emphasizes, "while we desire to devote ourselves as poor unworthy servants, to do God's will through his grace, nevertheless, no one shall thus imagine or think nor repeat about us that we set or seek our salvation anywhere other than in the grace of God and the merits of Christ alone."[72]

However, Dirk admits that human beings are sinners who cannot escape from the problem of sin as long as they exist on earth. Thus he says, "we confess ourselves as poor sinners and unworthy servants of the Lord and mourn with the prophet that our sins have gone over our heads and have become as a heavy burden upon us."[73] Human beings were born through the sinful flesh of Adam, bitten and poisoned by a serpent, and became partakers of Adam's sinful nature.[74] Dirk confirms this limitation of sinful man through the teaching of the Scripture. He points out that

---

69. Philips, "New Birth and the New Creature," 305.
70. Philips, "New Birth and the New Creature," 306.
71. Philips, "New Birth and the New Creature," 310.
72. Philips, "New Birth and the New Creature," 307.
73. Philips, "New Birth and the New Creature," 308.
74. Philips, "New Birth and the New Creature," 308.

the Scripture testifies that all persons are under sin, and he also points out that Solomon's prayer shows that there is no person who does not sin.[75] Dirk also claims that Job teaches that no one is clean before God.[76] According to Dirk, the greatest hope for humans with these limitations is the word of God. Of course, Dirk does not fail to mention that Jesus Christ alone is the only way of salvation and of healing for sinful humans. Dirk, however, believes that to live in this world, sinful human beings need to follow God's word, "God's Word preserves the people, those who trust upon the Lord," and that "God's Word is spirit and life and makes alive."[77]

Dirk's View of Sanctification

Dirk refers to the elect as "all those who are chosen out of grace from God in the sanctification of the Spirit and in the belief of the truth."[78] Sanctification is possible for the regenerated through spiritual fellowship with Christ; this fellowship refers to all participation in heavenly goods and gifts. For Dirk, sanctification is a synonym for holiness. Sanctification is God's ongoing work of sanctifying the chosen and it is also something that believers must continue to pursue. Thus, sanctification refers to the moral state of humanity in harmony with his legal status before God, and Dirk understands that sanctification is crucial for believers to see God.[79]

Dirk's understanding of sanctification can be divided into two categories. The first is sanctification as a change of Christian status. For Dirk, sanctification means the saved state of Christians. In this sense, sanctification for Dirk begins with regeneration and justification, events which take place at the moment of conversion. That is, the sanctification of a Christian means a state that belongs to the Lord, distinct from the world; this is the case because, as Dirk says, "he has now reconciled you with the body of his flesh by death, so that he should present you holy and blameless, without guilt before him."[80]

---

75. Philips, "New Birth and the New Creature," 308.
76. Philips, "New Birth and the New Creature," 308.
77. Philips, "New Birth and the New Creature," 309.
78. Philips, "Supper of Our Lord Jesus Christ," 121.
79. Philips, "About the Marriage of Christians." 567.
80. Philips, "New Birth and the New Creature," 313.

Second, Dirk argues that sanctification is something Christians must live out in their lives. Most notable in Dirk's view of sanctification is his communal understanding of it. Dirk believes that Christians are united as members of one body, and that "they also have the right and power with all the saints to enjoy all the divine things which Christ has instituted for us to the sanctification of his name and the promotion of faith and love."[81]

According to Dirk, even though "the congregation of Christ is the fellowship of the saints, who [are chosen] through the providence of God the Father, through the grace of Jesus Christ," it is also of great importance that they are sanctified as the body of Christ and that Christians are a united community.[82] In the sanctification of the Spirit, the congregation of God has fellowship with the saints, believes the truth, becomes one in the gospel, and remains in true peace.[83]

Dirk understands the subject of Christian sanctification in connection with the Triune God. First, sanctification comes from the Father's choice, the Father is the One who makes all good things happen to the saints, and the "God of all grace chastises [them] for [their] need, so that [they] might receive [H]is sanctification and live."[84] God's election to salvation makes it possible to live in the faith of the saints and to be sanctified in the Holy Spirit.[85] Hence, sanctified saints are not from Adam, but from God, the heavenly Father.[86]

Second, Dirk claims that sanctification is related to Christ. He points out that sanctification is from God for those who believe in Christ, saying, "for Christ is made from God to wisdom, righteousness, sanctification, and redemption for us."[87] Dirk argues that the incarnation of Christ and the ministry of the cross are both works of salvation and works for the sanctifying of humanity. Christ made humans holy and blameless by the reconciling work of the cross.

Finally, Dirk claims that the subject of sanctification is the Holy Spirit. In fact, for most of his discussions on sanctification, the work

---

81. Philips, "Supper of Our Lord Jesus Christ," 131.
82. Philips, "Sending of Preachers or Teachers," 220.
83. Philips, "Ban," 240–241.
84. Philips, "Three Admonitions: No. I," 388.
85. Philips, "Three Admonitions: No. I," 383.
86. Philips, "Incarnation of Our Lord Jesus Christ," 144.
87. Philips, "New Birth and the New Creature," 313.

of the Holy Spirit plays a very decisive role. First of all, the Holy Spirit plays a vital role in sanctification as one of the aforementioned categories of sanctification, the change of Christian status. All saved believers are God's chosen people, called by the blood of Jesus Christ, and they experience sanctification through the Holy Spirit. Dirk says that "all Christians are a separate people of God, chosen out of all peoples, bought with the precious blood of the Lamb, Jesus Christ, and sanctified through the Holy Spirit, to God as a sweet smelling savor and well-pleasing sacrifice."[88]

Furthermore, in Dirk's other category of sanctification, the changed life of Christians, the Holy Spirit appears to be more critical, because, for Dirk, the Holy Spirit is the subject of the Christian community's fellowship of saints. As mentioned earlier, Dirk tends to understand sanctification in a communal way, as the power or work of the Holy Spirit to encourage Christians to unite and live as a community.

Dirk's View of Unity with Christ

For Dirk, the concept of unity with Jesus Christ is a comprehensive term for salvation in general. Dirk uses the term in a broader sense, not in connection with a specific order of salvation, such as regeneration, justification, and sanctification. Although Dirk does not have an in-depth discussion of the features of unity with Jesus Christ, he makes clear that unity with Christ is essential to the salvation of believers. In other words, Dirk uses the concept of unity with Christ as the condition for the saved state of believers and as the condition for Christians to live as children of Christ.

Dirk believes that the external sign of saved children of God is true faith, new birth, and sincere Christlike living. Dirk, however, suggests unity with Christ as a condition for demonstrating external true faith.[89] The believers' unity with Christ makes this external sign possible. In addition, Dirk believes that to have faith is "to be united with Christ and be incorporated into him, yes, to be transplanted out of the fleshly nature of Adam and transformed into the spiritual heavenly divine nature of Christ."[90] In other words, to Dirk, the believers' unity with Christ is not

---

88. Philips, "New Birth and the New Creature," 297.
89. Philips, "Baptism of Our Lord Jesus Christ," 76.
90. Philips, "Baptism of Our Lord Jesus Christ," 276.

merely a change of their inner and spiritual state but also a source of a visible change of faith.

Dirk argues in his discussion of the Lord's Supper that the unity and fellowship of believers are portrayed and testified of through the bread and wine. Just as each grain and each grape changes form to become one loaf of bread and common wine, all Christians must be united with Christ and with each other, not remaining as individuals. Dirk's sense of unity with Christ here means having faith and receiving nourishment through Christ. It also means that the believers are transformed and changed into the nature and character of Christ and that God's chosen ones are justified and saved through Christ.[91]

For Dirk, being united with Christ is the condition of being part of a congregation of God. In other words, Dirk argues that being united with Christ entitles the person to be a member of his body as a saved person. For one who is united with Christ, "Christ is their Brother, Bishop, Mediator, Intercessor and Reconciler"[92]; moreover, Christ "desires to justify them and redeem all their frailties with his eternal sacrifice and steadfast prayer, and through the Holy Spirit reign and lead them into eternal glory."[93] Also, unity with Christ is the condition for believers' separation from all Gentiles. Dirk said that Jesus Christ brought his people who are united with him from all the Gentiles; "they were anointed with the oil of gladness, ate the heavenly manna, and drank the best wine in the sanctuary for a strengthening and eternal quickening of the hearts."[94] Thus the nature of those united with Christ is God's nature, and they love God's loved ones and live for God as God's possession.[95] They come to Jesus Christ, the shepherd of their souls, as the sheep hear and follow the shepherd's voice, and they enjoy true rest in God.[96]

Finally, Dirk associates the unity of believers with Christ with the covenant of God. That is, those united with Christ are those who are in the covenant of God. This is the same argument that the elect are in the covenant of God, and this argument proves that Dirk presupposes that those united with Christ are saved. Dirk says, "Now the covenant of God

---

91. Philips, "Supper of Our Lord Jesus Christ," 122.
92. Philips, "Supper of Our Lord Jesus Christ," 131.
93. Philips, "Supper of Our Lord Jesus Christ," 131.
94. Philips, "Concerning Spiritual Restitution," 340.
95. Phiips, "Three Admonitions: No. II," 403.
96. Philips, "Answer to Sebastian Franck," 453.

exists therein that we are children and inheritors of all his heavenly goods through faith in Jesus Christ. Through this covenant we are united with God. Therein and thereby God has accepted us and has chosen us to salvation in the sanctification of the Spirit and in the faith in truth, so that we should walk therein and serve him in the Spirit and truth."[97]

Dirk's View of Perseverance and Glorification

Even though Dirk's view of perseverance is not found prevalently throughout his writings, he has a firm understanding of the perseverance of the saints. In his works, he argues clearly that the grace of God protects and delivers his congregation. God is not affected by any interruption or the attack of all the wicked in the perseverance of his saints. God's perseverance is firm, and he preserves the elect according to his goodwill.[98]

Dirk states that those who are born of God and who become children of Jesus Christ receive the assurance of salvation by the Holy Spirit:

> Again, after the justified person has been born out of God, and thus has become [a] participant of the divine nature, 2 Pet 1:4, yes, after he is a member of Jesus Christ and one spirit with the Lord, and Christ dwells in his heart through faith, Rom. 12:4[-5]; 1 Cor.12:27; Eph. 1:23; 4:4; 1 Cor. 6:17, and the Holy Spirit has been given to him by God as a guarantee of salvation, 2 Cor. 1:22, therefore he may no longer be thus accused.[99]

Most notable in Dirk's argument for the perseverance of the elect is the concept that no one can charge against God's choice. In other words, since those who are in Jesus Christ no longer have condemnation, no one can change this fact or remove them from the way of salvation again.[100] Dirk suggests that many false prophets and false Christians try to lead the elect astray, but doing so is impossible. Dirk also believes that false Christians' activities will affect only the fallen, not the elected.

> False teachers can also sometimes indeed perform signs. One knows well how the Egyptian magicians withstood Moses and what they did through their magic, Exod.7:11[-12]; 2 Tim. 3:8. And Christ says that many false prophets and false Christians

---

97. Philips, "Frisian-Flemish Division," 501.
98. Philips, "Frisian-Flemish Division," 483.
99. Philips, "Tabernacle of Moses," 285.
100. Philips, "Tabernacle of Moses," 285.

shall arise [and] do great signs and wonders so that (if it were possible), even the elect should be led astray. Matt. 24:11. And Paul says, "The coming of the antichrist will happen according to the activity of Satan with all kinds of deceitful signs and wonders among those who will be lost," 2 Thess. 2:9[-10]. Therefore then, a Christian may not look upon the signs alone, but much more upon God's Word which is always certain and true, John 17:8.[101]

Dirk's doctrine of perseverance is included in his writings to encourage his congregations to keep their faith intact. This reflects the particular situation that he and his congregation were in at that time, one of persecution and suffering. In this situation, Dirk intends for his congregation to find hope for the future in his doctrine of perseverance. In other words, Dirk describes God as bringing the faith of his chosen people to the end and saving their souls.[102] Dirk asks "the eternal and only wise God [to] give us wisdom and understanding for it so that his highly praised name may be praised, the bound and restricted conscience may be unbound and freed, and the elect may be kept from all evil, comforted, and strengthened."[103]

Dirk makes minimal mention of glorification. He discusses glorification only two times in all his treatises. In one of these instances, he describes the glorification of Jesus Christ, and in the other, he explains that glorification by the Holy Spirit happens not only to Jesus but also to believers. Regarding the believers' glorification, he insists: "But this glorification of Christ through the Holy Spirit happens in his disciples who accept and keep his words in true faith, as he himself said, "I am glorified in them."[104]

Summary

This chapter explored Dirk's soteriology by examining various aspects of soteriology, including predestination, justification, conversion, regeneration, sanctification, perseverance, and glorification, aspects which are traditionally included in the order of salvation in Christian theology.

---

101. Philips, "Sending of Preachers or Teachers," 225.
102. Philips, "Frisian-Flemish Division," 493.
103. Philips, "Frisian-Flemish Division," 494.
104. Philips, "New Birth and the New Creature," 304.

In terms of predestination, Dirk's view does not deviate significantly from the Reformed tradition. Although he does not emphasize this aspect, he does reject any possibility of human choice, insisting that God's choice is the only way of salvation. The most mentioned concept in Dirk's discussion about salvation is the grace of God, and he acknowledges that all the processes of salvation are only made possible by it. According to Dirk, God's election began from the beginning and allows of no possibility that the elect will ever fall away.

With regard to justification, Dirk's views are similar to that of Luther. Justification in Dirk's thought is God's call to salvation in Jesus Christ, being chosen through his eternal love, and receiving God's justification for all who have faith in Jesus Christ. Dirk argues that God's justification is a one-time event performed at the beginning, and it is a definite event that cannot be changed by any person. Based on this idea of justification, Dirk opposes infant baptism because infants lack their own faith.

Dirk understands that conversion has a distinct component of repentance and faith but is tied to one event of repentance and faith. He logically distinguishes repentance from faith, but he does not make clear distinctions between the two in his writings. Dirk's most crucial point in the discussion of conversion is that repentance must be accompanied by substantial change, not merely by internal change and theological meaning.

Just as Harold S. Bender pointed out that the core of Anabaptist soteriology is regeneration, regeneration was more critical to Dirk than any other soteriological subject. Dirk directly discusses regeneration only among the many other salvation themes in *The New Birth and The New Creature*. The key message that Dirk stresses in this treatise is the practice of the faith of believers who have experienced the new birth, and he constantly insists that his readers live their lives as God's people.

In his discussion of sanctification, Dirk argues that sanctification is possible for the regenerated ones through spiritual fellowship with Christ. For Dirk, sanctification is meaningful as a change in the spiritual status of the Christian, and it is also meaningful because it enables believers to live as a united community. Dirk also understands the subject of sanctification from a Trinitarian perspective.

The phrase Dirk often uses to describe salvation is being "united with Jesus Christ." This term is comprehensive for salvation in general, and unity with Jesus Christ is a prerequisite for Christians to live as children of Christ.

Finally, there is little mention of perseverance and glorification in Dirk's entire writings, but Dirk has the idea that God preserves the elect to the end and insists that the glorification of Christ will happen to believers as well.

The Correlation of Dirk Philips's View of the Visible Church with His Soteriology

Although soteriology may not be the most critical theological theme for Dirk, it is noteworthy that Dirk conveys the message he most wants to teach his congregation throughout his soteriology. Dirk, while faithfully following the doctrine of soteriology in traditional Christian theology, pondered what God's salvation meant for believers living as the visible church in this world. For this purpose, he always mentions the relationship between doctrinal subjects and the believer's existence or practice in the discussion of salvation.

For Dirk, the congregation of God is a group of people who are justified by God. They are saved through God's justification. As mentioned earlier, Dirk's view is not very different from Luther's theory of justification. Dirk was familiar with Luther and his arguments, and it is clear that he was influenced by Luther's theology.[105] However, Dirk denounces the seeming contradiction between Luther's views of justification and his practice of infant baptism. Although Luther accused the Anabaptists of believing in justification by works only, from Dirk's perspective, Luther, who baptized unbelieving infants, was denying justification by faith. Dirk has a strong view that by understanding the subject of justification as God, no human can control human salvation through the form of infant baptism performed by the visible church. Moreover, Dirk objected to the visible church's acceptance of justification only as doctrinal or ideological. Dirk understands justification as an event that takes place at the beginning but connects the doctrine of justification with the life of believers on earth by mentioning that called believers should walk in spiritual life.[106]

What is impressive in Dirk's discussion of conversion is that it is indistinguishable from true repentance and the life worthy of that repentance, and that true repentance comes from abandoning the old man

---

105. Koolman, *Dirk Philips*, 71–72.
106. Philips, "Baptism of Our Lord Jesus Christ," 78.

and living life free from sin.[107] After believers are converted, they must live on earth, turn from sin, and live for Christ. In addition, it is worth noting that Dirk shares his discussion of conversion with that of baptism. Conversion is when an unbeliever is experiencing internal change, and baptism is a public confession of faith after receiving and having faith. Dirk shares these two different concepts because he understands that conversion leads to baptism, which in turn is part of the community of faith. Thus, to Dirk, the conversion of a person to live a proper life is no different from living as a member of the faith community. Newly converted people enter the faith community through their public confession of faith and live a new life on earth. For Dirk, conversion is significant in that it brings out external changes.

Dirk's view of sanctification shows how important the visible church is to him. Dirk argues that sanctification is an internal and spiritual change that takes place for believers, but his claim that sanctification of believers takes place within the community shows the role of the visible church in the sanctification of believers. For Dirk, sanctification was not enough to be regarded only as an event for the individual believer, but as a process that takes place together in the Christian community. In this respect, to Dirk, the visible church is the place where believers together completed their salvation, and the meaning of gathering believers together in the visible church can also be found in terms of sanctification.

Dirk uses the phrase "united with Christ" to point out the type of life believers should live in the visible church. As mentioned in this chapter, being "united with Christ" is used by Dirk as a general term for salvation. Although the term is used as a cause for the change of the believers' inner and spiritual condition, it is mainly used as a means of emphasizing the external sign of the saved children of God. Believers' unity with Christ is the source of their external signs as newborn children of God, creating a visible change of faith.

Finally, the most essential aspect of Dirk's relation to soteriology and the visible church is in Dirk's writing format. In other words, Dirk wrote a treatise on regeneration only among the various themes of soteriology. As mentioned earlier, Dirk deals with regeneration in a treatise entitled *The New Birth and the New Creature*, the main focus of which is the life of newborn believers as children of God. Dirk does not, of course, preclude an explanation of the theological and theoretical meaning of

---

107. Philips, "About the Marriage of Christians," 565.

regeneration, but the main purpose of the treatise is not to make readers understand the doctrine, but to encourage their lives as believers.

Dirk's discussion of soteriology emphasizes life as a Christian, as a child of God who has experienced a new birth. Dirk neither holds nor considers salvation without the fruit of the believer's life. Nevertheless, as discussed earlier in this chapter, Dirk does not lack strong views of soteriology. He does not consider any human possibility in the order of salvation but acknowledges that only God plans, directs, and completes salvation. Dirk followed a thoroughly Reformed tradition in which he developed his theology. Dirk, however, insisted that believers who were saved by God must continuously hold on to and pursue the divine nature through the Holy Spirit with God's renewal into his divine image.

Chapter 6

ANTHROPOLOGY

Introduction

THE LEADING NEO-ORTHODOX THEOLOGIAN Karl Barth argues that instead of using the expression "theology," it is better to use the term "theoanthropology." He claims that the reason for this is that the area of scholarship called theology is concerned with "God as the God of man," and deals with "man as God's man."[1] Barth's view indicates that theology and anthropology are intimately inseparable. As important as Barth was though, he was certainly not the first to argue in this way. Dirk's contemporary, John Calvin for example, knew the importance of understanding God in order to understand human beings. He argues that humans cannot separate knowledge of God and knowledge of humanity from one another, and that they cannot have an accurate knowledge of human beings without reflecting on the word of God.[2] Dirk also understands and explains man in terms of his relationship with God.[3] For Dirk, since the source of human existence is God, it is impossible to discuss human beings except in relationship to the Father, the Holy Spirit, and the Holy Spirit.[4] Therefore, if Dirk had encountered the term "theoanthropology" proposed by Karl Barth, he probably would have agreed.

1. Barth, *Evangelical Theology*, 11–12.
2. Calvin, *Institutes* I, i, 1–2.
3. Although Dirk did not write a treatise on anthropology, his views can be found from various subjects in his works. Dirk always describes man as God's people and relates his view of anthropology to other theological themes.
4. Philips, "Confession of Our Faith (Concerning) God," 62–66.

Dirk's anthropology, which is closely related to his ecclesiology, has certain specific features which will be examined in more detail in this chapter. His interest in people is expressed in them as making up the congregation of God. His anthropology is closer to practical anthropology than theoretical anthropology because he is concerned with people more in terms of their practical meaning than in terms of their theological meaning.

Although Dirk's *Enchiridion* is not organized systematically by doctrine, and while the topic mentioned most frequently in it is Jesus Christ, Dirk's redemptive-historical perspective of Creation-Fall-Redemption is also examined in some detail, in his discussion of human matters. Dirk discusses God in the first treatise of the *Enchiridion*. Subsequent treatises, *Creation, Redemption, and Salvation* deal with the work of Jesus Christ and the work of the Holy Spirit, after dealing with the creation and the fall of man. Since the other treatises of the *Enchiridion* deal with subjects related to Jesus Christ, it appears that the most important theological subject to Dirk was Christology. However, in a broad, comprehensive view of Dirk's theology, his understanding and discussion of Jesus Christ is directed to the holy life of believers as the congregation of God. His focus also concentrated on how the fallen human race will live on earth in the life that has been restored by Jesus Christ.

Hence, Dirk's discussion about Christ is the basis for further support of his redemptive-historical perspective, emphasizing the importance of Christ's ministry in the work of God's redemption. Nevertheless, his redemptive-historical perspective does not become the basis for his emphasis on Christology's superiority over other theological themes. After all, Dirk's anthropology is concerned with the role and position of human beings in a redemptive-historical perspective; it is also a discussion of the meaning, purpose, and values of human life changed by Jesus Christ.

In fact, a redemptive-historical perspective in dealing with anthropology was a preference in the Reformed theological tradition. A look at the anthropological structures of several scholars in the Reformed camp reveals that they have the same characteristics, including the structure of Creation-Fall-Redemption.[5] They dealt with human matters in the

---

5. This feature is found in the writings of many systematic theologians of the Reformed tradition. The theologians include Charles Hodge, Abraham Kuyper, Herman Bavinck, Louis Berkhof, Herman Hoeksema, William G. T. Shedd, and J. Oliver Buswell. In addition, this tendency is reflected in twentieth-century Baptist theologians Millard Erikson and Stanley Grenz. See Hodge, *Systematic Theology*, vol. 2; Kuyper,

redemptive-historical perspective and discuss anthropology between the doctrine of God and the doctrine of Jesus Christ. This tendency indicates that humankind is dependent on special revelation, and that humankind is decisively influenced by the work of Jesus Christ. It is also not much different from the concept of Theanthropology that Karl Barth mentions.[6]

The purpose of this chapter is to explore Dirk's anthropology. This chapter will discuss four of the following topics in Dirk's anthropology: the human creature; the human free will; sin, evil, and suffering; and human reason. The aim of this chapter is to argue that Dirk's anthropology has developed faithfully within the concept of Creation-Fall-Redemption. This chapter will also examine how Dirk's theological discourse on anthropology relates to the life of the congregation of God that constitutes the visible church.

Dirk's View of Human Nature

The Image of God

Dirk describes the nature of humankind before the fall in relation to the concept of the image of God. That is, the first human beings, Adam and Eve, were created in the image of God. Dirk is not interested in scientific questions about the nature of humans—for example, human beings with intellect, the use of language, the use of tools, and personal relationships. He merely describes humans in terms of the concept of the image of God.

To Dirk, Jesus Christ is the perfect human model created in the image of God. He believes that "[Jesus Christ] is the exact image of God."[7] Thus, the creation of humankind in the image of God means that the original creation was perfect. Dirk says, "[Adam and Eve] were created after the image of God, Gen. 9:6, and were made in his likeness, Gen. 5:[1], upright, good, and pure creatures of God, incorruptible and immortal, Wisd. of Sol. 2:23."[8]

Dictaten Dogmatiek, vol. 2; Bavinck, *Reformed Dogmatics*, vol. 3; Berkhof, *Systematic Theology*; Hoeksema, *Reformed Dogmatics*; Shedd and Gomes, *Dogmatic Theology*; Buswell, *Systematic Theology of the Christian Religion*; Erickson, *Christian Theology*; Grenz, *Theology for the Community of God*.

6. For Barth's concept of theanthropology, see Congdon, "Theology as Theanthropology," 30–66.

7. Philips, "Sending of Preachers or Teachers," 200.

8. Philips, "Congregation of God," 352.

Dirk then proceeds to examine the issue of how the image of God is related to the fall of humanity. Dirk makes no direct mention of whether humankind still possesses the image of God after the fall. Notwithstanding, Dirk uses Genesis 5:1 as a basis for referring to the image of God.[9] The story of the fall appears in Genesis 3; in chapter 5, Adam and Eve were created in the image of God, and later, Seth was born in the image of Adam. Logically, therefore, Seth was created in the image of God. However, because Seth was a child born after the fall of Adam and Eve, Dirk's use of Genesis 5:1 acknowledges that humanity still bears the image of God to some degree even after the fall.

Dirk, of course, acknowledges that the human body is entirely impure and corrupt.[10] He is familiar with the apostle Paul's confession, "I know that nothing good dwells within me, that is, in my flesh," and he knows that the human body has a limited, fallen nature unlike that of Jesus Christ.[11] Nevertheless, Dirk recognizes that the image of God in humans is destroyed but not entirely lost, and that the image of God must be renewed in humans.[12] Although Dirk uses the expression "the lost image of God," he does not consider the image of God completely lost. There is some enigma here, but at least, Dirk believes that "the lost image of God" has the potential for renewal and restoration, which means that humans turn away from the sins of the world.[13]

Dirk seems not interested in the Calvinist doctrine of total depravity. He did not use the terminology of the doctrine, nor did he participate in the debate concerning this doctrine. Nonetheless, it is worth mentioning that Dirk's view of the image of God does not result in his denial of the doctrine of total depravity. In fact, Calvin himself argued that there is some degree of *sensus divinitatis* in fallen humans.[14] Calvin believed that everyone is involved in doing business with God (*negotium cum Deo*).[15]

---

9. Philips, "New Birth and the New Creature," 294.
10. Philips, "Incarnation of Our Lord Jesus Christ," 145.
11. Philips, "Incarnation of Our Lord Jesus Christ," 145.
12. Philips, "Concerning Spiritual Restitution," 319.
13. Philips, "Concerning Spiritual Restitution," 320.
14. Calvin, *Institutes* I, iii, 1; I, iv, 4. Calvin also called it "the seed of religion" or "the worm of conscience" instead of *sensus divinitatis* (the sense of Deity). See I, iii, 3; I, iv, 1.
15. George, *Theology of the Reformers*, 197. Esther L. Meek describes this *sensus* in six arguments: (1) it is an awareness of divinity; (2) all human beings have it, believer and unbeliever alike; (3) it is naturally inborn, within the human mind; (4) it consists

In conclusion, the doctrine of total depravity and the concept of the total loss of the image of God have similarities, but cannot be identified as the same. In other words, Dirk's claim that humankind has the image of God even after the fall does not confirm whether he denied total depravity or not. Dirk insists, however, that the destroyed image of God must be restored in humankind, and through this restoration, humankind can live a life like Christ.[16]

For Dirk, the renewal of the image of God is not irrelevant to believers' lives.[17] Newly born believers are renewed in the image of God through Jesus Christ in the Holy Spirit. They are born again to the fellowship and likeness of Jesus Christ and so become the expression and image of the invisible God.[18] Thus, Dirk believes that a person who is renewed in the image of God is sanctified through the Holy Spirit,[19] and that "he is once again made in the image of God according to the inner person, in righteousness and truth."[20]

Human Constitution

Among the Anabaptist leaders, Balthasar Hubmaier probably has the most in-depth discussion of the human constitution. He described his trichotomist view in detail in his treatise *Freedom of the Will*.[21] Unlike Hubmaier, however, Dirk did not write about the human constitution as a specific treatise. As Robert Friedmann has said, "Anthropology, or the doctrine of man, is crucial also for the Anabaptists; but it remains our task to discover the proper formulation of it."[22] Dirk's view of humanity, as Friedmann suggests, is also mixed with his other theologies, and since it is not apparent, further research is needed for explanation. Among his writings and treatises which mention human constitution are *An Apology*

---

of an understanding of God's majesty; (5) it does not result from teaching or proofs; (6) it is ultimately unsuppressible (Meek, "Polanyian Interpretation of Calvin's Sensus Divinitatis," 10).

16. Philips, "New Birth and the New Creature," 295.
17. Philips, "Concerning Spiritual Restitution," 320.
18. Philips, "New Birth and the New Creature," 299.
19. Philips, "New Birth and the New Creature," 311–12.
20. Philips, "Answer to Sebastian Franck," 456.
21. For an English translation of the treatise, see Williams et al., *Spiritual and Anabaptist Writers*. See also Hubmaier, *Balthasar Hubmaier*.
22. Friedmann, *Theology of Anabaptism*, 58.

or *Reply*, *The Sending of Preachers*, and the first letter of *Two Additional Letters*.

Since Dirk did not speak directly on human constitution, it is not clear whether he has a trichotomist or dichotomist perspective. He does, however, make clear the distinction between body, soul, and spirit:

> Then the righteous shall shine like the sun in the kingdom of their Father, Matt. 13:43, then they shall sparkle as the stars like the brilliance of heaven eternally. Then they shall be completely blessed with body, soul, and spirit. Then we shall sit at the table with Abraham, Isaac, and Jacob in the kingdom of God and see that the unbelievers shall be excluded, Luke 13:27. Then shall happen what John wrote, see what love the Father has given us, that we are and are called his children.[23]

This is the only place in which Dirk refers to the body, soul, and spirit together, for elsewhere he refers only to body and soul or body and spirit. What is certain is that Dirk believes that humans are composed of the body as the material part and the spirit or soul as the non-material part.[24]

Although it is difficult to determine whether Dirk has theoretically and theologically distinguished the non-material part of man, the human spirit and soul, it is likely he did not focus on describing the terms' theological meanings, but instead regarded them as interchangeable terms, considering the use of "spirit" and "soul" interchangeably in the Scripture.[25]

Dirk's View of Human Free Will

In church history, the debate over the human role in salvation is constant. The Pelagian debate in the early fifth century highlighted a number of issues related to human nature, sin, and grace which never ceased in church history.[26] The Augustine tradition believed that human freedom was limited because human nature was damaged and corrupted by sin, and the Pelagian tradition believed that humans could take moral action

---

23. Philips, "Epistle to the Wife of I. the S.," 626.

24. Philips, "Epistle to the Wife of I. the S.," 628; Philips, "Apology or Reply," 189; Philips, "Sending of Preachers or Teachers," 231.

25. There has been discussion in the history of the church whether to view the human spirit and soul in two parts, but at least it is true that the Bible uses these two terms interchangeably. See Grudem, *Systematic Theology*, 472–82.

26. McGrath, *Christian History*, 79–80.

in their free will. The Pelagian tradition thus argued that human beings have the duty to be perfected through self-discipline.

The debate between the Augustine tradition and the Pelagian tradition has persisted since the fifth century, and the influence of the Pelagian controversy was large enough that the debate often appeared during the Reformation.[27] In this context, groups that emphasized even a little human responsibility did not escape the criticism of Pelagianism from their opponents. Anabaptists were not free from this criticism. Their opponents attacked the Anabaptists for overconfidence in human capacity and accused them of overconfidence in a human ability to restore the world and to save themselves.

Pilgram Marpeck, for example, who led the Anabaptist movement in southern Germany was attacked by Caspar Schwenckfeld. Schwenckfeld was a German theologian and one of the Protestant Reformers in Silesia. While Schwenckfeld agreed with Marpeck's claim that only faithful believers should be baptized, he attacked Marpeck's view as Pelagian that infant baptism was unnecessary to remove the original sin of infants because of Marpeck's claim that infants are sinless.[28] Luther also attacked the Anabaptist view of human responsibility, accusing Karlstadt, for example, believing that God could be pleased with works.[29] In a sermon, Luther also criticized the Pelagians and Anabaptists as trying to gain their own righteousness.[30] He also argued that Anabaptists were no different from Catholics in terms of works,[31] for though the Anabaptists rejected Roman Catholic works righteousness, they did hold to another works righteousness.[32]

Among Anabaptist leaders, Balthasar Hubmaier was probably the one who was most accused of Pelagianism. This probably happened because unlike other Anabaptist leaders, Hubmaier made his views on the issue very public when he published a treatise on free will, thereby

---

27. In this regard, the main controversy in the Reformation era would be that of Luther and Erasmus. Luther published *De servo arbitrio* (*The Bondage of the Will*, 1525) as opposed to *De Libero Arbitrio Diatribe Sive Collatio* (*Of Free Will*, 1524) of Erasmus. See Luther, *Martin Luther on the Bondage of the Will*; Erasmus and Luther, *Discourse on Free Will*; Oberman, *Luther*, 211–18.

28. Klaassen and Klassen, *Marpeck*, 362–63.

29. *LW* 40, 84–85.

30. *LW* 51, 384; *LW* 17, 256.

31. *LW* 40, 364.

32. *LW* 12, 273.

attracting much more critical attention from scholars on the subject, and as a result, he was stigmatized as being Pelagian as well.[33]

Although the Pelagian controversy was not a major issue for Dirk and his congregation, identifying whether Dirk is Pelagian or not is important in understanding his theology. To answer this question, one needs to note Augustine's and Pelagius' arguments. Indeed, the thought of Augustine has had a profound impact on the formation of the church and on Christian doctrine during the Middles Ages, as well as after the Reformation. The leaders of the Reformation, such as Luther and Calvin, accepted the thought of Augustine which emphasized original sin and salvation by the grace of God without any resistance.[34] The opponent of Augustine's theology was Pelagius. The main concern of the controversy between Augustine and Pelagius was how to understand the freedom of the human will in salvation.[35] Augustine believed that Adam's nature was corrupted because of sin, and as a result, his sin was passed on to all his descendants. Humans with original sin are no longer able to come to God by their free will, but they are able to go toward evil. Pelagius made an objection to the claim of Augustine that humans inherited original sin from Adam, for that doctrine seemed to deny human responsibility and effort. Pelagius believed that because all human beings have total freedom of the will, they are fully responsible for their sins. In addition, he claimed that obeying all God's commandments and being made entirely holy is the obligation of all Christians.[36]

The Pelagian controversy does not end with finding answers to the question of whether humans possess free will. According to Augustine, because there is no free will that leads to salvation, humans can be saved only by the grace of God. After all, the key point to this controversy is whether God or humans themselves have the initiative that leads to salvation. Therefore, to determine whether or not Dirk is following Pelagius,

---

33. Many studies of the twentieth century define Hubmaier as Pelagian and at least claiming to be semi-Pelagian. See Steinmetz, "Scholasticism and Radical Reform," 144; MacGregor, *Central European Synthesis*, 15; Davis, *Anabaptism and Asceticism*, 150–63; Kim, *Balthasar Hubmaier's Doctrine of Salvation*, 54–60.

34. MacCulloch, *Reformation*, 106–15; Eire, *Reformations*, 295–96; Brown, *Heresies*, 207.

35. Brown, *Heresies*, 200–207.

36. Kelly, *Early Christian Doctrines*, 361–66; González, *History of Christian Thought*, 2:29–33.

it is necessary to determine whether Dirk recognizes human initiative in salvation.

Dirk mentions the freedom of humans several times in his treatises, but he mentions free will only once:

> And then whenever unbelievers and idolaters see that others who pride themselves of the gospel and faith and reproached their idolatry and for a long time avoided it, now fall into it again, whether it happens out of free will or compulsion, then they are strengthened in their false worship and allow themselves to think that they are correct and boast of their substitute as the true worship, to the disdain of all pious Christians.[37]

However, even in this mention of free will, he refers to a claim concerning the fall of unbelievers, not to the salvation of humans. Even in this reference, Dirk does not see humans' corruption as resulting only from their free will, and his use of the expression "free will or compulsion" leaves room for blaming human corruption not solely upon human choice. In referring to human freedom, Dirk says that it is possible for humans to have free access to God through the Holy Spirit in Jesus Christ,[38] and he also argues that sinners can repent under the sovereignty of God, rather than turning away from sin by repenting themselves.[39] For Dirk, the possibility of salvation depends entirely on God, Jesus Christ, and the Holy Spirit, and he completely denies that a human has the possibility of saving himself. In this context, Dirk's understanding of free will is distinguished from that of Pelagius. Dirk recognizes quite clearly that human beings cannot do anything themselves in salvation, but are saved solely by the grace of God. In this respect, Kenneth's evaluation is correct, wherein he argues for a synergistic principle, where some Anabaptists see both divine grace and human effort in salvation. Kenneth's synergistic principle is different from Pelagianism and is to be found in the thought and writings of both Dirk Philips and Menno Simons, as well as in the Hutterite confession.[40]

Determining whether Dirk held to Semi-Pelagianism is more complicated. Semi-Pelagianism denies certain views of both Augustine and Pelagius. It denies Augustine's claim of the total bondage of the will, the

---

37. Philips, "Apology or Reply," 182.
38. Philips, "Our Confession," 68.
39. Philips, "Supper of Our Lord Jesus Christ," 124.
40. Davis, *Anabaptism and Asceticism*, 163.

priority and irresistibility of grace, and rigid predestination, but it also denies Pelagius' claim that humans are capable of being saved through free will.[41] Semi-Pelagianism argues that salvation can be achieved through the cooperation of God and humans, through both grace and free will. That is, human beings are not capable of fully achieving salvation on their own, but they naturally have the power to undertake a move toward believing in God to be saved.

One of the hallmarks of Dirk's movement, the Dutch Mennonite movement, and other Anabaptist branches is their emphasis on the lives of believers and God's work. This tendency is often closely reflected in their theology. Indeed, Hubmaier emphasized that believers must practice God's work, and this thought led to the conclusion that after human will is restored by God's grace, humans can follow God's will positively.[42]

Nevertheless, although Dirk, like Hubmaier and other Anabaptists, emphasizes the fruits of believers' lives, that does not mean that Dirk is Semi-Pelagian. Dirk, instead, stresses the lives of believers and argues that those who have experienced a new birth partake of divine characteristics because they are from God.[43] In this sense, it is clear that he believed that the restored man could follow God's will positively. He denies, however, that people can achieve salvation on their own, and that humans have the ability or even the possibility to move toward salvation. Dirk's view, as previously described is that in each aspect of salvation, people are completely passive and require God's calling and grace. Dirk's thought does not contain any elements that could be labeled as Semi-Pelagian, instead he believes that God has the initiative to save human beings, that people play no active part in the process of salvation.

Dirk's View of Sin, Evil, and Suffering

Sin

Dirk's discussion of sin is divided into three major phases. The first is that sin leads to a break in humankind's relationship with God. Second, since Adam and Eve committed original sin, the true nature of humankind

---

41. Erickson, *Christian Theology*, 91.
42. Kim, *Balthasar Hubmaier's Doctrine of Salvation*, 59.
43. Philips, "New Birth and the New Creature," 294.

tends to sin. The third is that God will make judgments based on human sin.

First, Dirk argues that sin has caused a total separation in the relationship between God and humankind. As the apostle Paul mentioned, because of the birth of the physical body, people are born with the nature of the children of wrath, and with sin under the curse of all the law.[44] As a result, Dirk believes that "all humanity [is] under sin and knows no one (except Christ Jesus alone) as entirely free from sin."[45]

Dirk understands the origin of sin in connection with Satan. It is by Satan that humans have sinned, and whoever sins is a child of the devil, not a child of God. Regarding a child of God, Dirk explicitly says, "he cannot sin because he is born of God."[46] Dirk's view led to much criticism,[47] and it is well known that Anabaptists, not only Dirk, were accused of being idealists for their pursuit of the pure church on earth.[48] However, it is not difficult to discern whether Dirk's straightforward claim was an explicit or substantive. Dirk makes an explicit claim that the children of God cannot sin, and at the same time he makes a substantive claim that humans are bound to sin. This means that Scripture says that anyone who does not do what is right is not God's and does not love his brother, but in the real life of many figures in Scripture, including the Apostle Paul, even those who believe in God struggle with the problem of sin.[49] Dirk emphasized believers' lives as children of God, not to deny the existence of sin in this world.

Dirk stresses that the Son of God has come to earth to solve this problem of sin.[50] The Son came to earth as a sacrificial offering to God the Father for the sins of the whole world, "with which sacrifice he has opened a new and living way to the holy of holies (that is, to the hiddenness

44. Philips, "Our Confession," 68.
45. Philips, "Tabernacle of Moses," 283.
46. Philips, "Ban," 242.
47. Dirk was attacked for a variety of reasons. Early in his ministry, he was attacked by "rebellious rebaptizers," and his perspective on sacraments was also targeted. In his debate with Adam Pastor, he was attacked for being a tolerant person; in particular, Dirk took a stand against Pastor's definition of human sin. In other words, Dirk strictly applied excommunication because he had a strict view of human sin. (Koolman, *Dirk Philips*, 10, 35–40, 138).
48. Estep, *Anabaptist Story*, 1–2; Dyck, *Introduction to Mennonite History*, 33–36.
49. Philips, "Tabernacle of Moses," 284–85.
50. Philips, "Ban," 242.

and fellowship of the divine and heavenly goods, yes, to heaven itself) for all those who believed in him."[51] Dirk likens the ministry of Jesus Christ to Moses and the Israelites in their escape from Egypt and crossing of the Red Sea in the Old Testament. The Red Sea symbolizes the blood of Jesus Christ, and the crossing of the Red Sea symbolically washed away all human sins; but Pharaoh and his servants were drowned in the Red Sea and annihilated, as the devil, sin, and death were destroyed by the blood of Jesus Christ.[52] By Christ's coming, human beings, who deserved God's judgment for their own sins, were made exempt from the judgement. Dirk illustrates this in the following extract:

> Should this sin now be paid, this death taken away, the righteousness of God be satisfied, and life be brought again to a dead humanity, then the son of the Most High had to appear and become human, Luke 1:31; Rom. 8:3, take our sins upon himself and die for us, Isa. 53: 8, and through his death and blood triumph against the devil, sin, death, and hell, 1 Pet 2:24; 3:18.[53]

Therefore, Dirk believes that believers in Jesus Christ must practice all ordinances in accordance with the gospel of God, abstain from sin, and keep all commands according to the word of God.[54]

Second, Dirk argues that humans are born with sin. Although Adam was born as a perfect being, after Adam's fall, the earth was soiled by sin, and all people have been cast under the curse, and their nature has been corrupted.[55]

Dirk argues that before sin, mankind, as described in Genesis 2, was the perfect figure of the image and likeness of God and was created for eternal life.[56] Although Dirk is silent about the reason or path of the first human's Adam's fall, and although he is silent about why the serpent approached only Eve, he makes clear the consequences of mankind's first sin. Since the original sin, humankind has been on the path of disobedience and has possessed the knowledge of good and evil. Dirk describes this as follows:

---

51. Philips, "Tabernacle of Moses," 269.
52. Philips, "Baptism of Our Lord Jesus Christ," 97.
53. Philips, "Concerning the True Knowledge of Jesus Christ," 162.
54. Philips, "Sending of Preachers or Teachers," 224.
55. Philips, "Incarnation of Our Lord Jesus Christ," 137.
56. Philips, "Baptism of Our Lord Jesus Christ," 77.

> [Because] they come to a knowledge of good and evil and step from simple ignorance into conscious wickedness, and they sin against the Lord through their own disobedience and transgression of the divine Word and command, then it is the proper and appointed time that they first be taught, yes, with the law of God be heartily admonished to penitence so that they amend themselves, lament their sins before God, confess, and bear remorse over them.[57]

Third, Dirk insists that God will make judgments based on human sin. According to Dirk, one important feature of God on this subject is that he condemns human disobedience and transgression. The righteousness of God does not compromise with evil and does not allow his children to be children of sin.[58] The sending of his Son to the earth, who suffered and was crucified for the sins of humankind, demonstrates God's firm and unchanging attitude toward sin, and sinners will see this strong wrath and unchanging zeal of God towards sin.[59]

Dirk, therefore, says that God will show his severe judgement and his earnest wrath over sin in the last days.[60] In the description of the Lord's Supper, Dirk speaks of the benefits of commemorating the Lord's suffering and death, including how much God hates sin: "so that we may concern ourselves heartily therewith, which is very necessary in order to come to our self-knowledge, to the true humility, to the pure fear of God, to the true remembrance of the suffering of Christ, and to the hatred of sin."[61]

Not everyone agrees on Dirk's view of original sin. Keeney does not take a stance on whether Dirk agrees or denies original sin.

> Indeed, S. Hoekstra and Karel Vos have claimed that Dirk denied original sin, apparently because Dirk spoke incautiously with respect to the consequences of original sin in children. If original sin implies a necessary guilt in all men from birth, and a consequent condemnation by God until they are forgiven after repentance, Dirk did deny originals. If, however, it implies

---

57. Philips, "Baptism of Our Lord Jesus Christ," 77.
58. Philips, "Concerning the True Knowledge of Jesus Christ," 163.
59. Philips, "Supper of Our Lord Jesus Christ," 124.
60. Philips, "Supper of Our Lord Jesus Christ," 124; Philips, "New Birth and the New Creature," 305; Philips, "Concerning Spiritual Restitution," 334.
61. Philips, "Supper of Our Lord Jesus Christ," 124.

a nature that is weak or corrupted so that it inevitably sins, Dirk would have accepted this definition.[62]

According to Keeney, although both S. Hoekstra and Karel Vos claimed that Dirk denied original sin, it is impossible to determine whether Dirk accepted original sin. Dirk obviously denied that the children are guilty because of original sin, but this argument is not enough to provide evidence that Dirk denied original sin.

> Therefore, no one may either accuse or damn young children on account of original sin except he denies the death, blood, and merit of Jesus Christ. For if children may be damned through Adam and on account of his transgression, then Jesus Christ has died in vain for them, Rom. 5:19, and the guilt of Adam that has come upon us and has not been paid for through Jesus Christ.[63]

As Hoekstra and Vos have argued, Dirk does take a negative stance against the idea of consequences of original sin in children, but this is not enough to prove that Dirk denied the doctrine of original sin. Dirk argues that original sin degrades all mankind, and that the only way to be freed from original sin is by the sacrifice of Jesus Christ on the cross. Dirk clearly teaches original sin, and that because of original sin, all people after Adam were "cast under the curse and corrupted in their nature."[64] He also believes, however, that it is invalid to argue a relationship between original sin and its effect on children, since they are unable to make profession of faith at a young age. Keeney's analysis was appropriate from this point of view, but it needed to be further refined. Dirk does not deny original sin, but denies some theories about original sin. In other words, Dirk admits that because of original sin, all mankind is cursed and inclined toward evil against God, but he rejects the claim that infants must receive baptism for salvation because of original sin.[65]

Dirk also discussed original sin in his treatise, *The Baptism of Our Lord Jesus Christ*, in which he refuted arguments in favor of infant baptism, saying that infant baptism had no spiritual or theological efficacy.[66] He also argued against explanations of the guilt of the infants, as well as explanations of their salvation, held by those who supported infant

---

62. Keeney, *Development of Dutch Anabaptist Thought and Practice*, 68.
63. Philips, "Baptism of Our Lord Jesus Christ," 92.
64. Philips, "Incarnation of Our Lord Jesus Christ," 137.
65. Philips, "Baptism of Our Lord Jesus Christ," 91.
66. Koolman, *Dirk Philips*, 69–70.

baptism. Dirk does not deny the consequences of original sin in children to deny the effect of original sin on all humankind, but to weaken the legitimacy of infant baptism.

Evil and Suffering

There is always suffering in human life, and the suffering of this world overflows. It is therefore natural for a human being in suffering to ask why he or she must suffer and what it means to endure it. Since Dirk and his community had to suffer persecution for their faith,[67] the understanding and even endurance of this suffering would have been very important in keeping their faith and community.

Before discussing Dirk's view of the problem of evil and suffering, it is necessary to look at the view of evil discussed in the Christian tradition. In this tradition, it has been understood that human beings have brought evil to themselves, and although God is the sovereign ruler over all things, the responsibility for evil lies with humankind. However, the question of theodicy still remains—even though the full resolution of this matter does not seem possible—that is, what the Almighty and good God is doing in the reality of evil and suffering. First, Augustine was a pioneer in the discussion of the problem of evil in the history of Christianity. The hallmark of his discussion is his decisive role in Christianity's acceptance of Neoplatonism. He regards evil as the privation of good (*privatio boni*), not a substantial (*substantia*) thing in itself; through this view he also avoided Manichaeism's dualism of good and evil.[68] Augustine recalls his conversion in chapter 7 of *Confessions*, saying that he could clearly see the unreality of evil thanks to the Platonists' books he read, through which he eventually overcame the teaching of Manichaeism on the origin of evil.[69] He says in *Against the Academics*, which he wrote after his conversion from Manichaeism, that he longed for truth not only by faith but also by understanding, and he found a way of understanding in Platonists that did not go against Christian holy mystery.[70]

---

67. Koolman, *Dirk Philips*, 5, 49, 60, 72, 88, 103, 104, 110–13, 117, 145.

68. Augustine, *Confessions* III, 12; V 10; 20; VII, 18–20. For the Augustinian tradition's view of the problem of evil, see Mathewes, *Evil and the Augustinian Tradition*, 5–9. Also see MacDonald, "Primal Sin," 110–39.

69. Augustine, *Confessions* VII, 9, 20–21.

70. Augustine, *Against the Academics*, 148–50.

However, Augustine's theory of evil is quite different from, at least, that of Plotinus, the proponent of Neoplatonism. In particular, their stance is vastly different in regard to the origin of evil. In *On the Free Choice of the Will*, written between 388 and 396, Augustine claims that the origin of evil lies in the free will of rational creation.[71] For him, evil is a phenomenon that occurs in the soul—voluntarily turning away from God—not something that exists outside the soul.[72] This position is also held in the later *Confessions* and *The City of God*.[73] On the contrary, Plotinus assumes the absolute evil which is entirely lacking in goodness, that is, the metaphysical evil that exists independently of the soul as evil itself, which is defined as the principle of evil that can explain why evil beings are evil.[74] According to Augustine, however, all that God creates, who is almighty and good, is good, and so long as matter is created, it is good, and therefore it cannot be the principle of evil.[75]

Calvin accepted Augustine's view of the problem of evil.[76] Although Calvin did not have as deep a philosophical discussion of evil as Augustine, he, like Augustine, tried to explain the existence of evil in the world without weakening the omnipotence of God.[77] Calvin's distinction in this discussion is that he emphasizes the incomprehensibility of God's providence over evil. In other words, evil is a hidden mystery that cannot be ultimately understood.[78] In a comment on the book of Job, which deals with the problem of the righteous suffering, Calvin says, "Hence the Book of Job, also, in humbling men under a conviction of their folly, feebleness, and pollution, always derives its chief argument from descriptions of the Divine wisdom, virtue, and purity."[79] For Calvin, the recognition of the incomprehensibility of God's providence before the reality of evil is the humble and right attitude of finite human beings.[80]

Although Dirk does not include a philosophical or theoretical discussion of the problem of evil and suffering, his view of the subject is not

71. Augustine, *Augustine*, 29–30, 42.
72. Augustine, *Augustine*, 70–72.
73. Augustine, *Confessions* VII, 5; 13, Augustine, *City of God*, 257–58.
74. O'Meara, "Metaphysics of Evil in Plotinus," 179–82.
75. Augustine, *Augustine*, 218–21, 249–53.
76. González, *History of Christian Thought*, 3:127.
77. González, *History of Christian Thought*, 3:143–146.
78. Calvin, *Institutes* III, xxi, 2.
79. Calvin, *Institutes* I, i, 3.
80. Calvin, *Institutes* III, xxiv, 8–11.

ANTHROPOLOGY 171

very different from Augustine or the that of the Reformed tradition. Dirk argues that the influx of evil into the world derives from the original sin of humankind, and that the event in which Adam and Eve ate from the tree of the knowledge of good and evil caused them to experience suffering in the life of this world.[81] In other words, Dirk believes that the existence of evil in this world stems from the choice of human beings who betrayed God's command, and that evil is the responsibility of humankind, not God. Dirk also claims that the influx of evil originating from Adam and Eve is maintained on earth by the devil's people.

> From this Adam and his wife, Eve, have come two brothers, Abel and Cain, Gen. 4:1, the one upright and the other godless. Abel was a child of GOD and a member of the Christian church; but Cain was a child of the devil and captured in his fellowship, 1 John 3:12. The pious and righteous one was hated by the evil and murderous Cain, and was murdered out of the envy of his evil heart. And this is a clear symbol and witness that from that time on two kinds of people, two kinds of children, two kinds of congregations have existed on earth, Matt. 23:34[-35]. They are, namely, God's people and the devil's people; God's children and the devil's children, John 8:44; God's congregation and the synagogue or assembly of Satan, Rev. 2:9; and that God's children must suffer persecution from the devil's children, 1 John 3:1. Christ's congregation must be oppressed, hunted, and killed by the anti-Christian assembly. Of this God has also given clear knowledge that he has set enmity between the snake's seed and the woman's seed, and that the snake's seed shall lie low or bite the seed of the woman in the heel.[82]

Dirk does not mention the personal suffering and evil that humans experience in life, but he clarifies how evil spreads in this world. Dirk claims that the suffering of the people of God represented by Abel comes from the people of the devil, represented by Cain; this suffering occurred after Adam and Eve's first sin.

Dirk's distinction from previous Christian traditions in terms of his view of human suffering is that Dirk does not give his congregations a merely theoretical discussion of the origin and reason for suffering; he discusses suffering mainly in order to ask them to endure suffering as Christians. Clearly, for Dirk, the suffering of this world begins with evil

---

81. Philips, "Baptism of Our Lord Jesus Christ," 77.
82. Philips, "Congregation of God," 353-54.

and begins with those who have betrayed God. However, in his discussion of how to deal with suffering, Dirk is not concerned with where evil has come from, but with how Christians should live in the reality of evil. For Dirk, "all Christians must suffer and be persecuted, just as Christ promised them and has also said: The world shall rejoice and you shall mourn, but your sadness will be turned into joy, John 16:33."[83] But Christian suffering is not meaningless; "they must go through much pressure and suffering to enter into the kingdom of heaven."[84] Although suffering for Christians has continued since the beginning of this world, Dirk believes that those who are glorified in the resurrection will have better joy rather than suffering in this world; Dirk refers to "the conflict and suffering of all the saints from the beginning of the world, from the time of righteous Abel until the present time. Thus you will discover how all God-blessed people had to suffer so much as the apostle to the Hebrews related, Heb.11:[35], namely, how the pious people of God were struck and did not accept deliverance, since they received the resurrection which is better."[85] For Dirk, the daily suffering in this world does not discourage saints, because their inner life is still renewed from day to day.

Dirk's View of Human Reason

Dirk did not ignore human reason, and saw human reason necessary to understand the word of God. Dirk, as it is well known, was opposed to spiritualists such as David Joris and Sebastian Franck,[86] so he opposed the position that the spiritualists insisted on, that of disregarding human reason and merely emphasizing an individual approach.[87] On the other hand, Dirk was also familiar with the teachings of humanism. As mentioned in the previous chapter, Dirk must have known at least some of Erasmus' teachings, as he sometimes introduced Erasmus' arguments.[88]

Although Dirk appears to have been influenced by the Mystics in the Lower Rhine, that influence is limited only to the Brethren of the

---

83. Philips, "Congregation of God," 373.
84. Philips, "Congregation of God," 374.
85. Philips, "Three Admonitions: No. I," 387.
86. Koolman, *Dirk Philips*, 29–31, 151–57.
87. Philips, "Answer to Sebastian Franck," 445.
88. Philips, "Baptism of Our Lord Jesus Christ," 101.

Common Life; it is true that Dirk's ideas are more influenced by Erasmus.[89] In fact, Erasmus influenced many Anabaptists in addition to Dirk; and therefore, as has been rightly argued, "Erasmus was at least partially responsible for the rise of Anabaptism."[90] Keeney describes Menno and Dirk's interest in humanism as follows: "The apparent fondness of the Dutch Mennonites for the writings of Erasmus seems to testify to this, although it may only be the plundering of the writings of a well-known countryman when he can be used to support their arguments."[91] In addition, Keeney argues that Dirk may have used Erasmus' translation of the Bible.

> Which Bible(s) did Dirk use? This becomes a particularly difficult question when, as indicated, he quoted from memory. Some references seem to be based on the Latin Vulgate text. He used Latin more often in his writings than Menno did. It would be surprising if Dirk, as a Frisian, would not have used the East Frisian Bible published by Bugenhagen in 1545, based on Luther's German Bible. It may also be assumed, though a detailed analysis was not made by us, that he used the famous Zurich or Christoffel Froschouer version, of which there were many editions and of which the Anabaptists were very fond. It would certainly have been available to him. It is likely that he also used the Greek New Testament of Erasmus.[92]

Perhaps the most widely known humanist work in sixteenth-century Europe is the *Enchiridion Militis Christiani* by Erasmus. In it, he argues that the church could be reformed by returning to the writings of the Fathers and to the Scripture.[93] In other words, Erasmus believes that a layperson could live a new life of godliness by reading the Scripture regularly, and on this basis the church could be renewed and reformed.[94] He believed that the future vitality of Christianity rested with the layperson, not with the clergy; and by emphasizing the subjectivity of religion, he believed that the layperson could confess their sins directly to God rather

---

89. Since Dirk was associated with Franciscans during his childhood and had a high level of education from them, it seems clear that he was influenced by the Mystics. See biographical outline in chapter 1 of this dissertation.

90. Friesen, *Erasmus, the Anabaptists, and the Great Commission*, 3.

91. Keeney, *Development of Dutch Anabaptist Thought and Practice*, 24.

92. Keeney, "Editors' Introduction," 14.

93. McGrath, *Reformation Thought*, 47; Eire, *Reformations*, 107–8.

94. McGrath, *Reformation Thought*, 47.

than relying on the system of the church.⁹⁵ Religion, therefore, is the matter of the individual's conscience and mind, and it is essential that lay people recognize their calling as Christians.⁹⁶

Erasmus' assessment of human nature and the will, however, tends to be overly optimistic. Accordingly, Zwingli's and Luther's criticism of Erasmus was a criticism of this optimism, with Zwingli publicly criticizing Erasmus in *Commentary on True and False Religion*,⁹⁷ and Luther also criticized him in his *On the Bondage of the Will*.⁹⁸ However, although Dirk did not openly criticize Erasmus, he did not agree with Erasmus' optimism. Obviously, he was part of the Erasmus-influenced Anabaptist group, but unlike Erasmus, he did not have a high view of human reason.⁹⁹ Though Dirk often describes human reason as something that leads against the word of God, he does not regard merely reading Scripture to be sufficient in understanding the word of God.¹⁰⁰ Dirk believes that the teachings from the Holy Spirit are true wisdom, rather than the knowledge and wisdom of the world that humans make themselves;¹⁰¹ this illustrates well what Dirk thinks of reason. Dirk argues that, contrary to what Erasmus expected, human beings cannot fully understand the Scripture and act according to it without the help of the Holy Spirit.

> Who [believers] pride themselves more of the gospel and Christendom, of true theology and knowledge of Holy Scripture than [do] the highly praised wise [ones] of the world, the perverse scribes who allow themselves to think, since they have studied in advanced schools (and, therefore, according to the common proverb, the more learned the more perverted they have become), so they alone are teachers and masters of Scripture and yet themselves have neither received nor taught the divine words of the first school primer? For they have not yet been in the school of Christ and they have not had the true master teacher, namely, the Holy Spirit, yes, have neither seen nor known [him]. But they speak about the Scripture which they

---

95. Eire, *Reformations*, 108–9.
96. McGrath, *Reformation Thought*, 48; Eire, *Reformations*, 109.
97. Zwingli, *Commentary on True and False Religion*, 9.
98. *On the Bondage of the Will* (*De Servo Arbitrio*) was published in December, 1525.
99. Friesen, *Erasmus, the Anabaptists, and the Great Commission*, 20–42; Murray, *Biblical Interpretation in the Anabaptist Tradition*, 42–45.
100. Philips, "Baptism of Our Lord Jesus Christ," 101.
101. Philips, "Sending of Preachers or Teachers," 199.

do not understand, and even when they already do understand something, they yet do not wish to act in accord with it, John 14:26; 15:26; 16:7.[102]

Summary

Although it is not known whether or not Dirk intended it, a characteristic of his anthropology is that it has a structure of "Creation-Fall-Redemption." Dirk discusses humanity in his collection of treatises, *Enchiridion*, in a large structure: humanity was created with the image of God; humanity has fallen by betraying God; and humanity can be saved by Jesus Christ. This tendency is found throughout his *Enchiridion*, especially in *Creation, Redemption, and Salvation*.[103] Based on this background, this chapter could be divided into four anthropological categories: Dirk's view of the human nature; Dirk's view of human free will; Dirk's view of sin, evil, and suffering; and Dirk's view of human reason.

Dirk's greatest concern in the discussion of the human creature is that humans are created in the image of God. Dirk believes that the creation of humanity in the image of God represents the perfection of God's human creation; he also believes that although humans have fallen, humans still maintain the image of God. According to Dirk, humans lost the image of God because of the fall, but he believes the image of God could be renewed. As for the constitution of humankind, it is not clear whether Dirk has a trichotomist or dichotomist perspective. Dirk, however, would have thought of soul and spirit as interchangeable terms.

Dirk's view of free will follows Augustine's tradition. Dirk believes that there is no human ability or possibility in salvation and that the possibility of human salvation depends entirely on the Triune God. Even though it is true that Anabaptists have historically been criticized for supporting the Pelagian tradition and for over-reliance on human abilities, Dirk at least disagrees with the claims made by those objectors.

It is clear that Dirk is against Pelagianism, but judging whether Dirk is following Semi-Pelagianism requires complex and careful attention. Semi-Pelagianism asserts that the grace of God and human free will must work together in salvation; it also believes that human beings are incapable of achieving complete salvation, but are capable of initiating

---

102. Philips, "Sending of Preachers or Teachers," 199.
103. Philips, "Our Confession," 68–71.

a move toward faith in God. In fact, Dirk seems to have a high view of human abilities because he always stresses the life of believers as saved. Dirk, however, believes that renewed human beings can follow God's will positively, but he does not claim that such human ability plays a specific role in salvation. Therefore, Dirk believes that in salvation, the human is passive and wholly dependent on the grace of God.

Dirk's discussion of sin can be divided into three concepts: first, sin leads to a break in a person's relationship with God; second, since Adam and Eve committed original sin, the true nature of humanity tends to sin; third, God will make judgments based on sin. Regarding original sin, there are claims that Dirk denied original sin, but they are not accurate judgments. Dirk clearly denies that infants are guilty because of original sin. However, because of his opposition to infant baptism, Dirk needed to deny that infants are corrupted by original sin; but he did not deny that all humankind is under the influence of the original sin. As for evil and suffering, Dirk follows Augustine's tradition. Dirk believes that the cause of suffering in this world lies in original sin, originating from Adam and Eve. Dirk, however, argues that the existence of evil and suffering in this world is not the responsibility of God; instead, it stems from the choice of humans, who have betrayed God's commands.

Dirk had a different perspective on the ability of human reason than that of the humanists, who had an overly optimistic view of the human will and human nature. Although Dirk did not ignore or consider human reason in understanding God's word, Dirk often expresses human reason as opposed to God's word, and he emphasizes teaching from the help of the Holy Spirit, not the idea that human reason is true wisdom.

The Correlation of Dirk Philips's View of the Visible Church with His Anthropology

Although anthropology and the visible church do not seem to be related to each other, the basis for forming Dirk's anthropology includes his view of the church. Dirk deals with human matters in the context of a relationship with God. He did not write a treatise on theological anthropology, but he describes various themes related to humanity in relation to God or to issues in the church. In other words, Dirk reveals his anthropology in the course of dealing with his other interests rather than describing anthropology first or as a separate, stand-alone issue.

An important part of Dirk's description of human creation is the concept of the image of God. Dirk believes that man was created in the image of God and that this image is maintained, not completely extinguished from man, even after the fall. But what is important to Dirk here is the concept of "renew." The image of God was given at the creation of man, but because it was distorted after the fall, it must be renewed to believers. Dirk sees the problem of human beings leaving God and living with sinfulness as a distortion of the image of God.[104] Therefore, the congregation of God is a gathering of those who have restored the image of God, and re-born believers are those who have restored the image of God through Jesus Christ in the Holy Spirit. For Dirk, however, the concept of restoring the image of God has more than a theological meaning. Those who have restored the image of God are theologically no longer of the world but of God, and their change includes ethical and moral change in this world. Dirk thus argues that believers can live Christlike lives in this world through the restoration of God's image.[105]

Dirk's discussion of human free will also reveals how important he values the lives of believers and the life of the visible church. As mentioned above, Dirk did not believe that human free will plays an active role in salvation, but he believes that it is possible and necessary to follow God's will positively after the human will is restored by the grace of God. Dirk's stance on free will makes it possible to expect a positive future for the life of the congregation of the visible church. In other words, Dirk emphasizes the lives of believers, and argues that believers are partakers of divine characteristics because they are from God and must live a life worthy of him. Thus, the free will of human beings who are saved is important for Dirk, not because it plays a role in salvation, but because believers who partake of divine characteristics play an important role in living their lives.[106] Dirk sees humans as completely passive on the issue of salvation, but considers them to be very active on issues of believers' lives. This understanding of Dirk's view of human will allows believers to emphasize the Christian's life as a member of the visible church, and it

---

104. Philips, "Concerning Spiritual Restitution," 319–20.

105. Philips, "New Birth and the New Creature," 295.

106. Dirk's view aligns with the Reformed view that Christians take part in sanctification—not regeneration and justification. Dirk and the Reformed view also believe that God, not man, is the author of sanctification. See Calvin, *Institutes* II, ii, 7; II, ii, 12; Owen, *Of the Mortification of Sin in Believers*, 532–37.

prevents the possibility that his emphasis on God's sovereignty in salvation is biased towards antinomianism.

In Dirk's anthropology, the theme most directly related to the visible church is the subject of evil and suffering. Although Dirk does not deepen the philosophical discussion of evil and suffering, he discusses evil and suffering in situations where he and his community had to respond to criticism, attacks, and persecution. In these situations, his main message is not to have a political and violent response to persecution in this world but to have a passive and nonviolent response. Dirk considers the value and meaning of dealing with violence nonviolently, rather than considering the causes and responses to violence ahead of him. For Dirk, the suffering in this world occurs to keep believers' faith, and it will be turned into a blessing. Believers will enter the kingdom of heaven through suffering, and they will receive greater rewards. This perspective of evil and suffering made it easy for Dirk and his congregation to understand and accept the situations they faced, and it laid the theoretical foundation for them to live as members of the visible church in persecution and suffering.

Finally, Dirk's disagreement with the humanists reveals how he understood the role of the Holy Spirit in the visible church. Of course, Dirk emphasized the lives of believers, but unlike humanists, he did not see human reason as positive. For Dirk, the interpretation and application of God's word are important, but they are impossible without the help of the Holy Spirit. The help and guidance of the Holy Spirit, therefore, are necessary for the life of the visible church and its members, and they are the key to sustaining them as saints. Dirk sees the ability of renewed human beings positively, but he sees no human ability without the help of the Holy Spirit.

Chapter 7

CONCLUSION

DIRK PHILIPS IS LESS known today than Magisterial Reformers such as Martin Luther, John Calvin, or even Ulrich Zwingli. Likewise, he is also not known as well as certain Anabaptist leaders, including Conrad Grebel, Michael Sattler, Balthasar Hubmaier, and Menno Simons. Nevertheless, this dissertation has argued that the influence of Dirk and his movement was never small. Although Dirk lived most of his life in the shadow of other leaders, he was a more systematic and analytical thinker than other leaders in his group,[1] and his hermeneutic of the Scriptures was more systematic in its explication than that of any other leader in the Anabaptist movement.[2] His pastoral influence may not have reached that of Menno, who was his former leader in the group, but his theoretical and theological influence surpassed that of Menno.[3] Therefore, this dissertation examines the theology and views of Dirk Philips, a relatively neglected early Anabaptist leader in the Netherlands, and it attempts to investigate important concepts in his theology. This dissertation analyzes four aspects of Dirk Philips's theology—his Christology, his ecclesiology, his soteriology, and his anthropology—and it examines their connection with his concept of the visible church. Therefore, a number of new insights into Dirk's theological positions are being argued for through this process of research and analysis.

The first new insight is that Dirk's various theological topics are connected to the theology of visible church, and within it the congregation of God. For Dirk, the purpose of theological writings was for the benefit of

1. Keeney, "Research Note," 558.
2. Schubert, "Dirk Philips' Letter and Spirit."
3. Shantz, "Ecclesiological Focus," 115–16.

the faith of the congregation of God. He wrote to admonish and to teach his congregation to live on earth with the word of God, with the identity of the people of God, and in the proper system of Christian belief.

As argued in the last section of each chapter of this dissertation, Dirk's main reason for discussing Christology, ecclesiology, soteriology, and anthropology is not to provide theological and doctrinal knowledge for members of the invisible church. Rather, it is to provide a system of beliefs for the holy and to distinguish the life of the congregation of God in the visible church.

In his Christology, Dirk argues that believers who have a true knowledge of Jesus Christ will live a new life of keeping his commandments. Similarly, in his ecclesiology, Dirk argues the qualifications of believers in the ordinance of the church, which informs his views of the conditions of the believers. Dirk's soteriological views favor the theme of regeneration over other themes, because he emphasized the concept of the new birth over other issues to be examined. Lastly, in his anthropology, Dirk most importantly argues that humans were created with the image of God, and he insists that believers must restore their lost image of God to live their lives as saved.

The second new insight is to provide a different perspective of Dirk and the Mennonites' theology. Many scholars have been interested in Dirk and Menno Simons' unique Christology, especially William Keeney, who argued that the most important themes of Dirk's theology are the word of God and the incarnation.[4] The primary reason that Dirk Philips's theology is known as Christology is because of his unique perspective on the incarnation, and because the largest portion of his writing is on Jesus Christ instead of other theological topics. This assessment assumes that the incarnation is the most important theological theme for Dirk.

However, Dirk's most important theological theme is ecclesiology, not Christology, because the basis for all of his theological discussions is the religious practice of members of the visible church. Dirk's discussion of Christology is closely related to the direction and quality of life for newly born-again believers in Jesus Christ. In other words, Dirk discusses Christology more than any other theological subject because a true knowledge of Christ is essential for believers to live as those who confess Christ as Lord.

---

4. Keeney, "Dirk Philips," 38.

CONCLUSION 181

This dissertation also found that Dirk did not adhere to the claims of Pelagius, nor was he Semi-Pelagian. In fact, as mentioned in the previous chapter, Anabaptists have been criticized by many for supporting Pelagianism. Anabaptists' tendency to emphasize practical matters and the fruit of the Spirit led to a stigma of Pelagianism and to the misunderstanding that they believed that human actions could lead to salvation. But this dissertation demonstrates that Dirk constantly insists that the initiative of salvation rests only with God, and Dirk believes that the possibility of human salvation depends entirely on God, Jesus Christ, and the Holy Spirit.

Dirk completely denies that human beings have the possibility of initiating salvation, proving that he has nothing to do with Pelagius' arguments, and he also sets himself apart from Semi-Pelagians by rejecting the possibility of human beings moving toward salvation. Dirk regards humans as passive in salvation and in need of the full grace of God, and he does not believe that human actions contribute in any way to salvation; but he does believe that human actions are meaningful for the life of saved Christian in this world.

The third new insight is that Dirk's soteriology takes the format of Creation-Fall-Redemption, which is the center of the Reformed worldview—although Dirk never used this distinction or this terminology. Of course, the redemptive-historical perspective of "creation, corruption, and redemption" was developed after Dirk, but at least this dissertation showed that Dirk's soteriology did not deviate from the Reformed tradition.

Dirk's view of free will follows Augustine's tradition. Dirk believes there is no human ability in salvation, and he believes that the possibility of human salvation depends entirely on the Triune God. Dirk's emphasis on the believer's practice does not lead to a high view of human ability in salvation.

As for Dirk's view of evil and suffering, this dissertation argues that they are in full agreement with Reformed understanding on those issues. Dirk believes that the original sin of Adam and Eve brought evil and suffering into the world. In other words, the original sin of man was the cause of the influx of evil and suffering into the world. Dirk thus places the responsibility of the existence of evil and suffering in this world on humans, and he claims that God is not responsible for human sin.

In developing the themes of this dissertation naturally leads to the following fourth new insight: Dirk does not support the Donatists' view of ecclesiology. This dissertation disagrees with the recent position taken by Alister McGrath in which he argues that Mennonites were supporters of the Donatist tradition. He claimed that the Anabaptists had an ecclesiology in the Donatist tradition, referring to Menno Simons as a representative figure.[5]

McGrath describes two aspects of the ecclesiology of the Donatist tradition. The first feature is their unique interpretation of two major related beliefs which are insisted by Cyprian of Carthage in *On the Unity of the Church*.[6] The Donatist tradition interpreted in light of Cyprian's two major related beliefs. The first belief is that when the bishop is apostate because of his lapse, he needs to be put out of the church and can no longer be recognized as capable of performing the sacraments. In Augustine, on the other hand, apostate bishops can be restored by repentance, and Augustine insists that they can continue to perform the sacraments. The second feature is that the Donatist tradition overlooks the great sin of schism, but in contrast, Augustine considers both schism and betrayal a great sin.

First, it is incorrect to evaluate the ecclesiology of the Anabaptists or Dirk Philips through the principle of "ignoring schism," the second feature of the Donatist tradition, according to McGrath. It also would not be appropriate to evaluate any Protestant sect through that principle. As matter of the fact, since Protestantism split from the Catholic Church, and since the Reformer Luther did not want to divide from the Catholic Church at first, but did eventually leave the Catholic Church, applying the "schism" criterion to Protestant groups leads to the conclusion that all Protestant groups have a Donatist tradition in their ecclesiology which recognizes the schism of the church. Besides, because McGrath himself sees Luther's rejection of Augustine's ecclesiology as being in support of Augustine's grace, McGrath also understands that not all Protestant

---

5. McGrath, *Reformation Thought*, 149–50.

6. McGrath sums up two major related beliefs: "First, schism is totally and absolutely unjustified. The unity of the church cannot be broken, on any pretext whatsoever. To step outside the bounds of the church is to forfeit any possibility of salvation. Second, it therefore follows that lapsed or schismatic bishops are deprived of all ability to administer the sacraments or act as a minister of the Christian church. By passing outside the sphere of the church, they have lost their spiritual gifts and authority. They should therefore not be permitted to ordain priests or bishops. Any whom they have ordained must be regarded as invalidly ordained; any whom they have baptized must be regarded as invalidly baptized" (McGrath, *Reformation Thought*, 144). Also see Cyprian of Carthage, "On the Unity of the Church."

groups could be free from the responsibility of preventing church schism.[7] Thus, with this second criterion, it would not be appropriate to distinguish whether Dirk and the Mennonites followed Augustine's ecclesiology or Donatus' ecclesiology.

However, the first feature of the Donatist tradition presented by McGrath sets a clearer standard. In other words, Augustine's and Donatus' views were different as to whether the administration of sacraments was valid if it was done by a bishop who had lapsed but had returned after repentance. Augustine supported the continuation of the administration of the sacraments by a bishop who was once apostate but who had repented and returned, while Donatus, in order to preserve the purity of the church, insisted that the baptism and ordination performed by a bishop who has become apostate are ineffective.

Dirk and his community were also believers who continually tried to create a pure church on earth. However, where Dirk and his followers differ markedly from the Donatist tradition is their attitude toward the repentant. Of course, Dirk is a strict figure in seeing church discipline as necessary to build community purity. For example, he believed that the wife of an excommunicated husband should be avoided[8] and that the Christian community should not have any covenant other than the teaching of the Scripture.[9] He was a very strict practitioner of the Scripture and a man of strict discipline for the pure church on earth. But where Dirk was most different from Donatus was in his treatment of the repentant. Donatus refused the ordination of the once apostate but returned Felix of Aptunga, while Dirk believed that if a brother who was once excommunicated from the community for sin repents, the community should accept him with love and care as before. Dirk saw the purpose of excommunication as keeping the church pure, while at the same time, it was also for the sinful brother to realize himself and to have pitiful repentance. Dirk insisted that believers should pursue a pure church but he did not claim to be ontologically consistent with the "invisible church" and the "visible church," and he did not argue against Augustine's concept of the "sinfulness of Christians." Therefore, Dirk's ecclesiology is not in the tradition of Donatus but is much closer to the Augustine tradition; but he emphasizes the lives of believers as the saved congregation of God.

7. McGrath, *Reformation Thought*, 143.

8. Philips, "About the Marriage of Christians," 568; Philips, "Omitted Writing about the Ban and Avoidance," 585–86.

9. Philips, "Short but Fundamental Account," 499–505.

Based on all that has been said, this dissertation argues that the central theme of Dirk Philips's theology is the good life of the congregation of God in the visible church; his theology is faithful to the Augustine tradition but does not allow the possibility of the indulgence of believers. In addition, in his discussion of the visible church, Dirk argues for his interest in the congregation of God as a practical outworking of the word of God.

BIBLIOGRAPHY

Althaus, Paul. *The Theology of Martin Luther*. Translated by Robert C. Schultz. Philadelphia: Fortress, 1966.

Armour, Rollin S. *Anabaptist Baptism: A Representative Study*. Studies in Anabaptist and Mennonite History 11. Scottdale, PA: Herald, 1966.

Augustine. *Against the Academics*. Translated by John J. O'Meara. Ancient Christian Writers 12. Westminster, MD: Newman, 1951.

———. *Augustine: On the Free Choice of the Will, On Grace and Free Choice, and Other Writings*. Edited by Peter King. Cambridge Texts in the History of Philosophy. Cambridge: Cambridge University Press, 2010.

———. *The City of God*. Edited by Hermigild Dressler. Translated by Grace Monahan and Gerald G Walsh. The Fathers of the Church: A New Translation 14. Washington, DC: Catholic University of America Press, 2008.

Avis, Paul D. L. *The Church in the Theology of the Reformers*. New Foundations Theological Library. Atlanta: John Knox, 1980.

Barth, Karl. *Evangelical Theology: An Introduction*. Translated by Grover Foley. 1st ed. New York: Holt, Rinehart and Winston, 1963.

Bavinck, Herman. *Reformed Dogmatics*. Edited by John Bolt. Translated by John Vriend. Vol. 3. 4 vols. Grand Rapids: Baker Academic, 2003.

Beachy, Alvin J. *The Concept of Grace in the Radical Reformation*. Bibliotheca Humanistica & Reformatorica 17. Nieuwkoop, The Netherlands: De Graaf, 1977.

Bender, Harold S. "The Anabaptist Vision." *Church History* 13.1 (1944) 3–24.

Bender, Harold Stauffer. "The Anabaptist Theology of Discipleship." *The Mennonite Quarterly Review* 24.1 (January 1950) 25–32.

———. *Menno Simons, Life and Writings*. Scottdale, PA: Mennonite, 1936.

———. "'Walking in the Resurrection': The Anabaptist Doctrine of Regeneration and Discipleship." *The Mennonite Quarterly Review* 35.2 (April 1961) 96–110.

Berkhof, Louis. *Systematic Theology*. 4th ed. Grand Rapids: Eerdmans, 1949.

Boyd, Stephen B. *Pilgram Marpeck: His Life and Social Theology*. Durham, NC: Duke University Press, 1992.

Brown, Harold O. J. *Heresies: Heresy and Orthodoxy in the History of the Church*. 4th ed. Peabody, MA: Hendrickson, 2007.

Buswell, J. Oliver. *A Systematic Theology of the Christian Religion*. Grand Rapids: Zondervan, 1962.

Calvin, John. *Institutes of the Christian Religion*. Translated by Henry Beveridge. Grand Rapids: Eerdmans, 1957.

Choi, Jung K. "The Centrality of Andreas Karlstadt in Shaping Anabaptist Soteriology." PhD diss., Dallas Theological Seminary, 2016.

Clasen, Claus-Peter. *Anabaptism: A Social History, 1525–1618: Switzerland, Austria, Moravia, South and Central Germany*. Ithaca, NY: Cornell University Press, 1972.

Colwell, John E. "A Radical Church: A Reappraisal of Anabaptist Ecclesiology." *Tyndale Bulletin* 38 (1987) 119–41.

Conant, Keith Ian. "The Marriage Views of Hans Denck, Dirk Philips, and Menno Simons." Master's thesis, Northeast Missouri State University, 1994.

Congdon, David W. "Theology as Theanthropology: Barth's Theology of Existence in Its Existentialist Context." In *Karl Barth and the Making of Evangelical Theology: A Fifty-Year Perspective*, edited by Clifford B. Anderson, 30–66. Grand Rapids: Eerdmans, 2015.

Cornelius, Carl Adolf. *Geschichte Des Münsterischen Aufruhrs*. Leipzig: Weigel, 1855.

Cyprian of Carthage. "On the Unity of the Church." http://www.newadvent.org/fathers/050701.htm.

Cyril of Alexandria. "Cyril of Alexandria's Second Letter to Nestorius." In *The Christological Controversy*, edited by Richard A. Norris Jr., 131–34. Sources of Early Christian Thought. Philadelphia: Fortress, 1980.

Davids, Peter H. "Anabaptist View of the Church." *Evangelical Quarterly* 56 (April 1984) 81–93.

Davis, Kenneth R. "No Discipline, No Church: An Anabaptist Contribution to the Reformed Tradition." *Sixteenth Century Journal* 13 (1982) 43–58.

Davis, Kenneth Ronald. *Anabaptism and Asceticism: A Study in Intellectual Origins*. Studies in Anabaptist and Mennonite History 16. Scottdale, PA: Herald, 1974.

Deppermann, Klaus. *Melchior Hoffman: Social Unrest and Apocalyptic Visions in the Age of Reformation*. Edited by Benjamin Drewery. Translated by Malcolm Wren. Edinburgh: T. & T. Clark, 1987.

Durnbaugh, Donald F. *The Believers' Church: The History and Character of Radical Protestantism*. Scottdale, PA: Herald, 1985.

Dyck, C. J. *An Introduction to Mennonite History: A Popular History of the Anabaptists and the Mennonites*. Scottdale, PA: Herald, 1967.

Dyck, Cornelius J. "The Christology of Dirk Philips." *The Mennonite Quarterly Review* 31.3 (July 1957) 147–55.

Eire, Carlos M. N. *Reformations: The Early Modern World, 1450–1650*. New Haven: Yale University Press, 2016.

Erasmus, Desiderius, and Martin Luther. *Discourse on Free Will*. Edited by Ernst F. Winter. New York: Ungar, 1961.

Erickson, Millard J. *Christian Theology*. 3rd ed. Grand Rapids: Baker, 2013.

Estep, William Roscoe. *The Anabaptist Story*. Grand Rapids: Eerdmans, 1975.

———. "The Ecumenical Implications of Menno Simons' View of the Church." *The Mennonite Quarterly Review* 62.3 (July 1988) 356–67.

Finn, Nathan A. "Curb Your Enthusiasm: Martin Luther's Critique of Anabaptism." *Southwestern Journal of Theology* 56.2 (2014) 163–81.

Franck, Sebastian. "A Letter to John Campanus." In *Spiritual and Anabaptist Writers*, edited by George H. Williams and Angel M. Mergal, 145–60. Philadelphia: Westminster, 1957.

Friedmann, Robert. "The Oldest Church Discipline of the Anabaptists." *The Mennonite Quarterly Review* 29.2 (April 1955) 162–66.

———. "On Mennonite Historiography and on Individualism and Brotherhood: A Communication from Dr Robert Friedmann." *The Mennonite Quarterly Review* 18.2 (April 1944) 117–22.

———. *The Theology of Anabaptism: An Interpretation*. Studies in Anabaptist and Mennonite History 15. Scottdale, PA: Herald, 1973.

Friesen, Abraham. *Erasmus, the Anabaptists, and the Great Commission*. Grand Rapids: Eerdmans, 1998.

Fulop, Timothy E. "The Third Mark of the Church? Church Discipline in the Reformed and Anabaptist Reformations." *Journal of Religious History* 19.1 (June 1995) 26–42.

George, Timothy. *Theology of the Reformers*. Nashville: B & H, 2013.

Goncharenko, Simon Victor. "The Importance of Church Discipline within Balthasar Hubmaier's Theology." PhD diss., Southwestern Baptist Theological Seminary, 2011.

González, Justo L. *A History of Christian Thought*. 3 vols. Nashville: Abingdon, 1970–75.

———. *The Story of Christianity*. 2 vols. in one book. 11th ed. Peabody, MA: Prince, 2010.

Grenz, Stanley J. *Theology for the Community of God*. Nashville: Broadman & Holman, 1994.

Grislis, Egil. "The Meaning of Good Works: Luther and the Anabaptists." *Word & World* 6.2 (1986) 170–80.

Grudem, Wayne A. *Systematic Theology: An Introduction to Biblical Doctrine*. Grand Rapids: Zondervan, 1994.

Harder, Leland, and Konrad Grebel. *The Sources of Swiss Anabaptism: The Grebel Letters and Related Documents*. Classics of the Radical Reformation 4. Scottdale, PA: Herald, 1985.

Harreld, Donald J. *High Germans in the Low Countries: German Merchants and Commerce in Golden Age Antwerp*. The Northern World. Leiden: Brill, 2004.

Hershberger, Guy F. *The Recovery of the Anabaptist Vision*. Scottdale, PA: Herald, 1957.

Hillerbrand, Hans Joachim. *A New History of Christianity*. Nashville: Abingdon, 2012.

———. "Origin of Sixteenth-Century Anabaptism: Another Look." *Archiv Für Reformationsgeschichte* 53.1–2 (1962) 152–80.

Hodge, Charles. *Systematic Theology*. Vol. 2. 3 vols. Grand Rapids: Eerdmans, 1952.

Hoeksema, Herman. *Reformed Dogmatics*. Grand Rapids: Reformed Free Publishing Association, 1966.

Hofmann, Melchior. "The Ordinance of God." In *Spiritual and Anabaptist Writers*, edited by George H. Williams and Angel M. Mergal, 182–203. Philadelphia: Westminster, 1957.

Holl, Karl. *The Cultural Significance of the Reformation*. Translated by Barbara Hertz Karl and John H. Lichtblau. Living Age Books 25. New York: Meridian, 1959.

———. "Luther Und Die Schwarmer." In *Gesammelte Aufsatze Zur Kirchengeschichte I:Luther*, edited by Karl Holl, 420–67. Tübingen: Mohr, 1932.

Holsinger-Friesen, Thomas. *Irenaeus and Genesis: A Study of Competition in Early Christian Hermeneutics*. Journal of Theological Interpretation Supplements 1. Winona Lake, IN: Eisenbrauns, 2009.

Hubmaier, Balthasar. *Balthasar Hubmaier: Theologian of Anabaptism*. Classics of the Radical Reformation 5. Scottdale, PA: Herald, 1989.

Hudson, Winthrop Still. "Who Were the Baptists?" *The Baptist Quarterly* 16.7 (July 1956) 303–12.

———. "Who Were the Baptists?" *The Baptist Quarterly* 17.2 (April 1957) 53–55.
Hullu, Johannes de. *Bescheiden Betreffende de Hervorming in Overijssel*. Deventer: de Lange, 1899.
Jay, Eric George. *The Church: Its Changing Image through Twenty Centuries*. Atlanta: John Knox, 1980.
Johnson, Todd E. "Initiation or Ordination? Balthasar Hubmaier's Rite of Baptism." *Studia Liturgica* 25.1 (1995) 68–85.
Joris, David. *The Anabaptist Writings of David Joris, 1535–1543*. Classics of the Radical Reformation 7. Waterloo, ON: Herald, 1994.
———. "Of the Wonderful Working of God." In *The Anabaptist Writings of David Joris, 1535–1543*. Waterloo, ON: Herald, 1994.
Karlstadt, Andreas Rudolf. *The Essential Carlstadt: Fifteen Tracts by Andreas Bodenstein (Carlstadt) from Karlstadt*. Classics of the Radical Reformation 8. Waterloo, ON: Herald, 1995.
Keeney, William E. "The Development of Dutch Anabaptist Thought and Practice from 1539–1564." PhD diss., Hartford Seminary, 1959.
———. *The Development of Dutch Anabaptist Thought and Practice from 1539–1564*. Nieuwkoop: de Graaf, 1968.
———. "Dirk Philips: A Biography." In *The Writings of Dirk Philips, 1504–1568*, edited by William E. Keeney, 19–47. Classics of the Radical Reformation 6. Scottdale, PA: Herald, 1992.
———. "Dirk Philips' Life." *The Mennonite Quarterly Review* 32.3 (July 1958) 171–91.
———. "Editors' Introduction." In *The Writings of Dirk Philips, 1504–1568*, edited by William E. Keeney, 11–15. Classics of the Radical Reformation 6. Scottdale, PA: Herald, 1992.
———. "Research Note: 500th Anniversary of Dirk Philips." *The Mennonite Quarterly Review* 78.4 (October 2004) 557–60.
———. "The Writings of Dirk Philips." *The Mennonite Quarterly Review* 32.4 (October 1958) 298–306.
"Keeney, William Echard (1922–2006)." *Global Anabaptist Mennonite Encyclopedia Online*. https://gameo.org/index.php?title=Keeney,_William_Echard_(1922-2006).
Keller, Amalie. "Ludwig Keller—Scholar with a Mission." *Mennonite Life* 8.4 (1953) 159–60.
Keller, Ludwig. *Ein Apostle Der Wiedertäufer*. Leipzig: von G. Hirzel, 1882.
Kelly, J. N. D. *Early Christian Doctrines*. 5th ed. San Francisco: Harper & Row, 1978.
Keyser, Marja. *Dirk Philips: 1504–1568: A Catalogue of His Printed Works in the University Library of Amsterdam*. Amsterdam: University Library of Amsterdam, 1975.
Kim, Changkyu. *Balthasar Hubmaier's Doctrine of Salvation in Dynamic and Relational Perspective*. Eugene, OR: Wipf and Stock, 2013.
Klaassen, Walter. *Anabaptism in Outline: Selected Primary Sources*. Classics of the Radical Reformation 3. Scottdale, PA: Herald, 1981.
———. "'There Were Giants on Earth in Those Days': Harold S. Bender and the Anabaptist Vision." *The Conrad Grebel Review* 12.3 (1994) 233–37.
Klaassen, Walter, and William Klassen. *Marpeck: A Life of Dissent and Conformity*. Studies in Anabaptist and Mennonite History 44. Waterloo, ON: Herald, 2008.

Koolman, J. ten Doornkaat. *Dirk Philips: Friend and Colleague of Menno Simons, 1504–1568.* Edited by C. Arnold Snyder. Translated by William E. Keeney. Kitchener, ON: Pandora, 1998.

———. "First Edition of Dirk Philips' Enchiridion." *The Mennonite Quarterly Review* 38.4 (October 1964) 357–60.

———. "Joachim Kükenbieter (Nossiophagus) Ein Lutherischer Eiferer Des Reformationszeitalters." *Nederlands Archief Voor Kerkgeschiedenis* 44 (1962) 157–76.

Koop, Karl, ed. *Confessions of Faith in the Anabaptist Tradition, 1527–1660.* Classics of the Radical Reformation 11. Kitchener, ON: Pandora, 2006.

Krahn, Cornelius. *Dutch Anabaptism: Origin, Spread, Life, and Thought (1450–1600).* The Hague: Nijhoff, 1968.

———. "Prolegomena to an Anabaptist Theology." *The Mennonite Quarterly Review* 24.1 (January 1950) 5–11.

Kreider, Robert. "Anabaptism and Humanism: An Inquiry into the Relationship of Humanism to the Evangelical Anabaptists." *Mennonite Quarterly Review* 26.2 (April 1, 1952) 123–41.

Kuyper, Abraham. *Dictaten Dogmatiek.* Vol. 2. 5 vols. Kampen: Kok, 1910.

Littell, Franklin H. *The Anabaptist View of the Church: An Introduction to Sectarian Protestantism.* Studies in Church History 8. Hartford, CT: American Society of Church History, 1952.

———. *The Anabaptist View of the Church: A Study in the Origins of Sectarian Protestantism.* Boston: Starr King, 1958.

Lohse, Bernhard. *Martin Luther's Theology: Its Historical and Systematic Development.* Edited and Translated by Roy A. Harrisville. Minneapolis: Fortress, 1999.

Longman, Tremper, III. *How to Read Genesis.* Downers Grove, IL: InterVarsity, 2005.

Luther, Martin. "The Babylonish Captivity of the Church." In *Reformation Writings of Martin Luther*, edited by Bertram Lee Woolf, 1:208–329. 2 vols. The Basis of the Protestant Reformation. London: Lutterworth, 1953.

———. *Martin Luther on the Bondage of the Will: A New Translation of De Servo Arbitrio (1525) Martin Luther's Reply to Erasmus of Rotterdam.* Edited by James Innell Packer and Olaf Raymond Johnston. Westwood, NJ: Revell, 1957.

MacCulloch, Diarmaid. *The Reformation.* New York: Penguin, 2005.

MacDonald, Scott. "Primal Sin." In *The Augustinian Tradition*, edited by Gareth B. Matthews, 110–39. Philosophical Traditions 8. Berkeley: University of California Press, 1999.

MacGregor, Kirk R. *A Central European Synthesis of Radical and Magisterial Reform: The Sacramental Theology of Balthasar Hubmaier.* Lanham, MD: University Press of America, 2006.

Marbeck, Pilgram, et al. *The Writings of Pilgram Marpeck.* Classics of the Radical Reformation 2. Scottdale, PA: Herald, 1978.

Mathewes, Charles T. *Evil and the Augustinian Tradition.* Cambridge: Cambridge University Press, 2001.

Mathison, Keith A. "The Lord's Supper." In *Reformation Theology*, edited by Matthew Barrett, 643–73. Wheaton, IL: Crossway, 2017.

McGrath, Alister E. *Christian History: An Introduction.* Chichester, UK: Wiley-Blackwell, 2013.

———. *Reformation Thought: An Introduction.* 4th ed. Malden, MA: Wiley-Blackwell, 2012.

Meek, Esther L. "A Polanyian Interpretation of Calvin's Sensus Divinitatis." *Presbyterion* 23.1 (1997) 8–24.

Miller, Marlin E. "The Church in the World: A Mennonite Perspective." *The Covenant Quarterly* 41.3 (August 1983) 45–50.

Murray, Stuart. *Biblical Interpretation in the Anabaptist Tradition.* Studies in the Believers Church Tradition 3. Kitchener, ON: Pandora, 2000.

Nestorius. "Dogmatic Letters of Nestorius and Cyril of Alexandria." In *Christology of the Later Fathers*, edited by Edward Rochie Hardy, 346–54. Louisville: Westminster John Know, 2006.

———. "Nestorius's Second Letter to Cyril." In *The Christological Controversy*, edited by Richard A. Norris Jr., 135–39. Sources of Early Christian Thought. Philadelphia: Fortress, 1980.

Oberman, Heiko Augustinus. *Luther: Man between God and the Devil.* New Haven: Yale University Press, 2006.

O'Meara, Dominic J. "The Metaphysics of Evil in Plotinus: Problems and Solutions." In *Agonistes: Essays in Honour of Denis O'Brien*, edited by John Dillon and Monique Dixsaut, 179–85. Aldershot, UK: Ashgate, 2005.

Owen, John. *Of the Mortification of Sin in Believers.* Grand Rapids: Christian Classics Ethereal Library, 2010.

Pater, Adrian J. "A Study of Selected Doctrines in Melchior Hoffman's Theology." PhD diss., New Orleans Baptist Theological Seminary, 1978.

Payne, Ernest Alexander. "Who Were the Baptists?" *The Baptist Quarterly* 16.8 (October 1956) 339–42.

Philips, Dirk. "About the Marriage of Christians." In *The Writings of Dirk Philips, 1504–1568*, edited and translated by William E. Keeney et al., 552–77. Harrisonburg, VA: Herald, 1992.

———. "Answer to Sebastian Franck." In *The Writings of Dirk Philips, 1504–1568*, edited and translated by William E. Keeney et al., 445–67. Harrisonburg, VA: Herald, 1992.

———. "An Apology or Reply." In *The Writings of Dirk Philips, 1504–1568*, edited and translated by William E. Keeney et al., 173–97. Harrisonburg, VA: Herald, 1992.

———. "The Ban." In *The Writings of Dirk Philips, 1504–1568*, edited and translated by William E. Keeney et al., 238–54. Harrisonburg, VA: Herald, 1992.

———. "The Baptism of Our Lord Jesus Christ." In *The Writings of Dirk Philips, 1504–1568*, edited and translated by William E. Keeney et al., 72–111. Harrisonburg, VA: Herald, 1992.

———. "Concerning Spiritual Restitution." In *The Writings of Dirk Philips, 1504–1568*, edited and translated by William E. Keeney et al., 316–49. Harrisonburg, VA: Herald, 1992.

———. "Concerning the True Knowledge of Jesus Christ." In *The Writings of Dirk Philips, 1504–1568*, edited and translated by William E. Keeney et al., 152–72. Harrisonburg, VA: Herald, 1992.

———. "A Confession about Separation." In *The Writings of Dirk Philips, 1504–1568*, edited and translated by William E. Keeney et al., 611–17. Harrisonburg, VA: Herald, 1992.

———. "Confession of Our Faith (Concerning) God." In *The Writings of Dirk Philips, 1504-1568*, edited and translated by William E. Keeney et al., 62-67. Harrisonburg, VA: Herald, 1992.

———. "The Congregation of God." In *The Writings of Dirk Philips, 1504-1568*, edited and translated by William E. Keeney et al., 350-82. Harrisonburg, VA: Herald, 1992.

———. "Epistle to Four Cities." In *The Writings of Dirk Philips, 1504-1568*, edited and translated by William E. Keeney et al., 476-88. Harrisonburg, VA: Herald, 1992.

———. "Epistle to the Wife of I. the S." In *The Writings of Dirk Philips, 1504-1568*, edited and translated by William E. Keeney et al., 619-31. Harrisonburg, VA: Herald, 1992.

———. "Evangelical Excommunication." In *The Writings of Dirk Philips, 1504-1568*, edited and translated by William E. Keeney et al., 591-610. Harrisonburg, VA: Herald, 1992.

———. "The Frisian-Flemish Division." In *The Writings of Dirk Philips, 1504-1568*, edited and translated by William E. Keeney et al., 468-551. Harrisonburg, VA: Herald, 1992.

———. "The Incarnation of Our Lord Jesus Christ, the Only Begotten Son of His Eternal and Almighty Father." In *The Writings of Dirk Philips, 1504-1568*, edited and translated by William E. Keeney et al., 134-51. Harrisonburg, VA: Herald, 1992.

———. "The New Birth and the New Creature." In *The Writings of Dirk Philips, 1504-1568*, edited and translated by William E. Keeney et al., 293-315. Harrisonburg, VA: Herald, 1992.

———. "Omitted Writing about the Ban and Avoidance." In *The Writings of Dirk Philips, 1504-1568*, edited and translated by William E. Keeney et al., 578-88. Harrisonburg, VA: Herald, 1992.

———. "Our Confession Concerning the Creation, Redemption, and Salvation of Humanity." In *The Writings of Dirk Philips, 1504-1568*, edited and translated by William E. Keeney et al., 68-71. Harrisonburg, VA: Herald, 1992.

———. "The Sending of Preachers or Teachers." In *The Writings of Dirk Philips, 1504-1568*, edited and translated by William E. Keeney et al., 198-237. Harrisonburg, VA: Herald, 1992.

———. "A Short but Fundamental Account." In *The Writings of Dirk Philips, 1504-1568*, edited and translated by William E. Keeney et al., 489-521. Harrisonburg, VA: Herald, 1992.

———. "The Supper of Our Lord Jesus Christ." In *The Writings of Dirk Philips, 1504-1568*, edited and translated by William E. Keeney et al., 112-33. Harrisonburg, VA: Herald, 1992.

———. "The Tabernacle of Moses." In *The Writings of Dirk Philips, 1504-1568*, edited and translated by William E. Keeney et al., 264-92. Harrisonburg, VA: Herald, 1992.

———. "Three Admonitions: No. I." In *The Writings of Dirk Philips, 1504-1568*, edited and translated by William E. Keeney et al., 383-97. Harrisonburg, VA: Herald, 1992.

———. "Three Admonitions: No. II." In *The Writings of Dirk Philips, 1504-1568*, edited and translated by William E. Keeney et al., 398-411. Harrisonburg, VA: Herald, 1992.

———. "Three Admonitions: No. III." In *The Writings of Dirk Philips, 1504-1568*, edited and translated by William E. Keeney et al., 412–26. Harrisonburg, VA: Herald, 1992.

———. "The True Knowledge of God." In *The Writings of Dirk Philips, 1504-1568*, edited and translated by William E. Keeney et al., 255–63. Harrisonburg, VA: Herald, 1992.

———. "An Unknown Letter of Dirk Philips." In *The Writings of Dirk Philips, 1504-1568*, edited and translated by William E. Keeney et al., 631–35. Harrisonburg, VA: Herald, 1992.

Philips, Obbe. "A Confession." In *Spiritual and Anabaptist Writers*, edited by George H. Williams and Angel M. Mergal, 204–25. Philadelphia: Westminster, 1957.

Philipsz, Dirk. *Die Geschriften van Dirk Philipsz*. Bibliotheca Reformatoria Neerlandica 10. Edited by Samuel Cramer and Frederik Pijper. 's-Gravenhage: Nijhoff, 1914.

Price, Theron D. "The Anabaptist View of the Church." *Review and Expositor: An International Baptist Journal* 51.2 (April 1954) 187–203.

Rempel, John D. "Christology and Lord's Supper in Anabaptism: A Study in the Theology of Balthasar Hubmaier, Pilgram Marpeck and Dirk Philips." PhD diss., University of St. Michael's College, 1988.

———, ed. *Jörg Maler's Kunstbuch: Writings of the Pilgram Marpeck Circle*. Classics of the Radical Reformation 12. Kitchener, ON: Pandora, 2010.

———. *The Lord's Supper in Anabaptism: A Study in the Christology of Balthasar Hubmaier, Pilgram Marpeck, and Dirk Philips*. Scottdale, PA: Herald, 1993.

Reymond, Robert L. *A New Systematic Theology of the Christian Faith*. Nashville: Thomas Nelson, 1998.

Richardson, Cyril Charles. *The Church through the Centuries*. New York: Scribner's Sons, 1938.

Riedemann, Peter. *Hutterite Confession of Faith: Translation of the 1565 German Edition of Confession of Our Religion, Teaching, and Faith by the Brothers Who Are Known as Hutterites*. Classics of the Radical Reformation 9. Scottdale, PA: Herald, 1999.

Rogers, Ronald David. "The Relationship of Soteriology and Ecclesiology in Sixteenth-Century Evangelical Anabaptism." PhD diss., Mid-America Baptist Theological Seminary, 1986.

Schubert, Aaron. "Dirk Philips' Letter and Spirit: An Anabaptist Contribution to Reformation Hermeneutics." *Religions* 8.3 (2017) 41–45.

Shantz, Douglas H. "The Ecclesiological Focus of Dirk Philips' Hermeneutical Thought in 1559: A Contextual Study." *The Mennonite Quarterly Review* 60.2 (April 1986) 115–27.

Shedd, William G. T., and Alan W. Gomes. *Dogmatic Theology*. 3rd ed. Phillipsburg, NJ: P & R, 2003.

Simons, Menno. "Admonition to the Amsterdam Melchiorites." In *The Complete Writings of Menno Simons, C.1496-1561*, edited by J. Denny Weaver, translated by Leonard Verduin, 1021–26. Scottdale, PA: Herald, 1986.

———. "The Blasphemy of John of Leiden." In *The Complete Writings of Menno Simons: C.1496-1561*, edited by J. Denny Weaver, translated by Leonard Verduin, 31–50. Scottdale, PA: Herald, 1984.

———. "Brief Confession on the Incarnation." In *The Complete Writings of Menno Simons, C.1496-1561*, edited by J. Denny Weaver, translated by Leonard Verduin, 416–54. Scottdale, PA: Herald, 1986.

———. "Christian Baptism, 1539." In *The Complete Writings of Menno Simons, C.1496-1561*, edited by J. Denny Weaver, translated by Leonard Verduin, 227-88. Scottdale, PA: Herald, 1986.

———. "A Clear Account of Excommunication, 1550." In *The Complete Writings of Menno Simons, C.1496-1561*, edited by J. Denny Weaver, translated by Leonard Verduin, 455-586. Scottdale, PA: Herald, 1986.

———. "Confession of the Distressed Christians." In *The Complete Writings of Menno Simons, C.1496-1561*, edited by J. Denny Weaver, translated by Leonard Verduin, 499-522. Scottdale, PA: Herald, 1986.

———. "Final Instruction on Marital Avoidance, 1558." In *The Complete Writings of Menno Simons, C.1496-1561*, edited by J. Denny Weaver, translated by Leonard Verduin, 1058-61. Scottdale, PA: Herald, 1986.

———. "Foundation of Christian Doctrine 1539-40." In *The Complete Writings of Menno Simons, C.1496-1561*, edited by J. Denny Weaver, translated by Leonard Verduin, 103-226. Scottdale, PA: Herald, 1986.

———. "Instruction on Discipline to the Church at Franeker, 1555." In *The Complete Writings of Menno Simons, C.1496-1561*, edited by J. Denny Weaver, translated by Leonard Verduin, 1041-43. Scottdale, PA: Herald, 1986.

———. "Instruction on Excommunication, 1558." In *The Complete Writings of Menno Simons, C.1496-1561*, edited by J. Denny Weaver, translated by Leonard Verduin, 959-98. Scottdale, PA: Herald, 1986.

———. "A Kind Admonition on Church Discipline 1541." In *The Complete Writings of Menno Simons, C.1496-1561*, edited by J. Denny Weaver, translated by Leonard Verduin, 407-18. Scottdale, PA: Herald, 1986.

———. "The New Birth c.1537." In *The Complete Writings of Menno Simons, C.1496-1561*, edited by J. Denny Weaver, translated by Leonard Verduin, 87-102. Scottdale, PA: Herald, 1986.

———. "Reply to False Accusations, 1552." In *The Complete Writings of Menno Simons, C.1496-1561*, edited by J. Denny Weaver, translated by Leonard Verduin, 541-78. Scottdale, PA: Herald, 1986.

———. "Reply to Gellius Faber 1554." In *The Complete Writings of Menno Simons, C.1496-1561*, edited by J. Denny Weaver, translated by Leonard Verduin, 623-782. Scottdale, PA: Herald, 1986.

———. "Sharp Reply to David Joris, 1542." In *The Complete Writings of Menno Simons, C.1496-1561*, edited by J. Denny Weaver, translated by Leonard Verduin, 1019-20. Scottdale, PA: Herald, 1986.

———. "The True Christian Faith, c. 1541." In *The Complete Writings of Menno Simons, C.1496-1561*, edited by J. Denny Weaver, translated by Leonard Verduin, 321-406. Scottdale, PA: Herald, 1986.

———. "Why I Do Not Cease Teaching and Writing." In *The Complete Writings of Menno Simons, C.1496-1561*, edited by J. Denny Weaver, translated by Leonard Verduin, 289-320. Scottdale, PA: Herald, 1986.

Snyder, C Arnold. *Anabaptist History and Theology: An Introduction*. Kitchener, ON: Pandora, 1996.

———, ed. *Later Writings of the Swiss Anabaptists, 1529-1592*. Classics of the Radical Reformation 13. Kitchener, ON: Pandora, 2017.

———, ed. *Sources of South German/Austrian Anabaptism*. Translated by Walter Klaassen et al. Classics of the Radical Reformation 10. Kitchener, ON: Pandora, 2001.

Stayer, James M., et al. "From Monogenesis to Polygenesis: The Historical Discussion of Anabaptist Origins." *The Mennonite Quarterly Review* 49.2 (April 1975) 83–121.

Steinmetz, David C. "Scholasticism and Radical Reform: Nominalist Motifs in the Theology of Balthasar Hubmaier." *The Mennonite Quarterly Review* 45.2 (April 1971) 123–44.

Tillich, Paul. *A History of Christian Thought*. New York: Harper & Row, 1968.

Troeltsch, Ernst. *Die Soziallehren Der Christlichen Kirchen Und Gruppen*. His Gesammelte Schriften. Tübingen: Mohr Siebeck, 1912.

van der Zijpp, Nanne. "Wismar Resolutions." *Global Anabaptist Mennonite Encyclopedia, Online*, http://gameo.org/index.php?title=Wismar_Resolutions.

Waite, Gary K. *David Joris and Dutch Anabaptism, 1524–1543*. Waterloo, ON: Wilfrid Laurier University Press, 2006.

———. "David Joris' Thought in the Context of the Early Melchiorite and Münsterite Movements in the Low Countries, 1534–1536." *The Mennonite Quarterly Review* 62.3 (July 1988) 296–317.

Walton, Zachary J. *John Howard Yoder. Radical Theologian*. Edited by J. Denny Weaver. Cambridge, UK: Lutterworth, 2015.

Warfield, Benjamin Breckinridge. *Calvin and Augustine*. Philadelphia: Presbyterian and Reformed, 1956.

Weaver, J. Denny. *Becoming Anabaptist: The Origin and Significance of Sixteenth-Century Anabaptism*. Scottdale, PA: Herald, 1987.

Williams, George Huntston. *The Radical Reformation*. Philadelphia: Westminster, 1962.

Williams, George Huntston, et al., eds. *Spiritual and Anabaptist Writers: Documents Illustrative of the Radical Reformation*. The Library of Christian Classics 25. Philadelphia: Westminster, 1957.

Williamson, Darren T. "Erasmus of Rotterdam's Influence upon Anabaptism: The Case of Balthasar Hubmaier." PhD diss., Simon Fraser University, 2005.

Wolters, Albert M. *Creation Regained: Biblical Basics for a Reformational Worldview*. Grand Rapids: Eerdmans, 1985.

Yarnell, Malcolm B., III. *The Formation of Christian Doctrine*. Nashville: B & H, 2007.

Yoder, J. H. "Kirchenzucht Bei Zwingli." *The Mennonite Quarterly Review* 31.1 (January 1957) 63–71.

Yoder, John Howard, and Michael Sattler. *The Legacy of Michael Sattler*. Classics of the Radical Reformation 1. Scottdale, PA: Herald, 1973.

Zijlstra, Samme. "Menno Simons and David Joris." *The Mennonite Quarterly Review* 62.3 (July 1988) 249–56.

Zwingli, Ulrich. *Commentary on True and False Religion*. Edited by Samuel Macauley Jackson and Clarence Nevin Heller. Durham, NC: Labyrinth, 1981.

www.ingramcontent.com/pod-product-compliance
Lightning Source LLC
Chambersburg PA
CBHW051739230426
43670CB00012B/2081